Reading the Gravestones
of Old New England

To persuade men to prepare for the great and interesting scene of exchanging worlds, though it is a work altogether reasonable, and essentially connected with the happiness of their immortal souls, has ever been found a difficult task.

—The Rev. Alvan Hyde

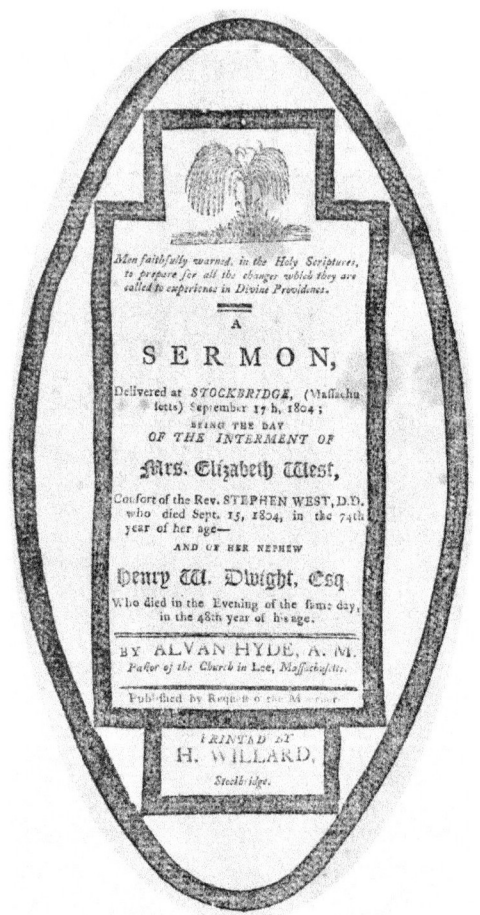

From the Rev. Alvan Hyde, *Men faithfully warned in the Holy Scriptures, to prepare for all the things which they are called to experience in Divine Providence; A Sermon Delivered in Stockbridge, (Massachusetts), September 17th, 1804; Being the Day of the interment of Mrs. Elizabeth West, Consort of the Rev. Stephen West, D.D. who died Sept. 15. 1804, in the 74th year of her age—And of her nephew Henry W. Dwight, Esq. Who died in the Evening of the same day, in the 48th year of his age* (Stockbridge, MA, 1804) (courtesy Williams College Archives and Special Collections; Williamstown, Massachusetts).

Reading the Gravestones of Old New England

John G. S. Hanson

McFarland & Company, Inc., Publishers
Jefferson, North Carolina

LIBRARY OF CONGRESS CATALOGUING-IN-PUBLICATION DATA

Names: Hanson, John G. S., author.
Title: Reading the gravestones of old New England / John G.S. Hanson.
Description: Jefferson, North Carolina : McFarland & Company, Inc., Publishers, 2021. | Includes bibliographical references and index.
Identifiers: LCCN 2021044606 | ISBN 9781476685458 (paperback : acid free paper) ∞
ISBN 9781476643298 (ebook)
Subjects: LCSH: Cemeteries—New England. | Epitaphs—New England. | Sepulchral monuments—New England. | New England—Social life and customs—To 1775. | BISAC: HISTORY / United States / State & Local / New England (CT, MA, ME, NH, RI, VT)
Classification: LCC F5 .H35 2021 | DDC 929/.50974—dc23
LC record available at https://lccn.loc.gov/2021044606

BRITISH LIBRARY CATALOGUING DATA ARE AVAILABLE

ISBN (print) 978-1-4766-8545-8
ISBN (ebook) 978-1-4766-4329-8

© 2021 John G. S. Hanson. All rights reserved

No part of this book may be reproduced or transmitted in any form or by any means, electronic or mechanical, including photocopying or recording, or by any information storage and retrieval system, without permission in writing from the publisher.

Front cover photograph: Center Cemetery; Lanesborough, Massachusetts (author's collection)

Printed in the United States of America

*McFarland & Company, Inc., Publishers
Box 611, Jefferson, North Carolina 28640
www.mcfarlandpub.com*

Table of Contents

Acknowledgments vii

Preface 1

Part I—Reading the Gravestones of Early New England 5

Part II—Categories of Epitaphs 47

The Classic 48

Scripture 56

Psalms and Hymns 70

English and American Poetry 100

The Graveyard School 148

Recurring but Unidentified 185

Bespoke 204

Sudden Death 230

Bibliography 241

Index 245

Acknowledgments

The work described in this book—searching for epitaph verse in disused graveyards, poring through books of transcribed inscriptions, searching for images and source texts on the internet—might sound like a solitary endeavor, but in fact it is quite a social undertaking. I have the benefit of collaborating with an extensive network of like-minded gravestone enthusiasts. Some study the iconography of the stones, others focus on individual carvers, still others are bringing much-needed attention to the graves of over-looked minority populations: enslaved people and freemen, Masons, Catholics, and Jews. Others are carvers themselves, or specialists in gravestone preservation. Many are fellow-members of the Association of Gravestone Studies (AGS), a diverse and congenial community of scholars, preservationists, and practitioners of funereal monuments.

I am grateful to all for their collegial insight and advice, but I must offer special thanks to Bob Drinkwater, who brought me into the AGS fold and has generously shared his deep knowledge of the stones and carvers of western Massachusetts, and Betsy and Al McKee, whose superb photographs of Connecticut River Valley stones are a constant source of new and interesting epitaphs. These fellow petrophiles have greatly encouraged me on my journey, and in return I try to provide helpful context and commentary on the verses they discover. It makes for a steady flow of stimulating discourse that has contributed to the breadth and depth of material in this study.

A significant portion of this project has entailed learning about the reading habits of early New Englanders and the written material available to them. In this I have benefited from the expert advice of rare book curators at the American Antiquarian Society and the Boston Athenaeum. I deeply appreciate their interest and support.

I have also been fortunate to receive many thoughtful comments from readers of this material and people who have heard me talk on the subject. I owe particular thanks to Barbara Palmer, who early on reminded me to read the verses through the eyes of those who chose them, not my own; Professor John Demos, who brought my attention to the importance of chronology and overlapping themes; my brother Charles, an accomplished scholar of colonial American religion who sharpened my understanding of the religious context of the times; Professor Herb Golder, who asked a question about Latin on these stones and published my response; and Maribeth Grennon Casey, whose opinion that the work was publishable gave me a much-needed boost of confidence.

I owe very special thanks to my friend Patrick O'Donnell, who took a deep interest in my work and told me I had to write this book. He then guided my progress with penetrating questions, discerning criticism, and insightful comments.

And most of all I am grateful for the unflagging support of my wife, Elizabeth, who has kept me company on many expeditions down the back-roads of New England in search of the next graveyard.

Note: Several passages in this book previously appeared as articles in *Arion: A Journal of Humanities and the Classics* (Trustees of Boston University, Winter 2020) and *AGS Quarterly* (The Association for Gravestone Studies, Spring 2020; Volume 44:1).

Preface

The graveyards of old New England are irresistibly fascinating. They appeal to the eye and the imagination, with their dignified stones standing or leaning in gray array, quiet abiding witnesses to the long histories of their towns. They provide a trove of useful information to historians, genealogists, and students of religious art. They also draw in visitors who find spiritual or philosophical comfort in contemplating lives and deaths from centuries ago, memorialized in granite or marble or sandstone.

For me, these graveyards hold an absorbing store of poetic messages from early New Englanders expressing their thoughts on what the Reverend Hyde called "the great and interesting scene of exchanging worlds." I started collecting epitaphs in these burial grounds when I was a kid, and through the years I kept asking myself, "Where did these verses come from, and how did they get on these gravestones?" Satisfying my curiosity on those two questions has become my infinitely rewarding avocation, leading me on a personal journey of heart and mind into the literary and spiritual world these people inhabited. The course of my studies has taken me down unexpected by-ways, introducing me to a marvelous range of devotional literature while opening a door into vanished but once-bustling scenes of commerce and competition in publishing and stone-carving.

My work typically starts with a slow walk through an old graveyard, taking pictures of interesting verse with my phone. To find these burial grounds, a good old-fashioned roadmap is an invaluable tool. Also, Findagrave.com usually lists all the cemeteries in a given town, with an on-line map to each. On other occasions, I will find something new in a book of inscriptions, or receive a message from a friend with an interesting epitaph attached. Then, like an eager lepidopterist with a netful of fresh specimens, I hurry home to search through my library and the internet to track down the original sources. There is a thrill-of-the-chase excitement that comes with each new discovery: An unexpected Bible verse! What, *another* Montgomery poem? Who on earth is Moscus? And who, for that matter, is the Reverend Collyer, and what *was* he doing in that bath-house? I hope I can convey the pleasure I feel each time I add another item to the collection, learn something new about the writings and publications of the age, encounter the unexpected life of a long-forgotten author, and add a little more to my appreciation of the literature these people read and how they brought their reading to bear on the occasion of a death.

The book is divided into two parts. Part I is the story of my years-long reader's walk among these gravestones. In it, I share some of the learning I have gained along the way: the identities of source texts and authors chosen for these stones; something of the tastes and beliefs of the people who did the choosing; some hypotheses on the various ways these texts were accessible to readers in remote towns and villages; a consideration of the decisions and transactions involved in turning words on a printed page into inscriptions in stone; some facts and informed speculation about the stone carvers and their role; a brief summary of the religious context of the times; and reflections on how the language and literature chosen for these epitaphs express these peoples' conflicted and evolving attitudes towards life, death, and eternity.

Part II is a compendium of noteworthy epitaphs, organized primarily by their sources, with a few thoughts and observations on each. In this section, I hope to share with you what I find interesting or distinctive about each verse's content, context, origins, and message.

As my collecting expanded into the body of work you now hold in your hands, two points became clear that I must state at the outset. First, this is not an exhaustive, quantitative analysis of the frequency or distribution of epitaphs in these graveyards. Such a study is beyond my capabilities, though it would be a worthy topic for a scholar to take up in a different book. The epitaphs I share here are those that attracted my interest, either for their language or their patterns of use.

Second, I have benefited greatly from reading the many erudite and often beautiful books written about the iconography of these gravestones and stories of the carvers who created them. Indeed, the illustrations in those books have provided me with many excellent epitaphs. But the fact is most of these books have relatively little to say about the verses themselves. This strikes me as an omission insofar as both the appearance and the content of an epitaph are integral elements of a gravestone's design. Another fine topic for another book.

Years ago, an essay in *Markers*, the annual journal of the Association for Gravestone Studies (AGS), called for "a study of epitaphs, their linguistic and literary effects, literary sources, and ... significance." A few years later, in her excellent Introduction to the Farber Gravestone Collection, Jessie Lie Farber posed the question "What is the source of the verses?" and answered, "This is a subject that invites research." This book, limited and idiosyncratic though it is, amounts to an attempt to begin to fill this lacuna.

In the pages that follow, I hope to show that these epitaphs constitute a written record of the literature these early New Englanders read and used in their efforts to find words to express their grieving. You will see how epitaph texts evolved from rigid Calvinist warnings to prepare for death and avoid the imminent danger of damnation (expressed using a fairly narrow range of Scripture verses, hymns, and devotional works), to a richer set of options including poetry and original composition—enabled by the increased availability of books.

You will note that the spelling, punctuation, and capitalization of the epitaphs as carved on these stones are often archaic or simply incorrect. In order to preserve the look and feel of the language of the time, I refrain from cleaning up or correcting these idiosyncrasies. On the other hand, the reader would soon grow annoyed were I to insert [sic] every time it could be called for, so I choose to omit the use of it altogether. Nor do I attempt to re-create the fonts used by the carvers, and their occasionally improvised line lengths. The reader will find ample images that illustrate the written composition of these stones.

Now I invite you to read and contemplate the words these people chose; admire the hand of the individuals who selected or composed these verses, recalling always that they were intended to be read by posterity—by us; and reflect upon what these very personal choices tell us about early New Englanders' changing and often conflicted attitudes towards life, death, and eternity.

Part I

Reading the Gravestones of Early New England

When I was ten or eleven years old, my father would sometimes drive his kids around the Berkshire Hills of western Massachusetts, exploring old graveyards and reading the inscriptions on the stones. We were most interested in gravestones from the late eighteenth and early nineteenth centuries, with their rounded tops and distinctive shoulders, decorated with carefully-carved winged death's-heads or staring angels' faces or hourglasses or stately willows weeping over urns. Some of the graveyards we visited were in the center of town, next to the old First Meeting House, with traffic whizzing incongruously past. Others were out along country roads, undisturbed except for the occasional pick-up truck or bicyclist going by. We sometimes found tiny overgrown family plots with a few tilting headstones, their iron fences rusted and falling from standing too long in the weather, far from any village, looking more a copse of woods than a proper burial ground.

I do not really have an explanation for my interest in this pursuit. Perhaps it was because my parents were both lapsed Episcopalians who raised a profoundly un-churched family. I suppose this graveyard reading provided my first window into the world of organized religion and spirituality. As I recall, my father was most interested in the bits of local history he could glean from the inscriptions—early family names, patterns of marriage, the range of professions, and hints of the social order suggested by different styles and degrees of decoration. I was absorbed by the verses carved on the stones, and would squat down to copy the most interesting ones in my awkward school-boy hand. Their words eloquently articulated concepts that I did not understand, so in his patient professor's voice my father satisfied my curiosity by providing rational explications of sin, repentance, and resurrection (he used much the same tone when answering our seasonal questions about nuances of the Christmas and Easter stories). My father knew all about these things thanks to his mid-western High-Church Episcopalian upbringing, an experience he did not intend to replicate for his children. Yet there he was, out in these peaceful graveyards, providing religious instruction to his kid after all. Life's little ironies. Whatever our motivations, these weekend excursions were some of my best boyhood times with my father.

I lost my enthusiasm for the project in my teens, having grown up a bit and acquired other, more worldly, interests. Decades later, while emptying my parents' house I found my old notebooks in a desk drawer and became engrossed all over again. This time my motivations are probably easier to understand. Many friends and family have exchanged worlds, in the words of the Reverend Hyde (including my father), and I have reached a point in life where the question of what to say in an epitaph is no longer hypothetical or aesthetic, but practical and personal. I am also a more educated and appreciative reader of the language and literature on these stones than when I was a kid.

My primary area for collecting remains what were small frontier towns in rural western Massachusetts—all towns named in this book are in Massachusetts except where otherwise indicated. I can find plenty of perfectly interesting epitaphs in the big towns along the coast (including Boston; Newport, Rhode Island; and New Haven, Connecticut), and you will read some of them in this book, along with verses from small towns across the Commonwealth and elsewhere in New England. But the rural towns and villages of western Massachusetts are where my journey of discovery first began, and the fact they were far from centers of publishing and learning in the eighteenth century makes the literature of their graveyards all the more interesting.

This is a singularly beautiful corner of the world, lush green in the summer, spectacularly red and orange and gold in the autumn, mesmerizing in the winter when the bare trees and sunlight and snow-cover combine to turn the hills purple. The landscape is defined by hills and valleys: the Taconic Range guarding the border between New York State and Massachusetts; the rocky ledges and wooded glades of the watersheds of the Hoosic and Housatonic Rivers with their small farm settlements, some of which grew to become market towns or mill towns or college towns; the great ridges

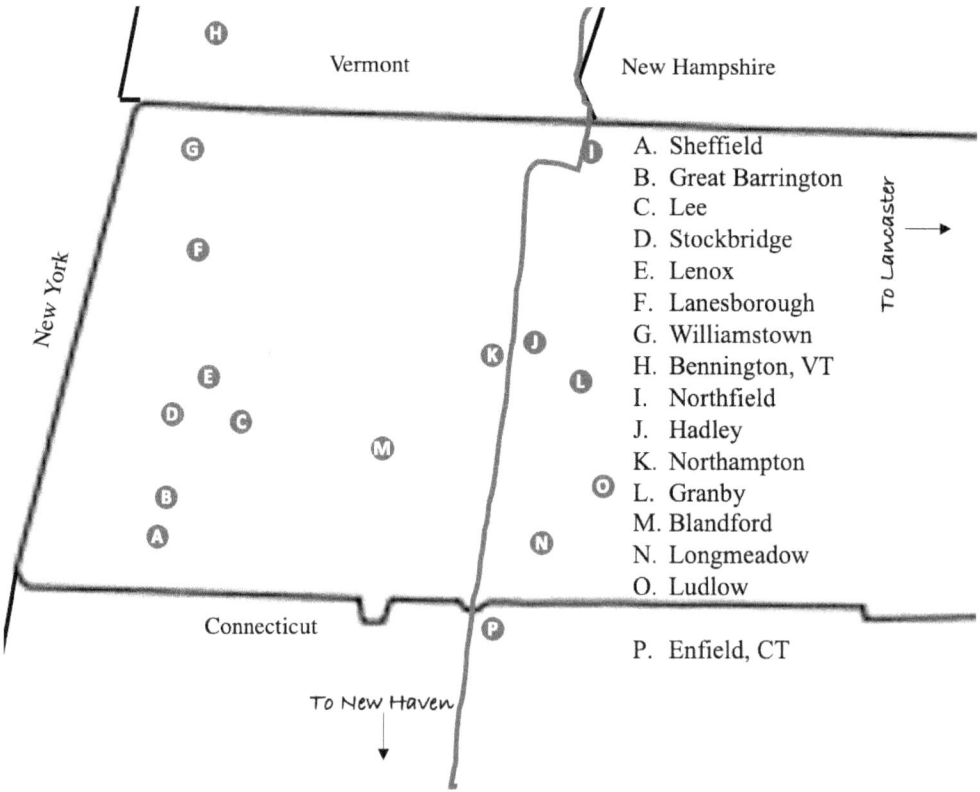

Location of graveyards referenced (partial).

of the Hoosac Range to the east eventually sloping down to fertile plains along the Connecticut River. Europeans settled the valley of the Connecticut first, with Puritans coming up the river from New London and New Haven to found Springfield, Deerfield, and Northampton. The Berkshires were remote in those early days, barely accessible beyond a daunting barrier of rocky hills, supporting mere outposts—missionary settlements among the Native Americans in Stockbridge, a fort to protect against the French and Indians in what became Williamstown. It took decades for land to be cleared, farms to be scratched out of the thin rocky soil, and villages to form. Today the region is fully connected to the world via Interstate highways; thousands of college students swell the populations of Williamstown, Amherst, Northampton, South Hadley, Pittsfield, Westfield, and Springfield; cultural tourists flock to innumerable museums and concert venues and historic properties; in Fall and Winter they and their leaf-looking and skiing counterparts spend bright merry nights in charming B&Bs, hip new hotels, or luxurious spa resorts. It has been a long time since life here was precarious, the landscape forbidding, and these towns remote—but it was thus when these epitaphs were carved.

Most of the epitaphs you will read in this book date from the last half of the eighteenth century through the first few decades of the nineteenth century. Earlier than that, the vocabulary of New England funerary practice was starker and less euphemistic than it became in later days. There were no cemeteries, there were burial grounds. The text on the stones is straightforward, "Here lies the body of...," with the date of death and perhaps the age of the deceased. If you had been killed by a native (not uncommon in these frontier towns) your grave marker might mention that fact. Later, by the mid–1800s, epitaphs tend to run to more mass-produced sentimental verse—though of course these have their own merit as choices made by the bereaved to express their feelings.

I still collect "in the field" as much as I can. There is nothing like getting out of the car exploring these old graveyards on foot, stone by stone. Nowhere else, in our overbuilt and wired modern world, can one come closer to experiencing New England village landscapes the way they looked in the late eighteenth century than by standing in the burial ground. Fifty years and more after I started, I still feel a sense of peace during a walk through these graveyards that I cannot express in words. I encourage you to turn off your smartphone and try it yourself. Go to a larger town like Longmeadow or Lenox and admire the stately stones in their well-ordered rows, adjacent to their equally fine churches. Visit tiny Blandford on its windy ridge, once a coaching stop halfway between the Connecticut River and the Berkshires, with its simple burial ground enclosed by a stone wall identical to those used to mark farmers' fields. Park your car on Jerusalem Road in Tyringham and look down across fields still cut for hay every year to the tidy burial ground nestled on its little knoll, a cast-iron fence all around, an old two-room schoolhouse off to one side, and the stately tower of the Meeting House rising above. Or walk into Lee's Old Center Cemetery on its tree-shaded hill up above town and church, and seek out the rows of early stones tucked in a far corner, past the spread of nineteenth- and twentieth-century stones that reflect the town's growth as a quarry and mill town. Get off the Massachusetts Turnpike in Ludlow and drive through the inevitable string of gas stations and fast-food joints until you spot the First Church. Look under the adjacent grove of trees to find the little graveyard. The day I visited, it was sadly neglected, the grass uncut, the stones lichen-crusted. But the gravestones of the earliest settlers still stand, with their carved stories of birth and marriage and death.* In Sheffield and Lanesborough the old cemeteries lie hard by busy Route 7, barely noticed by the cars roaring past. But enter, and after not many steps *you* will stop noticing *them*. See if you can find the Old Center Cemetery in Monterey. It is not so easy a task. Despite its name, the graveyard lies all by itself, quite surrounded by woods, set back twenty yards or so from a dirt road, not a house within a half-mile. But old maps of the town show an early church and a cluster of houses around the site, now long vanished.

Sadly, many of these stones are unreadable today due to weathering, acid rain, and neglect. Even epitaphs I transcribed in my childish fist are, upon my return to search them out again, illegible. And of course many epitaphs from the era are not just illegible but gone for good, through weathering, neglect, or vandalism. So I supplement my time in the graveyards with a variety of other sources of interesting verses. Town histories written in the late nineteenth and early twentieth centuries are an excellent resource. The books were often part of a town's centennial or sesquicentennial celebration; one way the proud authors honored their founders was to transcribe the carvings on their gravestones, an effort from which I benefited in studying epitaphs in Northfield, Longmeadow, and several other towns.

Other books are more exclusively focused on preserving the inscriptions for posterity. Thomas Bridgman published his fine *Inscriptions on the Grave Stones in the Grave Yards of Northampton and of Other Towns in the Valley of the Connecticut* in 1850, making his intention quite clear in the Preface: "The object of the Compiler in the work he has undertaken is to preserve in a durable form some most interesting but rapidly perishing memorials of our Puritan ancestors." Dorvil Miller Wilcox produced three such volumes for Lee between 1900 and 1910. In his Introduction to the final book, Wilcox gives an achingly precise description of the problem students of these early gravestones face:

> Anyone familiar with the old burial grounds of New England must realize how frail memorials in stone are in such a damp and frosty climate as ours. The yearly upheaval of the ground by frost causes the fall and fracture of some of the stones, and the weather of a century† almost obliterates some of the inscriptions.... A considerable number of ... stones, weakened by the disintegrating action of water and frost, have broken near the ground. Some of them have been reset, frequently with part of the inscription hidden in the earth, and some broken into fragments have been removed to the rubbish heaps. Some of those destroyed have been replaced by other memorials, usually of a more durable character, but more often the grave remains unmarked.

Wilcox is quite right on this last point. Whenever I am in one of these graveyards and see what appears to be a vacant section, I recall that in fact most filled up over time, necessitating new, later, cemeteries. There may no longer be gravestones above, but there is the dust of burials below.

Professional and amateur genealogists have published many volumes of gravestone transcriptions, though they all too often (for my purposes) content themselves

---

* The state of these graveyards can be a painful subject. Many towns work hard to keep them well maintained, but others, disappointingly, much less so. I always advocate for more and better preservation but recognize the headwinds posed by strained budgets and limited revenue for these villages and churches.

† Now more than two centuries.

with just the name-and-date information, ignoring any verse further down the stone. Not so Cynthia Tryon Hoogs, an intrepid researcher whose *Cemetery Inscriptions, Monterey, Massachusetts,* is invaluable in that it records verses that have since sunk below ground level and are now for all practical purposes lost forever. Similarly, I was thrilled to discover on-line a digitized version of Josephine C. Frost's one-hundred-page, type-written compilation of *Cemetery Inscriptions from Lanesboro[ugh], Massachusetts* (July 1910). She must have first transcribed all these verses by hand—what a labor of love! Frost (1864–1942) was a prodigious genealogist, writing or editing dozens of histories of various families. I find no Frosts in her index for Lanesborough; I do not know what brought her from her home grounds of New York and Long Island to the Berkshires.

For centuries, epitaphs have also attracted the attention of anthologists. I own several eighteenth-century collections of memorial verse whose subjects range from aristocrats and public figures to everyday people who happen to have noteworthy inscriptions. The common theme of most such volumes was summarized in an early example of the genre, James Jones's *Sepulchrorum Inscriptiones* (1727):

> The Monuments of the Dead are a Collection of all the sublimest Faculties the Living could excogitate, to perpetuate the Memory of their illustrious Ancestours; one may there read the various Compositions of many Nations, their different Turns of Fancy, all the promiscuous [sic] Humours and Inclinations peculiar to the several Branches of Mankind, the Grave and Serious, the Merry and Jocose…

These collections aim to interest, entertain, and to some degree instruct the reader. Another early anthologist, Thomas Webb (1775)—who incidentally cribbed a lot of his material from Jones and others—put it thus:

> The FIRST VOLUME includes all EPITAPHS distinguished by the Elegance, Delicacy, and Poetical Beauties of their Composition, or by the unaffected Piety, Christian Resignation, and pure Morality of their sentiments. In the SECOND VOLUME will be found such epitaphs as are remarkable for their Wit, Humour, Satire, or Singularity.

When I began this research, I expected to find many epitaphs from these early British collections being re-used in America; in fact this has proved to be quite rare. The modern descendants of these books are simple collations of "Quaint and Curious" verses that piqued the interest or touched the heart-strings of the editor. Few provide any real context or commentary.[*]

Another very valuable source for this book is the Farber Gravestone Collection, a superb assemblage of more than nine thousand high-quality photographs that can be studied on-line and searched by location, carver, and presence or absence of verse. The Collection includes photographs by Daniel and Jessie Lie Farber of Worcester; Harriette Merrifield Forbes, who worked in the 1920s mainly in Massachusetts; and Dr. Ernest Caulfield, a pediatrician who documented hundreds of Connecticut grave markers.

~~~

---

[*] A handful, however, have proven quite helpful. Two in particular stand out: Thomas Mann and Janet Greene's *Over Their Dead Bodies* (Brattleboro VT: Stephen Greene Press, 1962), a regrettably-named but delightful and instructive book, and Robert Pike's *Granite Laughter and Marble Tears* (Brattleboro, VT: Stephen Daye Press,1938), a truly beautifully-designed work.

To help manage this unruly collection, I began to sort the verses into eight categories that have proven useful for comparing and contrasting different types of epitaph, and assessing how these "genres" evolved over time. These working categories are: The Classic, Scripture, Hymns and Psalms, English and American Poetry, The Graveyard School, Recurring but Unattributed, Bespoke, and Sudden Death. Part II of this book presents noteworthy examples of epitaphs from these categories, with a few comments and observations on each; for now I will limit myself to an introductory overview of the categories themselves.

The Classic

Perhaps the most easily recognizable and most frequently chosen source text for epitaphs on the gravestones of early New England is one I have come to refer to simply as "The Classic." A perfect example, carved in simple block letters, can be found in Woods Cemetery in Monterey (formerly Tyringham), a tiny little hillock with some two or three dozen stones remaining upright, tucked in the bend of a little country road (Figure 1):

Figure 1. Deacon John Jackson stone (author's collection).

HEAR LIES THE
BODY OF DEACON
JOHN JACKSON
WHO DIED MARCH
13 ETH 1757 IN THE
54 YEAR OF HIS AGE

Behold And See
As You pass By
As You Are Now
So once Was I
As I Am Now
So You Must be
Therefore Prepare
To Follow Me

The Classic is not unique to New England. It was a popular trope in many early English and Scottish churchyards long before it appeared here; no doubt the early settlers brought it with them across the Atlantic. The church of Santa Maria Novella in Florence uses it in a fresco by Masaccio, *The Trinity* (ca. 1427). Beneath the kneeling donors is a skeleton painted on slab, with the epitaph "io fu gia quel che voi siete e quel chio son voi anco sarete" ("I was once what you are, and what I am you also will be"). The theme goes back to classical Greek and Roman tombs: "Viator, viator! Quod tu es, ego fui; quod nunc sum, et tu eris," or "Traveller, traveller! What you are, I was; what I am now, you also will be."

Much ink has been spilled, and many blogs written, trying to establish the origin of this quatrain—to no avail. No matter; what should command our attention is how often the theme was chosen and how many now-anonymous individuals customized the ur-text to convey a nuanced range of personalized images and emotions. After reading this epitaph and its closely related versions over and over, literally hundreds of times, I have come to appreciate two fundamental aspects of how the people of these small towns experienced life and death.

First, everyday life was a risky and uncertain proposition. Death was common and often quick. Infant mortality was high and medical care rudimentary. Every pregnancy posed a mortal risk for the mother, and every workday exposed men to the chance of death by a kicking animal, a falling load of wood, or a toppled wagon. So the message that death could come *at any time* was always apposite.

Second, to prepare for death was a specific, well-understood task. To die unprepared, in a state of sin, would result in eternal damnation in a very real, tangible Hell. The decades from roughly 1740 to 1820 were a time of conflict and upheaval in New England religious life (I will discuss the religious context of the times later in Part I). People disagreed fiercely on *how* to prepare for death. For some, preparation was a life-long process of painstaking adherence to Scripture and sermons through constant effort and will. For others, preparation consisted of a more immediate, emotional, and heart-felt experience of grace. But whichever camp you were in, there was no doubt at all about the *need* to prepare.

These attitudes were deeply ingrained in people's minds, repeated over and over in sermons and devotional reading. Let me provide just a few examples. First, rural New Englanders would be familiar with Jonathan Edwards's visceral warning to unregenerate sinners in his famous and much-reprinted sermon *Sinners in the Hands of an Angry God* (1741): "There is nothing that keeps wicked Men at any one Moment, out of Hell, but the meer Pleasure of GOD.... 'Tis nothing but his Hand that holds you from falling into the Fire every moment ... there is no other Reason to be given why you have not dropped into Hell since you arose in the Morning."

The same message is conveyed in much gentler language in James Hervey's enormously popular *Meditations Among the Tombs in a Letter to a Lady* (ca. 1746), a long and quite moving essay on the transience of life, death as the common fate of the high and low, and the vital importance of preparing oneself for the afterlife. Hervey offers the parable of a thoughtless jay bird's "idle business in dressing its pretty plumes" without a care in the world. In an instant, a passing sportsman shoots him and "lays the silly creature breathless on the ground." The moral of the story is: "Such, such may be the fate of the man who has a fair occasion of obtaining grace to-day, and wantonly postpones the improvement of it till to-morrow."[*]

In the 1780s the Rev. Samuel Hopkins, worried that belief in the risk of eternal damnation was waning among his parishioners, wrote a long tract to argue, in gruesome language similar to Edwards's, that unrepentant sinners will undoubtedly suffer forever. I read the Reverend Hopkins's work one summer afternoon in the comfort of the Boston Athenaeum's rare books library; imagine assigning yourself this devotional lesson of a winter evening in some drafty New England farmhouse:

---

[*] Hervey also describes what it means to suffer the agonies of Hell for all eternity, but it is thin beer compared to *Sinners in the Hands of an Angry God*. Hervey wanted to discomfit his readers, not terrify them. We will encounter Hervey's *Meditations* again in Part II.

> Don't forget a moment, in what an infinitely dangerous situation you are: On the brink of the bottomless pit, where are everlasting burnings; having nothing to secure you from sinking down to hell, being held out of it, only by the hand of him whose goodness you are abusing, and whom you are constantly provoking, in a manner dreadful to think of … [B]y this be warned to fly from the wrath to come. And remember, that the Lord Jesus Christ … now invites you to look unto him, that you may be saved from this infinitely dreadful, everlasting destruction, and you are called and commanded to repent and come unto him, that you may have eternal life. And it must therefore be altogether your own inexcusable fault, if you persist by refusing to obey his call: And your rejecting him, and thus going to hell, will necessarily render your punishment inexpressibly greater and more dreadful, than it would be, if there had been no Saviour, and you never had such an offer.[*]

Hopkins was a leading Calvinist theologian of his time. He was minister of the First Congregational Church in Newport, Rhode Island, when he wrote this, but earlier in life he had been minister in Great Barrington, so his preaching would have been familiar in the Berkshires.[†]

And in the early 1800s, the Rev. Alvan Hyde of Lee, a staunchly conservative clergyman, preached a funeral sermon urging his congregation to "prepare for all the changes which they are called to experience in Divine Providence," and to remember and apply the lessons of The Classic. Hyde says of the mourning friends and relatives of deceased:

> Let them not wait for louder warnings than those which are, this day, sounding in their ears, and which are to be viewed as a fulfilment of God's holy word. Their turn will also come, and prepared or not prepared, they must go when called. May the Lord give them all to realize their exposedness to death, and may he quicken them to have their lamps trimmed and burning.… God is speaking to us all,—and his language is,—*Be ye also ready*. Let us all seriously reflect on our condition as candidates for eternity. Our sands are swiftly running—eternal scenes are at hand. In a few days, it will be said of us, as it now is for our deceased friends, whose remains we are about to follow to the grave, that we are dead. Let us turn the present moments to the best possible account, and no longer boast ourselves of to-morrow.[‡]

All these lessons would be recalled to the reader's mind when she or he cast an eye on the lines "Prepare for death" on a gravestone.

Scripture

The Bible is a common and unsurprising source of epitaph texts for these gravestones. As mentioned, epitaphic verse of any sort is comparatively scarce in the seventeenth and early eighteenth century out in these hills. Short Bible verses were among the first enhancements to these spare memorials, providing a measure of grace. These passages would have been familiar to the deceased, their survivors, and

---

[*] Samuel Hopkins, *An Inquiry Concerning the future State of those who die in their Sins*
[†] It is worth noting that Hopkins left his pulpit in Great Barrington due to a combination of his flock disagreeing with his teachings and a lack of adequate compensation. Much the same thing happened to Jonathan Edwards in Northampton. Generalizations about the conflict between religious factions can be seen as the sum of a series of such specific disputes between an individual minister and his congregation.
[‡] Hyde, *A Sermon delivered … September 17th, 1804, being the day of the Interment of…Henry W. Dwight, esq.*

the community from a lifetime of church attendance. They were comfortably orthodox and also they were near to hand: a pulpit Bible could be found in every Meeting House, and most families owned one as well.* Bible verses also tend to be short and therefore not too expensive to add to a monument. As a result, you will find something from Psalms, Job, Ecclesiastes, Lamentations, or the Gospels in any of these graveyards.

Here is an early example, from Northampton's Bridge Street Cemetery, of a verse that was popular over many decades, Revelation 14:13:

> Here lies intered the body of
> the Revd. Mr. DANel BREWER,
> the late worthy Pastor of the first Church in Springfield,
> who departed this life on the 5th of Novembr 1733,
> in the 66th year of his age, and
> 40th of his Ministry
>
> *Blessed are the dead that die in the Lord,*
> *they rest from their labours, and their works follow them.*

This verse recurs often in the graveyards I have studied, and it was not limited just to ministers. Here it is a perfect choice to caption the life and works of the worthy the Reverend Brewer.

Most epitaphs that quote Scripture do so word-for-word, as does the Reverend Brewer's. Others show the work of writers who are comfortable adapting a Bible verse and turning it into an original composition. Here is an early example from the Hill Cemetery in Hatfield, on a stone noteworthy for a skull spewing leafy fronds from its teeth, like a medieval Green Man (Figure 2):

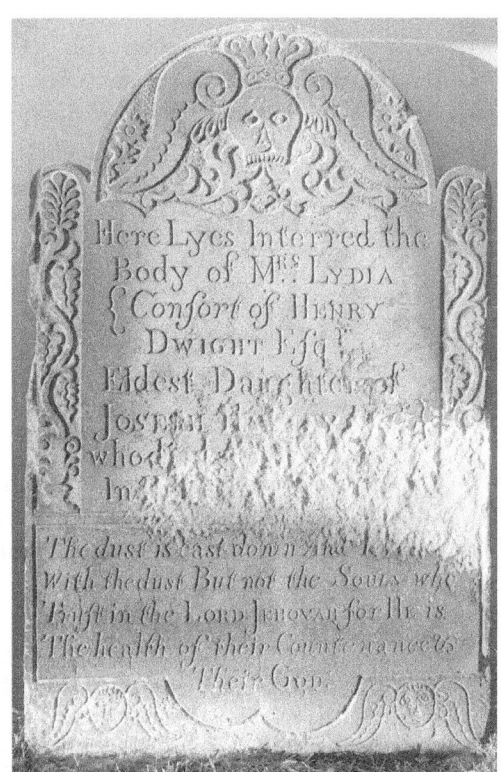

> Here Lyes Interred the
> Body of Mrs. LYDIA
> Consort of HENRY
> DWIGHT Esqr.
> Eldest Daughter of
> Joseph [illegible]
> who died [illegible but footstone
> shows 1748]
>
> *The dust is cast down and levelled*
> *with the dust But not the Souls who*
> *Trust in the LORD JEHOVAH for He is*
> *The health of their Countenance &*
> *Their GOD.*

Figure 2. Lydia Dwight stone (courtesy of American Antiquarian Society).

---

* I have a lovely small Bible, printed in Philadelphia in 1810, 3¼ x 5½ inches, just right for slipping into one's waistcoat or pocket for Sunday services. My antiquarian bookseller friends inform me that early editions of everyday Bibles are scarce nowadays—they were intensely used and many simply wore out over time.

This is a stirring composition. I had not known that Psalms 42 and 43 share the phrase "Why art thou cast down, O my soul? and why art thou disquieted within me? hope thou in God: for I shall yet praise him, who is the health of my countenance, and my God." Someone took these triumphal lines and combined them with the dramatic and (as far as I can tell) original image of one's own dust being thrown down and mingled with the dust of all who have died before.

Hymns and Psalms

The rich language of eighteenth-century hymns and various translations and adaptations of the Psalms provided another common source for epitaphs. Like Scripture, these verses would have been familiar to the deceased, their surviving families, the stone carver, and the minister. They were not used just in church, they were read, memorized, and recited as devotional literature in the home. In most cases we find a single verse of the hymn—not necessarily the most joyful, indeed often the most admonishing. But bear in mind that a single verse would likely have been enough for the devout contemporary reader to recall the whole hymn.

By far the most popular hymnodist I have read in these graveyards is Isaac Watts, who will be discussed in much greater detail in Part II. The earliest use of Watts I have found is "Great God, I own thy sentence just," whose first verse was used three times over fifteen years in the little village of Northfield, beginning with:

> Here lies buried Mrs.
> Anne Field wife of
> Mr. Moses Field
> Who decd Octobr ye 16 1755 in
> Ye 35 year of
> Her age.
>
> *Great God I own*
> *Thy Sentence Just*
> *I yield my Body*
> *To the Dust*

The text as it is carved on these stones might suggest that the faithful deceased is resigning him- or herself to inevitable mortality. But so long as the reader knows the complete hymn, then the message of imminent reunion with the Savior is clearly communicated:

> **Great God, I own thy sentence just,**
> And nature must decay;
> **I yield my body to the dust,**
> To dwell with fellow clay.
>
> Yet faith may triumph o'er the grave,
> And trample on the tombs
> My Jesus, my Redeemer, lives;
> My God, my Savior, comes.
>
> The mighty Conqueror shall appear
> High on a royal seat,
> And death, the last of all his foes,
> Lie vanquished at his feet.

> Though greedy worms devour my skin,
> And gnaw my wasting flesh,
> When God shall build my bones again,
> He clothes them all afresh.
>
> Then shall I see thy lovely face
> With strong immortal eyes;
> And feast upon thy unknown grace
> With pleasure and surprise.

"Yet faith may triumph o'er the grave / And trample on the tombs / My Jesus, my Redeemer, lives"—that is the uplifting message of confident faith we are meant to recall and take with us after reading Anne Fields's epitaph. I love Watts's flowing cadence, effortless rhymes, and vivid imagery, as in the fourth verse. The village kids must have loved singing it, and it was chosen in Hadley for Mrs. Sarah Montague (d. 1798, age 50). A similar Watts verse was chosen for the grave of a venerable church deacon in Lancaster's Old Settlers Burial Ground:

> ERECTED
> in memory of
> Dean. Josiah Ballard,
> who died Aug. 6th,
> 1799,
> in the 78th.
> Year of his age.
>
> *Let worms devour my wasting flesh,*
> *And crumble all my bones to dust.*
> *My God shall raise my frame anew,*
> *at the revival of the just.*

Both these hymns refer to a passage from Job 19: "For I know that my redeemer liveth, and that he shall stand at the latter day upon the earth: And though after my skin worms destroy this body, yet in my flesh shall I see God." The source for the Lancaster verse is the hymn "No, I'll repine at death no more":

> No, I'll repine at death no more,
> But with a cheerful gasp resign
> To the cold dungeon of the grave
> These dying, with'ring limbs of mine.
>
> **Let worms devour my wasting flesh,**
> **And crumble all my bones to dust,**
> **My God shall raise my frame anew**
> **At the revival of the just.**
>
> Break, sacred morning, through the skies,
> Bring that delightful, dreadful day;
> Cut short the hours, dear Lord, and come;
> Thy ling'ring wheels, how long they stay!
>
> …
>
> Haste, then, upon the wings of love,
> Rouse all the pious sleeping clay,
> That we may join in heav'nly joys,
> And sing the triumph of the day.

The appearance of the devouring worms is more than just fealty to the text in Job; the worms serve a dramatic purpose in the structure of the hymn. Re-read both texts and note how the verses of corruption and decay are immediately followed by images of sacred dawns and God's lovely face. This dramatic downward-then-upward contrast demonstrates Watts's consummate compositional skill.

When reading psalms and hymns on gravestones, it is important to know that this was an era of considerable dispute over the role of such texts in church services.* Early Calvinist practice was to recite or sing psalms, not hymns (because only the Word of God was appropriate in the service), with a leader declaiming each line and the congregation repeating it back (due to a lack of literacy and books). By the eighteenth century, literacy and book ownership were more common, and (championed by Isaac Watts) original hymns were coming into use—though not without controversy. The matter of what texts were acceptable to be sung could be a source of conflict between ministers and their congregations. Jonathan Edwards reportedly came home from a preaching trip to discover

> that his congregation had decided (without his input) to sing [hymns] from Watts … and "neglected the Psalms wholly." … Edwards negotiated to allow hymns in the Sunday afternoon services during the summer, while retaining the Psalms for Sunday mornings and other congregational exercises, but this was the first fault line to form between him and his congregation, a rift that would steadily widen until Edwards's dismissal….†

Still, amidst all the disputes, the beautiful rhymes and cadences of these psalms and hymns provided a rich source for expressing the deepest feelings of the people who lived and died in these small towns.

Poetry

Bibles and hymnals are unsurprising sources of epitaph texts. Less expected, perhaps, is poetry. I have found more than a century's worth of English and American poetry chosen for these memorials, from heroic to lyric to Augustan to Romantic to satiric. Some are the work of enduringly famous writers, like William Shakespeare, John Milton, Alexander Pope, Robert Burns, and Samuel Johnson. In fact, one of the unexpected rewards of this project has been encountering these familiar poets in a new and deeply moving context. For example, in Old Hadley Cemetery, a splendid graveyard tucked in among the cornfields on the fertile flatlands hard by the Connecticut River, there is a gravestone inscribed with both a fulsome eulogy and a passage from an elegy by Alexander Pope (1688–1744), a poet famous for his elegantly-rhymed "heroic couplets" (Figure 3):

---

* The study of which hymns and psalms were acceptable and popular at different points in early American religious history is a vast and specialized area of study. A good introduction to this topic is Allan I. Ludwig and David D. Hall, "Aspects of Music, Poetry, Stonecarving, and Death in Early New England," *Puritan Gravestone Art II: The Dublin Seminar for New England Folklife Annual Proceedings* (1978). And even these distinguished authors concede: "The bibliography on hymns and psalms in early America is copious. We can do little more than point the interested reader in the right direction." To which I can only say, "Amen."

† Christopher N. Phillips, *The Hymnal: A Reading History* (Baltimore, MD: Johns Hopkins University Press, 2018)

This monument is erected
in memory of the Hon.
Eleazer Porter, Esq. who for
many years served the Coun
ty of Hampshire in the important Offices of Chief Justice
of the Court of Common Pleas
and Judge of Probate, the
duties of which he performed
with the strictest fidelity.
He died May 27 1797. AE. 69

This modest stone, what few vain
marbles can
May truly say, here lies an honest man:
Calmly he looked on either life, and here
Saw nothing to regret or there to fear.
From nature's temp'rate feast rose satisfyd
Thanked Heaven that he'd liv'd and that
he died.

The source is Pope's *On Mr. Elijah Fenton at Easthamstead, Berks, 1729*:

Figure 3. Eleazer Porter stone (author's collection).

This modest stone, what few vain marbles can,
May truly say, Here lies an Honest Man;
A Poet bless'd beyond the Poet's fate,
Whom Heav'n kept sacred from the proud and great;
Foe to loud Praise, and friend to learned Ease,
Content with Science in the vale of peace.
Calmly he look'd on either life and here
Saw nothing to regret, or there to fear;
From Nature's temp'rate feast rose satisfied,
Thank'd Heav'n that he had lived, and that he died.

This is a fine memorial, and a tribute to Pope's popularity—Porter was clearly a man of considerable standing who merited an expensive gravestone and an extensive epitaph. In the last line Pope (and whoever composed this epitaph) beautifully articulates the perspective that death is a condition the just should welcome.

Other epitaphs originated in the work of poets who were renowned in their time and have since faded into obscurity. In some cases the neglect is justified, but you will meet several others who ought to be more widely read today, including no fewer than five accomplished women: Anna Laetitia Barbauld, Hannah More, Elizabeth Carter, Elizabeth Rowe, and Judith Sargent Murray. Still others were minor poets even in their day, and are entirely, and for the most part justifiably, forgotten today.

Consider this epitaph carved on an impressive table grave in Lanesborough Center Cemetery, by a poet of the somewhat middling rank, Thomas Campbell (Figure 4):

In memory of
Mrs. LAURA BURBANK
wife of
Doctor ASA BURBANK,
who died
November 1st 1811.
Age 25 years.

Cold in the dust this perished heart may lie
But that which warmed it once shall never die,
That spark unburned in its mortal home,
With living light eternal and the same,
Shall beam on Joy's interminable years,
Unveiled by darkness unassuaged by tears.

This is almost a direct quotation from Campbell's *The Pleasures of Hope* (1799). The person who selected this text (perhaps the bereaved widower was a reader of poetry in addition to being a doctor) slightly altered it, or had access to a slightly altered text. The original passage reads:

Figure 4. Laura Burbank stone (author's collection).

> **Cold in the dust this perished heart may lie**
> **But that which warmed it once shall never die,**
> **That spark unburned in its mortal frame,**
> **With living light, eternal, and the same**,
> Shall beam on Joy's interminable years,
> Unveiled by darkness unassuaged by tears.

Campbell (1777–1844) is hardly a canonic writer, though he did produce several stirring patriotic war songs, including *Ye Mariners of England, The Soldier's Dream, Hohenlinden* and in 1801 *The Battle of Mad and Strange Turkish Princes*. Little read today, he nonetheless merited burial in the Poet's Corner of Westminster Abbey. *The Pleasures of Hope* is a book-length poem, didactic and full of references to contemporary political events (the French Revolution, the partition of Poland, the abolition of slavery). Its success was instantaneous, and it was widely anthologized. But Campbell lacked the energy or motivation to follow it up, and his career languished—as it does to this day.

Still, the fact that it appeared in distant Lanesborough a mere dozen years after its publication is a tribute to the appeal its rhetoric and lofty sentiments once held. And for all these writers whose names have faded with time, the fact remains that they were published, read by the souls whose dust lies in these graves, and popular and relevant enough to be carved on their stones.

I also find American poetry chosen for these rural epitaphs, though not as early as English poetry and not nearly as often. I'm not sure why this is the case. Perhaps because the colonies looked to England for "real," proper literature. It may have simply been that there were so many more English writers to read and choose from. The scribbling legions of Grub Street produced a constant stream of occasional poems (written to memorialize or comment upon significant events), odes on the death of the great and good, and elegant formal epitaphs. This was also a great era for compilations and anthologies of English poetry. Whatever the reason, I have still to find such renowned early American poets as Anne Bradstreet, Edward Taylor, and Phillis Wheatley in these graveyards, nor have I been able to source any epitaphs to the many funeral broadsides or sermons published in the era. The American works that do appear are, to a one, obscure today but evidently were distributed and read in their day, at least by some.

The range of poetry these early New Englanders incorporated into their reading habits and epitaph selections is impressive. The number and variety of texts indicate that popular reading at the time was broad and deep, and also demonstrate how thoroughly poetry became acceptable for use on gravestones. These stones are a perpetual record of people using an expanding universe of words to express their emotions on matters literally of life and death.

The Graveyard School

The most unanticipated pleasure of my journey has been encountering the elegant, sometimes sublime, and too-often overlooked work of the Graveyard Poets. This enormously popular school of writers played a significant role in the literary and spiritual life of the late seventeenth and early eighteenth centuries. They composed contemplative, introspective, elegiac poems using several recurring tropes—an evening visit to a graveyard or a crypt, allegorical characters whose names define their (one-dimensional) characters, and observations of natural phenomena (a storm, nightfall, fields and farms)—to illustrate religious lessons in an easy, accessible way.* Their common themes, which fitted perfectly with the prevailing religious sentiment of the day, were the inevitability of death, the uncertainty of its timing, its leveling effect on all rank and privilege, the consequent vanity of our mortal ambitions and pursuits, and the supreme importance of living virtuously in order to secure eternal happiness.

Highly popular in its time, Graveyard poetry is not so widely read today. You might be familiar with Thomas Gray's *Elegy Written in a Country Churchyard* ("the paths of glory lead but to the grave") but few outside the academy read Thomas Parnell, Robert Blair, or Edward Young for pleasure or edification. I concede that at their worst these works can be formulaic and redundant, but at their finest they merit a better reputation. The Graveyard Poets, many of whom were also clerics, created deeply moving and often engrossing expressions of faith, sorrow and hope that gave colonial New Englanders a literature for their devotional reading that went far beyond the standard fare of Calvinist sermons and religious tracts.

Here is one frequently-chosen example, a passage from Edward Young's masterwork *The Complaint, or Night Thoughts on Life, Death and Immortality* (1742), that was used twice in Northampton, once in nearby Deerfield, then farther east in Brookfield, all over a span of thirty years (Figure 5):

> Here lies interr'd
> the Remains of
> Col°. SETH HUNT
> Who died Dec 28th,
> 1779. AEtat 31.
>
> *Why all this toil for triumphs of an hour,*
> *What, tho' we wade in wealth, or soar*
>   *in fame,*
> *Earth's highest station ends in, "Here he lies";*
> *And dust to dust concludes her noblest song.*

The original text (from *Night the Fourth*—the book consists of nine *Nights*) is:

Why all this toil for triumphs of an hour,
What, though we wade in wealth, or soar
    in fame?
Earth's highest station ends in, "Here he
    lies,"
And "Dust to dust" concludes her noblest
    song.

Figure 5. Seth Hunt stone (courtesy of Betsy and Al McKee).

---

* Indeed, in some ways the Graveyard Poets prefigure the Romantics, who used similar observations of nature to reveal even farther-reaching emotional truths.

I hear an echo of Thomas Gray in this passage. And there is great poetic power in Young's swift modulation between our heavy, material wading in a pile of metal coins; then soaring into the heights of fame; and finally back to earth and dust—always with the comforting implication that the deceased has lived nobly.

The works of Young and the other Graveyard Poets became part of the closet devotions of contemporary readers, a meditative pass-time conducted in private to improve one's spiritual condition. Choosing one of these poems, which emphasize the joys of salvation more than the risk of damnation, for the epitaph of a departed loved one shows an attitude towards death in which fearful anticipation has diminished and been replaced by acceptance and even longing.

Recurring but Unattributed

This category consists of epitaphs that appear over and over in these graveyards, across many miles and many years, but for which I cannot determine a particular author or source. These texts were evidently printed, widely distributed, and read by the people that chose these epitaphs. I have pored over many eighteenth-century almanacs, epitaph collections, and anthologies of "quotable" poetry, but nowhere have I found these specific verses.

One representative illustration of the type is "Friends & Physicians." The earliest I have found it chosen is in Lancaster's Old Settlers Burial Ground:

> Memento Mori
> ERECTED
> In Memory of M^r. WILLIAM FIFE,
> Who departed this life, May y^e
> 5th. 1790, in ye 74th
> Year of his Age.
>
> *Friends and physicians could not save,*
> *My mortal body from the grave,*
> *Nor can the grave confine me here,*
> *When Christ shall call me to appear.*

It was frequently chosen in Lee; here is just one noteworthy example, from the Center Cemetery (Figure 6):

> In memory of
> Mr. Jonathan Thach-
> er, son of Mr Jethro &
> Mrs. Hannah Thacher,
> who died at Alford, Dcr
> 14th 1807, of the kick of an
> horse, in the 28 year of his age.
>
> *Friends nor Physicians could not save,*
> *My mortal Body from the grave,*
> *Nor can this clay confine me here,*
> *When Christ shall call me to appear*

The Rev. Alvan Hyde, the conservative minister of Lee's First Congregational Church (a post he held for forty-one years), presided at Jonathan Thacher's funeral.

Note the harsh contrast between the relatively benign verse that a bereaved survivor chose for the unfortunate Jonathan's memorial, and the message of the Reverend Hyde's funeral sermon. Hyde sternly admonishes Thacher's survivors to be grateful to God for the lesson death teaches them:

> Never forget ... the goodness and mercy of God ... to show you so much kindness in your affliction. Now, you have one earthly tie less to attach you to this world. May this great loss ... influence you to meditate on your own departure from this world, more frequently, and with more satisfaction.[*]

In reading these epitaphs I always remind myself that the people who chose them inhabited an entirely different world than mine, and I try to hear these lines with their ears. Nonetheless I find it hard to believe that Jonathan Thacher's mourners found much solace in this message, or rejoiced to have one less loved one attaching them to this world. Surely they found more comfort in this simple quatrain, popular to the point of becoming a cliché, that at least reassured them the deceased had friends, was attended to by physicians who did all they could, died full of confidence in the Resurrection, and will surely rise again.

Figure 6. Jonathan Thacher stone (author's collection).

The identical verse is found over and over, in numerous cemeteries, across many years, with only slight variations. Given the geographic breadth of its occurrences between 1751 and ca. 1850, the verse must have been anthologized and widely distributed for a century—but no trace remains today in print, only in granite and marble.

To me, the epitaphs in this category (and there are many) evoke a vivid scene of writing, printing, distributing, and reading this genre of literature—a literature whose source texts appear to have vanished. I am convinced there once existed some sort of anthology of "verses appropriate for epitaphs" that contained these recurring but unidentified texts. Carvers might have used it as catalogue or sample-book, the minister might have kept a copy in his library for comforting bereaved parishioners, or traveling booksellers may have pedaled it to religious farmwives as material for their private devotions. And yet this is mere speculation on my part. I have not been able to locate such a book. It remains my personal White Whale as a researcher and book collector.

---

[*] Alvan Hyde, *A Sermon, Preached at Lee, Massachusetts, December 20th, 1807: Being the Next Lord's Day After the Interment of Mr. Jonathan Thacher, who Departed this Life December 14th, 1807—Aged 27 Years.*

Bespoke

Some of the most engaging and revealing epitaphs I have collected, the ones that make me think hardest about the people who created these memorials, are verses that do not recur at all and do not rely on any identifiable source text. I call this category "Bespoke" because as far as I can tell these compositions are unique to one individual's grave, the work of a single writer—usually (though not always) unknown. As noted already, many epitaphs consist of Bible verses, psalms or hymns, and poems that were modified by an unknown hand. The verses in this category, in contrast, are entirely (or almost entirely) original. We can only speculate on who composed the text and their relationship to the deceased.

In the Buckminster Cemetery in Barre we find this tender long farewell to a beloved daughter of the Soule family of stone carvers (Figure 7)*:

> Memento Mori
> In Memory of
> Susanna Soule Who was Born at
> Plimpton Feb^{ry} ye 24th 1741
> and Dec^d here Novem^r y^e 3^d 1771
> In the 30th year of her Age ~
>
> *This pleasant Child in Whom We did
> delight
> Lies here in dust Now Buried from our
> Sight.
> Her tunefull Voice that did Delight our ear
> We Now on Earth Shall no more Ever hear
> But Still we hoope and trust she^s gone to
> Sing
> Eternal praise to the Eternal King
> With Holy pious Job then let us Say
> the Lord he gave the Lord he takes away
> Twa^s God who call^d her hence Let us be Still
> and Learn Submission to his Holy Will
> She was with us but now She^s Callrd away
> Her glass was run She must no Longer Stay
> She^s gone She^s gone and never must return
> Untill the Glorious Resurrection Morn.*

Figure 7. Susanna Soule stone (courtesy of American Antiquarian Society).

I have not been able to find any of these lines used elsewhere, so I conclude it is original and bespoke for this grave. It certainly has the ring of a highly personalized message. I am not a genealogist, but it appears Susanna did not marry, and predeceased her parents (she was the child in whom *we* delighted). The emphasis on her tuneful singing is another sign this verse was composed for a specific individual, and the expression of hope that she is now singing in Heaven is quite moving. The reference to Job, the orthodox sentiment that her death was God's will to which we must submit, and the metaphor of the hourglass that has run out, are all familiar. But the mournful repetition of "she's gone, she's gone" is well

---

* As mentioned in the Preface, I have chosen neither to correct the archaic or incorrect spelling, punctuation, and capitalization of these epitaphs, nor do I insert [sic] every time it could be called for.

composed and truly poignant. This is a fine piece of writing and a highly articulate expression of her parents' grief.

Here is another example, a compelling memorial composed for a grave in Monterey's Chestnut Hill Cemetery, a disused but still well-tended little patch of land protected by an old stone wall (Figure 8):

In memory of Mr.
JOHN JONES
who died March 6, 1798
in the 75 year of his age

Poor house of clay oh how it empty lyes
The furnitures removd to Paradise
Angels have hence conveigh'd the sowel mind
Naught but the cabinet is left behind
Oh mind your latter ends deaths sometimes late
But who could e'er his life perpetuate
Be faithful you who Sion's walls do keep
Watchmen themselves must once be laid to sleep.

Figure 8. John Jones stone (author's collection).

The first quatrain is a sustained conceit for the body and soul (house, furniture, cabinetry) that I have not encountered anywhere else. It may not be a Shakespearean sonnet, but the writer must have known them, and demonstrates both wit and craftsmanship in trying to emulate them. I am not certain about "sowel," but I do find that spelling as an old Scottish variant for "soul," which seems roughly to fit.

Then come two lines that remind us a bit of The Classic—not everyone dies young (John Jones is seventy-five, after all) but none of us can control how many days we have. The last two lines are evocative of the Old Testament, echoing (but not quoting) Psalm 127:

> Except the LORD build the house, they labour in vain that build it: except the LORD keep the city, the watchman waketh but in vain;

and also Isaiah 62:

> I have set watchmen upon thy walls, O Jerusalem, which shall never hold their peace day nor night: ye that make mention of the LORD, keep not silence.

This is an altogether impressive literary accomplishment that merits our appreciation of the anonymous writer's skill and range of inspiration.

There are many more examples of such bespoke epitaphs in Part II. Each is a testament to the literacy and literary sensibility of an anonymous author. Some may be closer to folk art than high literature, but they are acts of individual creativity and often indicate a well-read writer. Each also evokes for me the friendship or kinship that must have existed between the writer and the deceased, centuries ago. Never forget, these were two individuals who were once just as alive as you and I are today. They knew the same news, endured or enjoyed the same weather, and lived in the same community; a community now utterly vanished from the earth.

Sudden Death

This very arresting type of epitaph, often bespoke, records sudden or violent death. Here the emotion brought on by the loss of a loved one is too raw, too immediate, to be expressed in a hymn or Bible verse or comforting piece of poetry. The shock of the event is memorialized in stone to make future readers viscerally aware that in the midst of life, death is always just a moment away. Consider this fearful epitaph that appears on a child's gravestone in Ludlow Center Cemetery (Figure 9):

In Memory of Chester
the Son of M^r. Asa & M^{rs}.
Sarah Dodge who Died
Sept^m 11th 1805. Aged 3
years 4 Months & 18 days

*With disentary & with worms
God did Death licence give;
To take away my prescious soul
and say I should not live.*

Figure 9. Chester Dodge stone (courtesy of Betsy and Al McKee).

I have not found another use of this text. It has the ring of hymnody; perhaps it is from a hymn whose later verses praise God's wisdom and assure us that young Chester's soul is in paradise. But try as I might to read this with the sensibility of the grieving Dodge parents, it sounds angry at a God who has personally given permission for Death to kill this child by hideous disease.

In Hampden Old Cemetery, this stone provides two gruesome descriptions of a single death (Figure 10):

In Memory of
Mr. ISAIAH LEACH
aged 30 years
Whose lamentable Death was occasion'd
by rolling a large Log from his
Sled which went directly over him;
He lay alone in this most
distressing situation about an hour
before he was discovered.
This dreadful Catastrophe
happened on Jan^{ry} 31st 1816

Ah hapless man crush'd 'neath the pond'rous load,
Quick from his wounds the crimson torrent flow'd:
Long time he lay prone on the chilling ground,
Ere friends arrived to dress the fatal wound.

This is a compelling composition, telling the same story twice in almost identical terms, first in prose and then in rhyme. The prose version reads like a newspaper item, and it specifies the rolling log as the instrument of the fatal wound. The poetic version is more dramatic, depicting the crimson torrent on the cold ground and introducing the friends who tried to save him. Someone worked long and hard to find the words to memorialize an extraordinary tragedy.

~~~

Figure 10. Isaiah Leach stone (courtesy of Betsy and Al McKee).

Accessing the Texts

So much, for now, for the major categories of epitaphs. Now to get at some questions that arose as my appreciation for this range of sources grew. First of all, how did so many, and such different, texts make it from the pages of books onto tombstones in rural New England? This turns out to be a fascinating thread on which to pull. Scripture, psalms, and hymns are easy to account for—as already mentioned, Bibles and Psalm books and hymnals were widely available and could be found in many homes. Other texts could be obtained through a variety of local sources. Ministers had libraries stocked with the devotional books they had studied at Harvard or Yale, and often owned a wider range of books. In Old Bennington, Vermont, the Rev. Jedidiah Dewey's epitaph includes a passage from Shakespeare; it is easy to suppose that he owned an edition of the Bard's works. In Monterey, the staff of the Bidwell House museum informed me that the Rev. Adonijah Bidwell's library included two books containing texts that appear on epitaphs in Part II: *Elegant Extracts*, edited by Vicesimus Knox and Watt's *Lyric Poems*. In Longmeadow, the 1819 probate records of the Rev. Richard Storrs show that he owned several books whose contents appear in these epitaphs, including Young's *Night Thoughts*, John Logan's *Sermons*, two volumes of Milton, two volumes of Watts, and William Cowper's *The Task*.

There were also lending libraries. At the American Antiquarian Society, I found this delightful description of a colonial woman who inherited her deceased husband's share of the Union Library in Hatfield, Pennsylvania:

Margaret Rees's literary tastes were wide-ranging. She read epic poetry, history, biblical commentary, devotional works, letters, and novels. In August 1764, she borrowed Milton's *Paradise Lost*.... In November, she borrowed Milton's *Paradise Regained*, *Cato's Letters*, and two volumes of Matthew Poole's *Annotations upon the Holy Bible*. After keeping Poole's *Annotations* for over a month, she exchanged it for Alexander Pope's *Works*. In 1765, she borrowed such diverse works as.... Henry Fielding's *Tom Jones* [and] Elizabeth Rowe's *Letters*.... In 1766, she borrowed James Hervey's *Meditations*.... However broad, Margaret Rees's tastes were not unusual. Many American women of the 1760s read similar books. Rowe and Hervey were the two devotional writers most popular among women during the last three decades of the colonial period.*

In addition, many colonial families owned at least a few books of improving and devotional reading, along with their Bible and Psalm or hymn books. Literacy rates were high (though spelling was erratic by today's standards), and if a farming household rose above subsistence living, they were apt to buy books and almanacs, and subscribe to newspapers. Some books were expensive, of course, with illustrations and ornate bindings, but printers also created cheap editions with an eye towards the less affluent market.

Two popular contemporary anthologies of poetry contain many of the verses that appear on these gravestones. *Elegant Extracts*, first published by Vicesimus Knox in 1791 as a companion to a similar volume of prose extracts, was an enormously popular work that went through many editions, and could be found in many households in early New England. Knox (1752–1821) was an Anglican priest, educator, and author of a wide range of essays, novels, sermons, and treatises. Lindley Murray's *The English Reader* (1799) was also widely read and went through many editions. It appears on the shelf-list of at least one early New England personal library. Murray (1745–1826) was a botanist, writer, and distinguished collector of theological and philological books. He designed *The English Reader* specifically to "assist young persons to read with propriety and effect." New England readers may well have found inspiration for an epitaph in the pages of Murray and Knox.

A good friend and regular correspondent whom I met through AGS shared library inventories preserved in probate records and the shelf-lists of several historic houses from the Longmeadow area. The Aaron Colton estate inventory of 1778, I learned, includes several books whose contents appear on local gravestones: a large Bible, Watts's *Psalms* and *Sermons*, and Flavel's *Works* (along with a beaver hat, a powder horn, sheep shears, and various bedsteads and blankets). The shelf-list of the Josiah Day House in West Springfield includes Watt's *Hymns and Spiritual Songs* and two editions of his *Psalms of David*, Lindley Murray's *English Reader*, and works by Hannah More, William Dodd, and Richard Baxter, all writers we will encounter in Part II.

The New England Primer could also be found in many homes and most schools in the region, and many of its words appear in these graveyards. First published in 1687, the *Primer* became an essential text in early New England education. It was part of the spiritual and literary fabric of its time; some two million copies were sold in the

---

* Kevin J. Hayes, *A Colonial Woman's Bookshelf* (Knoxville, TN: The University of Tennessee Press, 1996). We will encounter Milton, Hervey, Pope, and Rowe in Part II. To the extent that Margaret Rees's reading habits were comparable to those of people in rural New England, the overlap of her reading list and their epitaph texts is suggestive.

course of the eighteenth century, and it remained in print well into the 1800s. In its pages, children would learn their alphabet and their religion by reading such edifying lessons and verses as:

> In *Adam's* Fall
> We Sinned all.

or

> I in the Burying Place may see
> Graves Shorter there than I;
> From Death's Arrest no Age is free,
> Young Children too may die;

I have already mentioned that in my judgment there is evidence, though as yet no proof, of another relevant book, an anthology of *Verses Appropriate for Use as Epitaphs* which might have been owned by ministers and stone-carvers. This may never have existed, but it would account for the epitaphs that occur again and again, many miles and many years apart.

As for the distribution of the texts, the decades in which these epitaphs were chosen saw the growth of an extensive network of printers and traveling salesmen hawking broadsides, almanacs, newspapers, agricultural journals and affordable books throughout these towns and villages.* Many of these books were given as gifts. In an early version of direct marketing, the Rev. William Dodd (whom we will meet in Part II) makes this clear in the introduction to his *Meditations*, saying he wrote the book "with a design to be published in a small volume, proper to be given away by well-disposed persons at funerals, or on any other solemn occasion." In at least one recorded instance, his commercial strategy worked: a copy of the Reverend Dodd's *Reflections on Death* is inscribed "This book given to Mrs. Mercy Davis at the funeral of Elizabeth Coburn."† In the same spirit, Watts wrote that children should be given copies of his books as a reward for memorizing and reciting his *Psalms*.

I found another connection between children and these epitaphs, this one completely unanticipated, in the needlework samplers of young girls. A 1921 collection of *American Samplers* by the Massachusetts Society of Colonial Dames of America lists one hundred and fifty samplers containing reflections on death and sorrow stitched between 1713 and 1830. Many of these quote verses by Hervey, Pope, Matthew Prior, James Montgomery, and (always) Watts that also appear in burial grounds—stones and samplers drew from a common body of literature. In the same collection are

---

* I found a wonderful passage explaining why some Calvinist ministers approved of their flock supplementing traditional devotional texts with Graveyard poetry. It also sheds light on this distribution network:

... devotional writers might as well supply poetry which would help bring their readers closer to God. It was better to provide people with religious verse than to let them read the ballads and "filthy songs" which they were used to reading.... Cotton Mather wrote: "I am informed, that the Minds and Manners of many People about the Countrey are much corrupted, by foolish Songs and Ballads, which the Hawkers and Pedlars carry into all parts of the Countrey. By way of Antidote, I would procure poetical Composures full of Piety, and such as may have a Tendency to advance Truth and Goodness, to be published, and scattered into all Corners of the Land."

† Kevin J. Hayes, *A Colonial Woman's Bookshelf*. Hayes also makes the insightful point: "Inscriptions in surviving copies of these works provide key evidence concerning book circulation and its relation to mourning.... Books about how to cope with death, the inscription indicates, often were presented during times of mourning."

verses that could serve quite well as epitaphs, but which I have not found on a gravestone. Consider what this glimpse reveals about the home life and reading of these girls, and imagine young Prudence or Meribah or Esther working hour after hour, carefully absorbing, then sewing, such lessons as:

> *When I am dead and in my grave*
> *And all my bones are rotten,*
> *When this you see, remember me*
> *That I mant be forgotten*
> (1739)
>
> *While God doth spare*
> *For death prepare* (1780)
>
> *When I am dead and worms me eat*
> *here you shall se my name complete*
> (1787)
>
> *Remember maid for die thou must*
> *And all thy glory turn to dust.*
> (1793)

One fascinating window into the relationship between domestic reading and these epitaphs was opened for me by Elizabeth Pope at the American Antiquarian Society. She shared her work on the commonplace book kept by a colonial Rhode Island woman, Mary Hascall, over the years 1732–1767. In this book, a self-sewn sheaf of pages, Mary Hascall wrote down her favorite passages from Watts, Hervey, and Elizabeth Singer Rowe (as well as miscellaneous prayers, psalms, and sermons) to express her feelings on occasion of the deaths of three children and her husband. I do not know if the Hascall graves still stand, or if they have epitaphs. And we do not know whether Mary owned any of these authors' books. But she had access to the texts, she wrote down passages that were meaningful to her, and had them at her fingertips when she needed them.

In the antiquarian collections of the Boston Athenaeum I found another instance of epitaphs in a commonplace book, this time in cosmopolitan Boston. Ephraim Eliot (ca. 1762–1827) was the son of the Rev. Andrew Eliot, pastor of the New North Church in Boston. Ephraim graduated from Harvard College in 1780 and became a doctor. He wrote a book on the physicians of Boston, and also kept an extensive journal-cum-commonplace book. In it, Dr. Eliot transcribed several humorous epitaphs that evidently captured his fancy, including:

A Burlesque epitaph upon Ezekiel Little, said to have been written by John Devotion

> *Beneath this stone Ezekiel Little lies,*
> *Little he was, in everything but size.*
> *His mammoth carcase fills this spacious hole*
> *But in a nutshell sleeps his Little soul.*

An EPITAPH on a remarkable SLEEPER

> *Know though, who dost these hallow'd hillocks tread ---*
> *Here likes John H----, dear lover of his bed,*
> *Who often lull'd in Indolence's lap,*
> *Told the twelve strokes, and yawn'd for t'other nap;*
> *Full forty years on earth resided John,*

> *Yet, strange to tell, ne'er saw the rising sun;*
> *And it most griev'd him as he dying lay ---*
> *To think he'd rise again on judgment day!*

Eliot also copied this more serious epitaph, and added a personal anecdote and reflection upon the text:

> Epitaph on an Infant
>
> *To the dark & silent tomb*
> *Soon I hasten'd from the womb.*
> *Scarce the dawn of life began,*
> *E'er I measured out my span.*
> *I no smiling pleasures knew,*
> *I no gay delights could view;*
> *Joyless sojourner was I*
> *Only born to weep & die.*
>
> *Happy infant!—early blest!*
> *Rest—in peaceful slumber rest!*
> *Early rescued from the cares*
> *Which increase with growing years*
> *No delights are worth thy stay,*
> *Smiling, though they seem, & gay!*
> *All our gaiety is vain*
> *All our laughter ends in pain.*
>
> If this is true, & who can deny it? does it not prove the absurdity of mourning for the dead? especially those who are received to happiness in infancy?—
>
> A few days ago I saw a funeral—or rather two—The circumstances as I heard them were singular—Mrs. Lane had been sick of a fever for three weeks—her mother, advanced in age, did not leave her—Asking the Doctor, one day, how he thought the disease would terminate, she was told, that her daugher could live but a short time. God grant, she exclaimed, that I may go first! A few mornings after—the old lady arose, well as usual, but in a short time was siezed [*sic*] with apoplexy & died—Three hours after her daughter died—was it not a singular mercy?

What a memorable, candid, window into the spirituality of a city doctor around the turn of the eighteenth century. I do not know on which graves these epitaphs appear, if any. Nor can I connect any one book in the libraries mentioned above to any one gravestone. But taking it all together, I am convinced many of the epitaphs collected here were favorite passages saved or memorized by early New Englanders from their religious services or devotional reading or even occasional leisure reading, and stored up against the inevitable occasion of death.

Choosing the Epitaph

Having categorized the texts carved on the stones, and examined the various ways in which these texts were available, let us turn to the question of who chose the epitaph. It is a matter worthy of consideration, even if we are largely confined to speculation. The deceased may have made the choice on some occasions, but not often, I suspect. Death could come quickly and prematurely in these towns. Some tough old citizens who survived their threescore and ten years may have planned their own

Part I—Reading the Gravestones of Early New England

funerals, right down to the design of the gravestone and the choice of epitaph. But I doubt that the young woman who died in childbirth, or the toddler who fell victim to a smallpox epidemic, or the farmer killed by the kick of a horse, had planned ahead and made a personal selection of memorial verse. So it would have fallen to their bereaved survivors, or their minister, or the carver hired to produce the gravestone. I can't say for certain; the contemporary probate records I have studied document the cost of the gravestone and the carving, but not the choosing of the text.

Reflect, in this context, on an epitaph in the Old Cemetery in Bernardston (Figure 11):

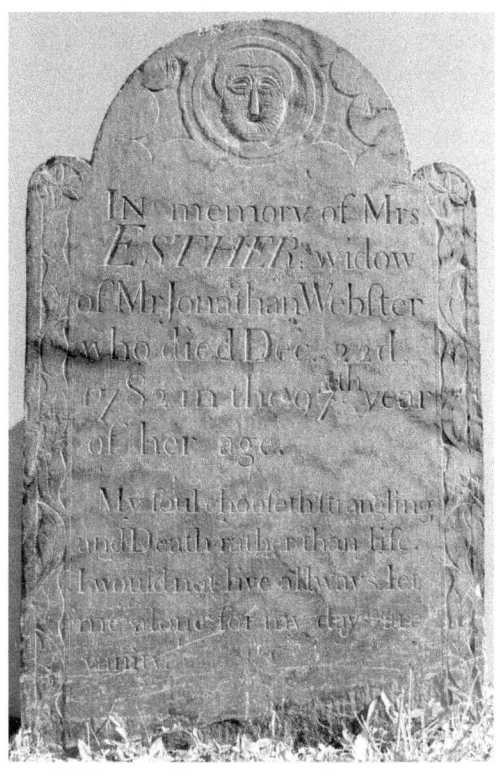

> IN memory of Mrs.
> ESTHER: widow
> of Mr. Jonathan Webster
> who died Dec. 22d,
> 1782 in the 97th year of her age.
>
> *My soul chooseth strangling
> and Death rather than life.
> I would not live allways: let
> me alone for my days are
> vanity.*

The verse is from Job 7; here it is in context:

> 13. When I say, My bed shall comfort me, my couch shall ease my complaint;
> 14. Then thou scarest me with dreams, and terrifiest me through visions:
> 15. So that **my soul chooseth strangling, and death rather than my life.**
> 16. I loathe it; **I would not live alway: let me alone; for my days are vanity**.

This is a startling choice for the epitaph of a ninety-seven-year-old woman. Job 7 is a sustained lament over the futility of life. Are we, the readers, meant to understand that Widow Webster had come to believe her days were vanity, and that she yearned for death? That in her nineties, she had nightmares and was terrified by visions when she thought of the comfort of lying down? Perhaps, but mightn't this be a case of the local minister seizing an opportunity to reiterate a cautionary piece of Calvinist instruction for the edification of old Esther's survivors and neighbors?

Figure 11. Esther Webster stone (courtesy of American Antiquarian Society).

Or consider another selection from Job chosen for the grave of the young son of the local minister in Montague's Old South Cemetery (Figure 12):

> In Memory of
> Mr. Zenas Son
> of the Revd Judah
> & Mrs Mary
> Nash who died
> July 29th 1777 in

ye 10th Year of
his Age.
*Thou Destroyest
the hope of Man.*

The verse is from Job 14, an intense disquisition on the finality of death. Verse 1 famously states "Man that is born of a woman is of few days, and full of trouble," while Verse 10 says that in comparison with a cut tree, that might yet grow back, "man dieth, and wasteth away: yea, man giveth up the ghost, and where is he?" The full text of Verse 19 reads: "The waters wear the stones: thou washest away the things which grow out of the dust of the earth; and thou destroyest the hope of man." This is surely a doleful lesson for a minister to choose for the grave of his own son. I might have expected a warning about the risk of death at any time, or gratitude that the child was spared the sorrows of our mortal world. This does not sound like the choice of a consoled, or consoling, father.

Figure 12. Zenas Nash stone (courtesy of American Antiquarian Society).

This question of who chose the text will arise often in Part II, almost always as a matter of tantalizing uncertainty. But never forget that at some point, a living person chose each and every text in these graveyards. The bereaved survivors must have given it careful thought: To commission a gravestone was in every sense a serious and momentous undertaking. The change from life to eternity was a matter of constant consideration and dreadful import. The epitaph was intended to be read by people who had known the deceased and by unknown future readers. For these reasons, we should consider the question of choosing each time we read an epitaph.

The Timing of the Transaction

Thinking about actual people commissioning these memorials and choosing the texts made me curious about how much time they had to attend to this significant task. How long after the death of the loved one did it take to have a completed, carved tombstone raised? The short answer is that there was usually an interval of several months or even years between death, interment, and the erection of a completed gravestone. Gravestone scholars note that carvers often back-dated their work—few stones were bought and paid for within a year of the inscribed death date, most were paid for after more than two years, and a reasonable percentage could be back-dated up to ten years. There are many contributing factors for this. In the case of a married couple, the first to die might have to wait for the second's death before a joint stone was carved. After a sudden and unexpected death, it took time for a stone to be ordered, the carving completed, and payment made. Finally, the cost of the gravestone and accompanying carving was considerable; the survivors may well have needed time to save up sufficient funds for a proper memorial. In the interim, a simple post or wooden marker would serve as a place-holder.

I first found myself thinking seriously about this interval when reading Solomon Glezen's stone in Stockbridge Cemetery:

> Erected to the Memory
> of SOLOMON GLEZEN
> who, made Prisoner by the
> Insurgents, fell at the Bat-
> tle in Sheffield Feb. 27th
> 1786 in the 26th year of
> his age.
>
> *Oh for a lodge in some vast Wilderness*
> *Some boundless contiguity of Shade*
> *Where rumor of oppression & deceit*
> *Of unsuccessful or successful War,*
> *Might never reach us more.*

We will have more to say about this choice of verse in Part II, but for now take a moment to admire this fine, handsomely-carved stone (Figure 13). The source of Glezen's epitaph, William Cowper's *The Task*, was published in 1785, a short interval in which to have made it across the Atlantic, over the Hoosac range, to be read in Stockbridge. Taking together the quality of the carving and the time required for this text to reach Solomon's friends and family as they searched for the right words with which to mourn his violent death, I infer there must have been a material delay between his death and the completion of the stone.*

I had a similar thought when I encountered this memorable epitaph, fraught with drama and historical interest, in Lancaster's Old Settlers Burial Ground:

> DEO PATRIAE AMICIS
> In Memory of Mr.
> WILLIAM HARRIS
> who fled from ye destruction
> of Charlestown, A.D. 1775,

Figure 13. Solomon Glezen stone (author's collection).

---

* A further piece of evidence was pointed out by an attentive reader and scholar of colonial history: The Battle of Sheffield took place in February 1787, not 1786. Evidently, by the time Glezen's friends got around to raising this memorial, someone had forgotten or mistaken the date of his death. I leave it to the genealogists to fret about how many other such errors are preserved in stone in these graveyards.

> where he was Public School
> Master 11 Years: and came
> to this town, where he died,
> Octr 30th, 1778, aged 34
> Years & 3 months: he left
> behind a Wife & 4 children,
> who raised this stone to perpe
> tuate ye memory of a man
> justly beloved.
>
> *O ye whose cheek ye tear of pity stains*
> *Draw near with pious reverence & attend;*
> *Here lie ye loving Husband's dear remains,*
> *The tender Father, & the generous Friend;*
> *The pitying heart that felt for human woe;*
> *The dauntless heart oppos'd to human pride;*
> *The friend of man to vice alone a foe,*
> *"For e'en his failings lean'd to virtue's side."*

This is an almost word-for-word rendition of *On My Ever-Honored Father,* which the Scottish poet Robert Burns composed on the occasion of his father's death in 1784.

So how did a Burns epitaph written in 1784 seemingly make its way to distant Lancaster, six years earlier, in 1778? With a little imagination we can place ourselves quite close to the widow Harris and her plight. Her husband dies, leaving a relatively young widow with four children. They had moved quickly from Charlestown to Lancaster, away from friends and family, just three years earlier, so she may be short on resources and cannot afford a gravestone right away. With the passage of time, her fortunes improve—perhaps she remarries?—and she can consider paying for a proper memorial to her late husband. And somewhere along the way, she encounters an edition of Burns's poem. It may be ten or more years since William Harris's death, but at long last his widow is able to provide him with a fitting, personalized, enduring monument.

Observe, by the way, the vocabulary of the Harris and Glezen stones; they are "to the memory of" and "in memory of." Certainly these phrases occur all the time in these graveyards, and I had always assumed they implied a proximate (in time) emotion, a natural next step after grief: "Abigail (or whoever) is no longer among us to speak with and enjoy; from now on we must remember her instead." But taking into consideration the interval of time between death and the completion of the inscription, isn't it possible that her memory is already fading, and needs to be recalled—if not among her immediate survivors, then for the wider community? This thought became a conviction when I read this stone in Lanesborough Center Cemetery:

> THIS MONUMENT
> BESPEAKS A TEAR IN
> FULL REMEMBRANCE
> OF THE AMIABLE
> MRS. ABIGAIL
> CONSORT OF CAPT.
> NATH. B. TORRY
> WHO DEPARTED
> THIS LIFE JAN. 22

Part I—Reading the Gravestones of Early New England 35

1789. IN THE 32.
YEAR OF HER AGE.

First of all, this is an exceptionally beautiful piece of carving, with a winged angel holding an hourglass and a trumpet emerging from a flowering plant (perhaps a lily?) that is growing in a handled pot (Figure 14). There is a lot of text, in multiple fonts, all of which indicate that this was a carefully planned and executed commission. Next, consider the statement that "this monument [speaks] in remembrance" of Mrs. Torry. It sounds as though time has passed since her death. This monument, this particular stone, has been commissioned and carved and raised to revive her memory, after an interval, not just to invoke it near the time of her death.

Any remaining doubt became certainty one cold, gray February morning when I read this stone in the Church on the Hill Cemetery in Lenox:

Figure 14. Abigail Torry stone (author's collection).

September 25
AD. 1778 deceasd
JOHN COLLINS
Esq. in the 40 year
of his age.

Here Fraternal Tears have flow'd
Conjugal Affection here has mourn'd
Here Filial Love has heav'd a sigh
Our Father's gone beyond the sky.

This Monument of Fraternal Affection was erected AD 1803 by Mr. Lemuel Collins.

This one stone, at least, was commissioned and carved some quarter-century after the subject died. Apparently John Collins's affectionate surviving brother had the means to provide the unnamed wife and family with a proper memorial for their deceased husband and father.

Across all these graveyards and memorials, I am sure that there was a wide range of intervals between death and the completion of a stone. But clearly, the bereaved often had ample time in which to consult their minister, their stone carver, and their books, in order to choose an epitaph that met their emotional and devotional needs.

The Carvers

I have touched several times on the possible role of the stone carver in creating these epitaphs. Let me take a moment to provide a little background on these interesting craftsmen before we immerse ourselves in their work. The lives and styles of early stone carvers are topics of much specialized study, intimately entwined with that of the evolution of gravestone iconography. Beginning with Harriette Merrifield Forbes's groundbreaking book *Early New England Gravestones and the Men Who Made Them*, several outstanding books have been written about carvers from eastern Massachusetts, Rhode Island, and Connecticut. In 1966, Allan Ludwig published *Graven Images*, a superb and seminal study of early New England gravestone iconography that provides considerable information regarding carvers. Since the 1970s, largely in the pages of *Markers* (the annual journal of the Association forGravestone Studies), a robust body of scholarship has developed regarding the carvers of the Connecticut River valley and the hill towns to the west. In the pages of these illuminating articles, full of insightful commentary on carving styles and painstaking reviews of probate records and newspaper advertisements, a vibrant world of craft and commerce comes to life. The development of the carving industry was tightly linked to the economic development of a region (fast-growing towns provided more customers, while more isolated villages were less attractive markets) and also to improvements in transportation (once high-quality stone could be shipped from distant quarries, carvers were less reliant on whatever local material was at hand and the quality of their product improved). Networks of like-minded carvers, sometimes collaborating, sometimes competing, shared innovations in style and technique to satisfy and shape the tastes of their customers—like painters in quattrocento Italy or Golden Age Amsterdam, if on a somewhat different scale.*

It is difficult to generalize about even this relatively small population of craftsmen. They were as individual as you and I, after all, though they shared a common trade. But let me try to paint a picture of the industry at the time. For one thing, gravestone-cutting was not necessarily a full-time trade. Probate records and family genealogies show that these carvers also worked as masons, builders, and joiners; one was a blacksmith, another a coffin-maker. Like most everyone at the time, from the minister to the inn-keeper to the doctor and lawyer, they also did some farming in order to supplement their incomes.

Some of the carvers were itinerant craftsmen who moved around in search of business—their telltale designs and dates allow scholars to track their peregrinations pretty accurately. There were also journeymen, skilled carvers who did not care to go into business on their own but hired themselves out to more established shops. These established businesses were often a family enterprise, sometimes running to multiple generations. Their owners stayed in one area and did work in many surrounding towns. Carvers had to own specialized and therefore valuable tools like stone hammers, adzes, gouges, writing chisels, compasses, and rubbers for smoothing stone slabs. These feature prominently in their probate records (along with the occasional inventory of uncarved gravestones). Above all, I came to appreciate that

---

* Some carvers resembled these artists in the irregularity of their personal lives, too. James Wilder of Lancaster fathered eight children by his wife and another by a distant cousin, who sued him for child support and won. Samuel Dwight made his name in Vermont but was originally from Connecticut and briefly attended Yale, until he skipped town, abandoning his first wife. Nancy Jean Melin, "Samuel Dwight: Vermont Gravestone Cutter" in *Markers IV: The Journal of the Association for Gravestone Studies; David Watters, Editor* (Lanham, MD and London; University Press of America, 1987); Laurel Gabel and Theodore Chase, "James Wilder of Lancaster, MA"; *ibid*.

it was a competitive business. There was always the risk of someone with new styles or new sources of stone coming along to sway customers' tastes and disrupt the local market.

Fortified with all this excellent research, I tried to identify any linkages between carvers and the epitaphs they carved. Are there, I wondered, discernible patterns of epitaph and carver? For example, if a carver owned an anthology of epitaphs and was in a position to suggest its verses as samples to his customers, I would expect to see certain "house stock" epitaphs repeated frequently on the stones he produced. On the other hand, if epitaph choices were primarily made by the bereaved survivors or their ministers, and the carver was thus largely an order-taker, I would expect to see few repetitions within a carver's body of work, and little overlap with other craftsmen (limited to random chance in the case of Scripture and hymns, and the influence of anthologies in the case of poetry).

I began by examining account books from two carving shops: John Stevens in Newport, Rhode Island; and Ithamar Spauldin in Concord, Massachusetts. The Stevens book is especially suggestive. I first read it at the American Antiquarian Society, in a beautiful over-sized facsimile edition published by the Preservation Society of Newport County. This unique document contains columns of long-hand revenue and expenses for the shop, notes on the weather, occasional poetry, and also several epitaphs. Two are Isaac Watts poems (not hymns), another is by the poet Elizabeth Rowe, the others appear to be bespoke. Three of these bespoke epitaphs include names: "An Epotaph [sic] on Doctor Frankland Morton," "An Epotaph on Edward Wanton," and "An Epotaph on Mr. Wm. Sanford." Two of these—Morton and Sandford—appear as written on local gravestones (though with Stevens's erratic spelling corrected). I cannot tell if Stevens was the author, or if he was taking down an order. I have not been able to match his Watts and Rowe entries to actual graves.[*]

I read the Ithamar Spauldin account book in the cozy confines of the Special Collections room at the Concord Public Library. In a neat eighteenth-century hand, Spauldin, a working stone-mason for whom carving tombstones was just one part of his business, meticulously records his daily and weekly jobs: laying bricks for Josh Jones, building a wall for Steven Minot's mill-dam, re-building chimneys for the Buttricks, repairing the school-house, building a hearth for Peter Wheeler and an oven for Asa Heywood. He also records his trips to the quarry in Harvard where he got his slabs for gravestones. Often, the day's entry is simply "In ye shop all day"—presumably carving.[†]

Spauldin's book contains a mother-lode of information for scholars of gravestones. His records confirm the often significant lag between death and the completion of the commission that we just discussed. He documents his costs of raw materials and cartage. He also matter-of-factly notes the prices he charges his

---

[*] The Stevens shop, by the way, is very much a going concern as a carving business, working on everything from gravestones to public monuments. I was recently in correspondence with the current proprietor to ask if he could shed any further light on the relationship between the carvers, the customers, and the choice of epitaph in the eighteenth century. Regrettably he could not—but did make clear that today the customer provides him with the desired text.

[†] He also earned money by trading in lumber and occasionally renting his horse to townspeople wanting to ride to Boston. He was not above taking a well-earned break; the phrase "did but little in the afternoon" appears from time to time.

customers for a completed gravestone—from $2 to $14, with many about $7. He also notes that he charges an extra 16 cents per line for "poetry." But he is maddeningly (for my purposes) silent on what that poetry is, and where it came from. None of the verses he carved are listed. He added a tidy catalogue of the books he owned, and while they reflect an impressive taste in literature (including Sterne's *Tristram Shandy*, Chesterfield's *Principles of Politeness*, *The Authentic Key to Masonry*, Paine's *Age of Reason*, *Female Policy Detected*, Johnson's *Dictionary*, and a cookbook, among others), there is not a single volume that would have enabled him to suggest an epitaph verse for a customer. I conclude that in the case of Ithamar Spauldin, the carver was an order-taker of his customers' choices for gravestone "poetry."

In contrast, I was thrilled to stumble across an article in an 1907 trade journal, *The Monumental New*s, about an eighteenth-century hand-written commonplace book of epitaphs owned by an English carver:

> Mr. Frank Watts, a monument dealer of London, sends us an interesting and unique old book of hand-written epitaphs, that was used several generations ago in the business now conducted by Mr. Watts before epitaph books began to be printed. It is an historic old volume, faded and ragged with age, and contains some of the originals of the quaint old English epitaphs, many of which have been copied all over the world and may occasionally be seen in the old cemeteries in this country.

The book contained versions of The Classic, a Pope epitaph, and a range of verses not found in New England. How I yearn to find an equivalent manuscript in the archives of a New England carver!*

Dissatisfied with the fragmentary and inconclusive evidence of these first-hand accounts, I determined to use the Farber Collection of gravestone images (which, as mentioned above, is marvelously searchable), to analyze hundreds of epitaphs carved by identified stone cutters, starting with the most prolific carvers whose work appears in western New England.† This is not a perfect methodology, I admit. The Farber Collection does not necessarily capture all the works of an individual carver, and my AGS correspondents inform me that the Farber attributions are not always accurate. Recent research has added a much greater degree of precision to the stories of the carvers.

With those caveats, for now I can only sigh and say that I cannot reach a definitive conclusion. The evidence points to "all of the above." Each carver's body of work includes examples of The Classic, hymnody, poetry, recurring-but-unattributed, and bespoke. To my surprise, several of the carvers do not appear to have used scripture. But *every*one has something by Watts. Several carvers feature a dozen different Watts passages (some used just once, others recurring two or three times). Yet only a small handful of Watts quotations are common across different carvers. For the most part, they or their customers seem to have had their own favorites.

A range of poets appear. Young and Pope are used by several of the carvers, but no single Young and Pope quotation is used by two different carvers. Other poets appear only once, including Hervey, Rowe, Baxter, Samuel Crossman (*Hope in Death*), Joseph

---

* The AGS research on the probate records of carvers provides a wealth of information about their tools and personal effects, but nothing about any books they owned.

† The carvers examined include Elijah Sikes, Ebenezer Drake, Ebenezer Janes, James Stanclift, John Dwight, John Ely, Nathaniel Phelps, Roger Booth, one known as "Drinkwater's Swift River Carver," and the Soule and Stebbins families.

Addison (*Rosamond*),* Judith Sargent Murray (*Elegiack Lines*), as well as Virgil and Horace. I am left with the unsatisfyingly vague impression that these carvers were conversant with a common body of works by Watts, Young, and Pope and might choose their own favorites to recommend. In addition, it appears that epitaph texts were often provided to the carvers by their customers, who themselves demonstrated a variety of personal preferences gleaned from a (roughly) shared pool of writers and books.

Each carver also makes use of recurring-but-unattributed epitaphs, enough to support, but not prove, my conviction that there was an anthology containing these verses. But the choices from this category vary widely from carver to carver, and some make extensive use of them while for other shops they are just one-offs.

A few of the most prolific carvers do repeat texts that are unique to them, suggesting (though again not proving) they had their own "house stock." For example, while Ebenezer Janes made frequent use of common recurring-but-attributed epitaphs, The Classic, and a dozen common Isaac Watts verses, there is one verse that appears on his stones four times between 1790 and 1792, for both men and women (I will use the "she/her" version here), that does not appear elsewhere; it appears to be unique to Janes's shop:

> *She's gone and left this mortal Stage*
> *Tho while in life adorn'd Her Age*
> *She patiently Resign'd Her breath,*
> *And now Her body sleeps in Death.*
> *Her Soul is gone we hope and trust*
> *To be with Christ among the blest*
> *To see His face forever nigh*
> *And sing His Praise Eternally.*

Whether Janes composed it, or whether it originated with one customer and others admired it, I cannot say.

Similarly, the Stebbins family stones display a little of everything, with many recurring-but-unattributed verses, a rich variety of passages from Scripture, and several different poets. As with Janes, there also are verses that the Stebbins shop carved more than once that do not appear anywhere else:

> *Stones round us teach*
> *ye living all must die*
> *O die to sin*
> *or die eternally*

and

> *Ye living men see here*
> *your end,*
> *To Jesus voice pray*
> *now attend;*
> *Your days your years*
> *how swift they fly.*
> *Beware be wise prepare to die.*

---

* I had never heard of this work by the famous and prolific essayist. I learned that Addison wrote the libretto to *Rosamond*, an opera so spectacularly bad that it essentially killed the art form in England. The fault, I gather, lies more in the music than in Addison's words. Still, it makes for an unusual and unexpected choice of epitaph text.

So again, these may have been unique to the Stebbins shop. I like the message that the stones have a lesson to teach us, and also the rhythm of "Beware, be wise." Whoever composed this had some literary skill.

Finally, here is one more example from the hand of John Ely that appears twice on his stones, and nowhere else:

> *A coffin, sheet & grave's*
> *my earthly store:*
> *Tis all I want: & Kings*
> *will have no more.*

This is a well-constructed, compact lesson, well worth our contemplative consideration.

I will continue to explore this subject, but I expect no, or few, "Eureka" moments. Rather—and this is no bad thing—I anticipate the evidence will keep pointing to a busy world of craftsmen and bereaved customers working with a wide but shared range of source texts to choose the words that express deeply felt emotions, and to create monuments that record these in perpetuity.

The Religious Context

I hope that all this information and informed speculation on the sourcing, choosing, and carving of these epitaphs will enhance the reader's appreciation of the verses themselves in Part II. Before we proceed, however, there are two fundamental aspects of the religious context of the time that are worth keeping in mind. First, as mentioned earlier in the context of The Classic, these gravestones were carved during an era of tremendous upheaval in New England religious life, indeed of open warfare among New England's ministers. Starting around 1740, a wave of itinerant evangelical preachers began traveling across rural New England. Their popular preaching exacerbated long-simmering tensions between "Old Light" and "New Light" ministers. Volumes have been written about these conflicts, to which I cannot do full justice here. One scholar described the essential distinction between the two camps thus:

> [The Old Light] intellectualist tradition ... emphasized the "understanding" and strict clerical control over congregations... [The New Light] tradition ... emphasized the "affections" and favored more active lay involvement in church affairs. For four generations these rival impulses had coexisted in the colonial pulpit, but under the press of the new revivals they separated into opposite and irreconcilable positions.[*]

Old Light ministers denounced the New Lights from their pulpits, and vice versa. Whole communities separated from their churches and formed new congregations. One scholar makes a point that informs our appreciation of these epitaph

---

[*] Harry S. Stout, *The New England Soul: Preaching and Religious Culture in Colonial New England* (New York and Oxford: Oxford University Press, 1986). Interested readers can also consult Richard D. Birdsall, *Berkshire County: A Cultural History* (New Haven, CT: Yale University Press, 1959); David D. Hall, *Worlds of Wonder, Days of Judgment: Popular Religious Belief in Early New England* (New York: Alfred A. Knopf, 1989); David E. Stannard, *The Puritan Way of Death: A Study in Religion, Culture, and Social Change* (New York and Oxford: Oxford University Press, 1979); and Douglas L. Winiarski, *Darkness Falls on the Land of Light: Experiencing Religious Awakenings in Eighteenth-Century New England* (Williamsburg, VA: Omohundro Institute of Early American History and Culture, 2017).

choices, arguing that "the real winners in the debates ... were neither the Old Light nor the New Light ministers but the laity. As censures grew and separations proliferated, ministers on both sides learned that ... their strength did not lie in the formal sanctity of their office ... [but] on the trust and voluntary support of their congregations." Ludwig makes a related point in *Graven Images*. Regarding the increased use of symbols on gravestones, he writes: "[When the Puritans] came to bury their wives and husbands and children, they could not be satisfied with the colorless doctrines their ministers intoned at the grave. Their love could not be reduced to the cold incision of a name on a boulder..." As with decoration, so too with epitaphs. As the struggle between Old and New Light beliefs raged, these gravestones show ordinary people empowered to choose personally meaningful expressions for their bereavement from a range of sources that ranged well beyond Bibles, psalters, and hymn books.

A second point to remember as you read these verses is the deeply conflicted attitude of New England Puritans and their Congregationalist descendants towards the prospect of death. As one scholar argues, "[T]he Puritans were gripped individually and collectively by an intense and unremitting fear of death, while simultaneously clinging to the traditional Christian rhetoric of viewing death as a release and relief for the earth-bound soul."* These contrasting attitudes are clearly revealed—for eternity—in the verses selected for carving onto their gravestones. "[T]he shift ... from fearful anticipation to eager longing for death ... runs through virtually all the available materials on death and dying during this period, from poetry to sermons, from journals to Sepulchral art...," and also the epitaphs collected here.

Consider a pair of contemporaneous epitaphs (and you can find many other examples in Part II). First, this passage from a John Wesley hymn was chosen in a little family plot in Hancock. See how it positively celebrates death as welcome improvement over our sorry mortal condition (with an allusion to Paul's *Epistle to the Romans*, Chapter 7):

> In memory of
> REUBEN ELY
> who died July 18th
> 182*
> in his 74th (?) year
>
> *His earth is afflicted no more*
> *With sickness or shaken with pain*
> *The war in the members is o'er*
> *And never shall vex him again*

Yet not thirty miles away, in Lee's Center Cemetery, the pure unvarnished version of The Classic was still in use well into the 1830s:

> SALLY
> wife of
> Edward Prichard
> died
> July 8, 1836; in the
> 37. year of her age.

---

* David E. Stannard, *The Puritan Way of Death*

> *Stop travler as you pass by*
> *As you are now so once was I*
> *As I am now soon you shall be*
> *Prepare yourselves to follow me.*

Over and over these gravestones reveal the competing and contrasting attitudes of the Congregationalist descendants of the early Calvinists. Some eagerly anticipate eternal happiness; others are still rooted in a lifetime of sermons on humankind's depravity and the likelihood of imminent damnation. Both are clearly expressed and carved for eternity on these gravestones.

~~~

To conclude this discursive introduction to the contemplative pleasures of reading these epitaphs, let me emphasize that as much as I enjoy uncovering the source texts and speculating about how they got there, I am always mindful of the fact that every single epitaph was chosen on an occasion of utmost gravity and importance, the death of a beloved individual person. Selecting the words for a gravestone was a profound and personal decision, in effect the commissioning of an original work of art (whether consciously or not, and quite likely the only work of art they ever commissioned). Do not think I idealize these people—no doubt some of these gravestones were carved for misers or drunkards, hard masters or unfaithful spouses, spiteful neighbors or impious wretches, then as now. But in most cases, tears were shed on the very spot where we stand today and read. And in *every* case these words were meant to be read. We owe the deceased, their survivors, and the carver the respect of taking each text seriously and considering how it was intended to be understood by townspeople, friends, family—and passersby like us.

For example, go ahead and permit yourself the pleasure of reading aloud this memorial from Lancaster's Old Settlers Burial Ground:

> In Memory of Mrs.
> Rebekah ye wife of Mr.
> Philimon Houghton,
> Who died Febry. ye 15th,
> AD: 1766, AEtatis 26.
>
> *Now sleeps, God rest her Soul;*
> *A virtuous wife Her hapless Husband's*
> *only Pride in Life.*
> *Triumphant mount where*
> *Happy Plannets role, And open Paradise to her*
> *Immortal Soul*

I have not been able to source these lines. The "happy planets roll" phrase is familiar from hymnody, and someday I may find a hymn that provides a basis for this epitaph. It may also be an original composition—there is something a little awkward in the scansion, and a bit unpolished in its shift from an exhortation to the departed Rebekah ("triumphant mount"), then to some unnamed angel ("open Paradise to her") within a single sentence. But no matter; we don't need deep textual analysis to hear the sincere, articulate, mournful voice of a husband who deeply loved a real woman named Rebekah Houghton who died too soon.

We can appreciate the same individuality and emotional immediacy in this infant's memorial in the New Hebron, Connecticut, Cemetery (Figure 15):

> Here lies enter'd
> the Remains of an
> Infant, daugher of
> Leonard E. & Betsey
> Lathrop who died
> Feby. 6th AD. 1795
> Aged three days.
>
> *so goes the Comedy of
> Life away, The curtain
> falls too soon, & Death
> concludes the Play.*

This is a startling choice for a newborn's grave. Consider the difference between the vocabulary here—the Comedy of Life, the falling curtain—and the blunt language of *The New England Primer*, which was still in use in 1795. And notice the absence of any orthodox Christian comfort in the resurrection, nor warning to prepare for eternity. Instead we are presented with an altogether secular metaphor in an almost fatalistic tone. This one leaves me wondering who composed it, and who chose to send this message, in perpetuity, from this little grave.

Figure 15. Lathrop Infant stone (courtesy of Betsy and Al McKee).

Reflect, too, how over time the epitaphs reveal a steady opening of possibilities for expressing attitudes towards the essential matters of death, the afterlife, love, and grief. Here are two epitaphs, composed some thirty-six years apart. The first is from the Colchester, Connecticut, Burying Ground:

> [Illegible]
> died Jany 22
> 1762 in ye 48
> Year of his age
>
> *Death ye Great
> Tirant Conquers
> all ye Race of Man
> Sense Adams Fall*

This is a fearful little couplet in the pure Calvinist vein, its simple language providing an unyielding reminder that we are categorically depraved, cursed by Adam to be born in a state of sin. Compare that choice of epitaph to this in Granby's West Cemetery a generation later (Figure 16):

In Memory of M^r. Noah
Ferry. Who Died Nov^r, 4th
1798. Aged 86

===

Experience, His Wife
Died Novr, 4th 1794
Aged 84 years.

===

Behold and see [illegible] *wonder here*
This Coupel liv.^d Near sixty Years
In wedlock band^s now yeald to Death.
Eighty odd year^s from their birth.

Here is a glass where You may see
From Death arrest no age is free:
Let each one read that passeth by
the Longest Liver must surely Die.

This is a lovely piece of work, an affectionate tribute to a couple who were married for sixty years and died four years apart, on the same day of the year. Close reading only deepens our appreciation. The first line may well have been taken from John Dowland's song, *Behold a Wonder Here*. Dowland (1562–1626) was a celebrated Renaissance musician and composer, whose works continue to

Figure 16. Noah and Experience Ferry stone (courtesy of American Antiquarian Society).

be played and adapted today. This is as close to a pure love poem as I have seen used anywhere in these graveyards:

Behold a wonder here —
Love hath receiv'd his sight,
Which many hundred years
Hath not beheld the light.

Such beams infused be
By Cynthia in his eyes,
At first have made him see
And then have made him wise.

Love now no more will weep
For them that laugh the while,
Nor wake for them that sleep,
Nor sigh for them that smile.

So pow'rful is the beauty
That Love doth now behold,
As love is turn'd to duty
That's neither blind nor bold.

Thus beauty shows her might
To be of double kind,
In giving Love his sight
And striking Folly blind.

The next three lines sound like the work of a family member or close friend. They could be the sentiments of the widowed Noah, in the few years after his wife's death, as he pondered the imminence of his own.

Mind you, there is still the familiar cautionary message from The Classic. The second quatrain opens with a riveting conceit: the gravestone (on which you are reading this message) is a mirror in which we see our own inevitable death. This is a significant enhancement to the usual first line of The Classic. We are no longer mere readers, being hailed as strangers passing by. Now we are peering into a mirror—and see Death peering back at us. This is the only time I have encountered these lines; they are a tribute to the imagination and creativity of an anonymous writer working among the gentle hills and fields of Granby.

That creativity continues into the next line, where again the standard formula of The Classic is enriched, in this case with a line from *The New England Primer*. The irony here, which was surely recognized by whoever made use of the line, is that the original verse was written as a lesson for children about early death. On the Ferry gravestone, however, the lesson is inverted: although death *may* come at any moment, even to the young, this couple lived well into their eighties. Yet we still must not take too much comfort, for they too had to die eventually.*

Finally, compare the tone and emotion of the Ferry epitaph to the message that Reverend Alvan Hyde of Lee preached in his 1804 sermon. Addressing the "afflicted friends" of a husband and father who died at age forty-eight, Hyde tells them:

> Long have you been warned to prepare for the scene, which is now opened to you, under the righteous providence of God.... It has pleased God to make many widows in the world, and to deprive many children of kind and affectionate parents.... God has taken away the head of your family; but the trial has been accompanied with peculiar mercies. You had opportunity to see your dear companion satisfied with living, and apparently rejoicing that he was in the hands of God. The world, in his view, had lost its importance.... But, the God in whom you profess to believe has done perfectly right.... He has brought you under his mighty hand, and he alone can support and comfort you. If, in his great mercy, he should see fit to do this, he will give you a sight of your own ill desert and his justice—he will give you submission;—and what better thing could he do for you?†

With no disrespect to the Reverend Hyde's beliefs or his authority, I think most bereaved spouses can derive more comfort from the Ferrys' verse than his sermon. Their epitaph teaches submission, but it does not make any attempt to give the reader a sight of her or his ill desert. Those eight short lines marvelously encapsulate the age's flux in attitudes towards death, weaving together multiple source texts to re-phrase the stern old Classic message with more allusive and poetic diction, and adding to it a very human expression of the virtues of married love.

We can read here evidence in stone of the passing of the old Calvinist rules. Ordinary people are choosing personal expressions for their bereavement from an expanding range of sources. It was not a sudden change; as we have already seen,

---

* I won't go so far to as claim that the author of this epitaph was consciously borrowing from Marcus Aurelius (II.14 "The longest-lived and the shortest-lived man, when they come to die, lose one and the same thing")—but given his or her potential familiarity with Dowland, the *Primer*, The Classic, and other poetic imagery, I would not rule it out.

† Hyde, *A Sermon delivered ... September 17th, 1804, being the day of the Interment of...Henry W. Dwight, esq.*

dramatically different attitudes overlapped for years. But over time we can observe change taking hold in these communities. Just as the iconography on the stones shifted slowly from Death's heads and coffins to soul effigies and willows weeping over urns, so too epitaph texts evolved from rigid Calvinist exhortations to prepare for death and avoid the imminent danger of damnation (expressed using a fairly narrow range of Scripture verses, hymns, and warning texts), to a richer set of options including poetry and original composition—enabled by the increased availability of books.

These were not, on the whole, especially famous or gifted or consequential people. Yet they found memorable words to express their feelings of faith, sorrow, and hope. The cumulative record of their choices, carved on these gravestones, comprises a profound body of literature that we do well to explore and appreciate.

Part II

Categories of Epitaphs

For each category, the reader is referred back to Part I for a short overall introduction.

Within each category, the examples are given in roughly chronological order of the date of death. My aim is to provide the reader with a sense how certain themes and sources evolved or overlapped over time, with a category and between categories.

The Classic

You will likely find this text in any early graveyard you care to visit, usually more than once in each graveyard, and often with slight variations. It is the cornerstone of any collection of typical New England epitaphs. The verse is so recognizable and so ubiquitous that Robert Frost incorporated it into one of his poems, *In a Disused Graveyard*. One perfect example, carved in simple block letters, is in New Marlborough's Old Center Cemetery—a fascinating graveyard, still in use, lying along a dirt road a short way from the center of the old village. The oldest portion consists of two impossibly steep little hillocks that must have challenged early sextons and mourners:

HEAR LIES THE
BODY OF M^r.
ELI FREEMAN
WHO DIED DECEMBr
THE 5TH AD 1760 IN
THE 38TH YEAR
OF HIS AGE

Behold And See
As You Pass By
As You Are Now
So Once Was I
As I am Now
So You Must Be
Therefore PrePare
To Follow Me

As mentioned in Part I, nothing could be more central to the lessons these gravestones teach than this often-repeated call to prepare, and its nuanced variations. A friend who studies the work of stone carvers in central New England shared this positively ominous variation from the New Hebron, Connecticut, Cemetery (Figure 17):

Figure 17. Ebenezer Haughton stone (courtesy of Betsy and Al McKee).

In Memory of Mr. Ebe-
nezer Haughton. ye 3rd. Son
of Mr. Ebenezer Haughton
y^e 2nd. & Mrs. Temperance
his wife, who died
May 15th 1788. In the
25th Year of his Age.

Step in and See as you pass by
As you are now so once was I
As I am now soon you must be
Prepare for death and Follow me.

That invitation from the dead to "step in" is dreadful.

Here is a very early and very stark warning in the Longmeadow Cemetery, presented as a message from a child (Figure 18):

Here Lyes
The Body of
Mr^s. Elizabeth keep
Who died the 29
day of July anno
1720 in the 12 year
of her age [H?]*ear you*
young so Am i
Ther
fore al prepare to die
The finest flesh is but dust—
Prepare,—for follow me you must.

Figure 18. Elizabeth Keep stone (courtesy of Betsy and Al McKee).

Obviously this verse was not created by poor twelve-year-old Elizabeth.* These words were put in her mouth by someone else as a lesson to the living. It might have been the minister, to judge by their tone—these are words of someone accustomed to deference on matters of religion. Indeed, the first line commands the attention of young readers in particular.

Note that it uses the present tense—you are young and so *[a]m* I—not the more common past tense ("as you are now, so once *was* I"). Where The Classic addresses itself to a single passing reader, this epitaph calls to al[l] young readers to prepare to die. These elements reveal a local author taking a core text and adapting it to convey a personalized message in response to the untimely death of Elizabeth Keep.

The message is no less compelling on the grave of one who lived to old age, as seen here in the old Center Cemetery (now called Fairmont Cemetery) in Lee:

---

* Note that young Elizabeth was presumably not married. At the time, "Mrs." could be used as an abbreviation "Mistress," or young woman, as well as for our current usage referring to a married woman.

> In memory of Mrs. Elisa-
> beth Jenkins Consort of
> Mr. Ebenezer Jenkins (late of
> Barnstable deceased) who died
> Octr 28th 1788 aged 91 years
>
> *Behold my friends while passing by*
> *This stone informs you where I lie*
> *Tho I have lived to ninty one*
> *Yet you may die while you are young*

I can hear old Mrs. Jenkins's voice warning us that she may have lived a long time, but only by the grace of God—she could just as easily have died young, and so might we.

Here is another example from the venerable Center Cemetery in Northfield:

> Here lies intered
> The body of Mr
> Ebenezer Field
> Who departed
> this life April
> 9th 1759
> Aged 42 years
>
> *Come Mortal man*
> *And cast an eye*
> *Come read thy doom*
> *Prepare to* Die

There is notable literary skill at work here, if on a limited scale. There is a solemn weight to the voice that summons us as readers to "Come.... Cast.... Come." Each line calls upon the reader to respond, and the force of the command grows with each line: "Come here, look, read, prepare for *death* (italicized by the stone carver for emphasis)." This little quatrain pulls us in and does not release us.

In contrast, a comparable text in the Old Deerfield Burial Ground does provide a release, if only temporary. Here we are called to consider the grave then told to "go thy way."

> Samuel Bordwell
> 1771 in the 86th Year of his Age.
>
> *Come hither Mortals, cast an eye*
> *Then go thy way, prepare to Die,*
> *Here read thy Doom*
> *For Die thou must,*
> *One Day like me be turn'd to dust.*

The deceased is on to us; he knows that, left to our own devices, we would go on our way and return to our hurrying business once we have paid our respects. But we are admonished not to forget what we read here. No matter how afield we travel, we must prepare ourselves to one day meet the fate here foretold.

A husband and wife buried in the Northfield Center Cemetery, who died sixteen years apart, display another pair of creative, revealing variations. The first is The Classic plain and simple; the latter is more consciously poetical:

In Memory of
Hepsibath Belding
wife to Lieu^t
Jonathan Belding She died
Decembr the 29 1761
in the 66 year
of her age

Reader behold as you pass by
As you are living so once was I
As I am now so you must be
Prepare for death & follow me

And then:

In Memory of
Lieu Jonathan Belding
Decd January ye 6 1778
in the 83 year of his age

Reader behold and shed a tear
Think on the dust that slumbers here
And when you read the State of me
Think on the glass that runs for thee

Do you hear how much richer the imagery of the verse has become over sixteen years, with the reader's tear, the slumbering dust, the running hourglass? These embellishments do not so much soften the message as incorporate a more poetic style and sensibility.

In Lancaster's Old Settlers Burial Ground there is a long, embroidered variant in the same vein:

In Memory of Mrs.
Martha Wilder, Wife of
Mr. Gardner Wilder, who
died March ye 7th, ADomi.
1764, Aged 27 years

My Loveing friends, as you pass by,
On my cold Grave but cast your Eye;
Your Sun like mine may set at Noon,
Your Soul be call'd for Very soon;
In this dark Place you'll quickly be;
Prepare for death & Follow me.

This same verse is also to be found in East Bridgewater, Canton, Attleborough, and Brattleboro, Vermont. So here we see the work of an enterprising original writer who re-cast The Classic to express its core message with deliberately poetic touches: the loving friend, the cold grave, the metaphor of the sun setting at noon, the darkness of the place we are bound for. This poet's whose work was evidently popular enough to be reproduced and distributed throughout New England.

I admire the composition of this short version from the Bow Wow Cemetery in Sheffield.* Note how the choppy scansion reinforces the blunt message, which in turn

---

* The cemetery derives its odd name from the adjacent road. I have no idea whence the road derives *its* name—a notorious stray dog, perhaps?

is highlighted on the stone by a little pointing hand or manicule that the carver included for emphasis and, perhaps, as a demonstration of his skill. The whole stone is truly a fully-integrated work of art (Figure 19):

In Memory of.
Mrs Anner. Wife
of Mr John Olds
Died Sept^r: 30th
1777: in the: 44th
Year of her Age.

This is my Cry.
Prepare to Die:
If you Don^t hear
There's cause to fear.

The following epitaph from the Westfield Old Burying Ground is a complex composition. It begins with the timeless theme that Death is the great shared destiny of all men, regardless of station in life. The next four lines are a lovely bit of hopeful

Figure 19. Anner Olds stone (author's collection).

poetry which I have not seen elsewhere. But the final coda that brings us sharply back to the unsoftened message of The Classic:

In Memory of
ELISHA PARKS Esqr
who died April 11th, 1778
in the 54th Year
of his Age.

The Great, the Good, the Wise, the Just
must all in time be turned to Dust.
Then learn to quite terrestrial Ties,
that you may soar above ye skies,
& there enjoy the blissful Favour
Of Jesus Christ our Lord & Saviour

Halt *passenger—Observe*
the contents: regard the date:
& Promise not on tomorrow.

The bold-faced **Halt** is the carver's. These last lines are written in an entirely different voice from the opening verse, as if a second speaker is addressing us. I hear an echo of Proverbs 27:1—"Boast not thyself of tomorrow; for thou knowest not what a day may bring forth." All in all, this is the work of a skilled writer.

Another remarkably developed articulation of The Classic is in the Forest Hill Cemetery in East Derry, New Hampshire:

Momento Mori

ERECTED
In memory of
M^r. Robert Gilmore
who Departed this Life
Sept. 3rd AD 1782
In the 85th year
of his age.

Death steady to his purpose from ye womb,
Pursues till we are driven to ye tomb.
O, reader wisely lay this thought to heart,
And seek an interest in ye better part.
Then when you close in death your mortal eyes,
Your soul may rise and reign above ye skies.

I am struck by the power of the opening couplet, with the image of Death already in steady pursuit of us even as we enter this world. Not relentless, not furtive, just steady and purposeful.

This gravestone from the East Randolph, Vermont, Cemetery provides an idiosyncratic, almost didactic version:

In Memory of Samuel
J. York, Son of Mr.
Joseph and Elce York
Who by the Kick of
a Horse died Novr. 13th
1795 In the 14th year
of his age

The fate of me, it argues fair,
That you should all for death prepare.

I love the rational, almost detached tone of "it argues fair." At the same time the message of "prepare to die" is poignantly enforced by the age of the deceased and the circumstance of his death. This is not great poetry, but it contains a few simple touches that lend resonance to the couplet. First, the use of the first person voice—an obvious dramatic construct, since poor Samuel did not compose this himself, having died suddenly from the kick of a horse. The words were written for him by parents or a minister or someone near the funeral process. But the device works and holds our attention. Admire, too, the nice balance of "me" in the first line with the anonymous "you" of the second line. This message is not for "friends," not a specific "reader," but all of us, whoever we may be, for ages to come.

I read another interesting variation chosen for a grave in the Congregational Church Cemetery in Brandon, Vermont:

in MEMORY of
Mr. Solomon Hinds.
who died. April 28
1798 aged 28 years
& 17 days.

All you who read with little care,
And go away & leave me here.

54　　　　　　　　　Part II—Categories of Epitaphs

> *Should not forget that you must die*
> *and be intom.d as well as I*

Pause and re-read this slowly, to hear the author's distinctive voice. Note how the first couplet does not command the reader to behold. On the contrary, it somewhat bitterly recognizes that we as readers are just glancing with a minimum of attention, as we pass by. In a similar vein, the second couplet is not a confident command to prepare, but an almost regretful imprecation not to forget. I can almost see the author shaking his head ruefully.

At about the same time, a chilling version was chosen three times in Amherst West Cemetery (Hannah Kellogg, d. 1812; Sarah Cowls, d. 1814; and Elizabeth Cooke, d. 1819). All three texts are identical; this strongly suggests a single carver, who had a copy of this epitaph in some sort of commonplace book or sample book to which he returned several times:

> *My children dear, this place draw near*
> *A mother's grave you see,*
> *Not long ago I was with you,*
> *And soon you'll bee with me.*

Here the deceased mother forgoes the instruction to prepare for death, but it is pretty clearly implied. Not many mothers today would choose an epitaph that invites her children to come close to her grave and consider their imminent death. Though mind you, this message was composed in an age of frequent death and open coffins.

This version is in Hadley, where the voice of the deceased strongly admonishes the reader. It also contains a good amount of pertinent biographical information.

> Rev. Jonathan Smith,
> Was settled in the ministry in
> Chilmark, Martha's Vineyard, Jan. 23, 1788
> Was dismissed by his desire on account of ill health,
> Sept. 4th, 1827,
> And died in Hadley, his native place,
> April 14, 1829, AE 31[*]
>
> *Reader, pause at this stone,*
> *Know that thou art mortal,*
> *And raise now one penitential*
> *Cry for Mercy in thy dying hour.*

The late minister's command that the reader raise a cry for mercy is deeply affecting. I have found no source and no other uses of this verse, suggesting a local, individual author. In this instance, I suppose the Reverend Smith might plausibly have composed his own epitaph: Knowing himself to be in failing health, perhaps he composed this "sermon" so it could be preached in perpetuity to congregations of future readers.

What does the enduring relevance of this theme, in its pure form and its many

---

[*] A keen-eyed reader observed that these dates make no sense: If the Reverend Smith died in 1829 at the age of 31, then he was born in 1798, a decade after got his pulpit on the Vineyard. But this is what my source (Bridgman) tells me. Until I get to Hadley myself to inspect the stone, I will posit that Bridgman made an error and Smith's age at death was 61; born in 1768, and ordained at the age of 20. Such are the travails of one who must often rely on secondary sources!

variations, tell us about the people who selected these epitaphs? Clearly the message was of urgent importance to them, and they wanted the reader to respond. I believe the reason The Classic remained so relevant for so long is that it resonated deeply with the ways many of these people experienced life, death, and religion. As mentioned in Part I, life was self-evidently precarious and the need to prepare one's soul was paramount. The Classic conveys this message simply, clearly and memorably. Of course other contemporaneous epitaph choices reflect other attitudes towards what Hyde called "the great and interesting scene of exchanging worlds." Not every grave exhorts us with the warning of The Classic. But when it *was* chosen, its meaning was recognized and understood.

Scripture

As mentioned in Part I, The Bible is a common and unsurprising source of epitaph texts in these burial grounds. For example, Revelation 14:13 was especially popular over many decades. In the Monterey Woods Cemetery an almost illegible stone has the verse more fully rendered:

> [Sacred?]
> to the memory of
> ISAAC GARFIELD
> who died ? 22d
> 1792
> in the 7 [illegible] Year
> of his Age
>
> *Blessed are the dead which die*
> *in the Lord from henceforth: Yea,*
> *saith the Spirit, that they may rest*
> *from their labours; and*
> *their works do follow them.*

The same verse was used in the Longmeadow Cemetery on a stone carver's grave:

> In Memory of
> Mr. ELIIAH BURT
> who died
> April 5 1820 in the
> 78th year of his age.
>
> *Blessed are the dead which*
> *die in the Lord that they*
> *may rest from their labours*
> *and their works do follow them.*

What an apt choice: the carver can rest from his labors beneath an enduring example of his life's work. The same verse was chosen in a tiny family plot in Hancock as late as the 1860s:

> Sarah Sweet
> Born Feb. 25.
> 1779;
> Died April 28
> 1860

Scripture

*Blessed are the dead which
die in the Lord from henceforth
Yea, saith the Spirit, that they
may rest from the labours:
their works do follow them.*

Is this not an altogether perfect verse for a Congregationalist epitaph? It affirms that the worthy are at rest after the struggles of life, and will be blessed in the hereafter. The survivors are comforted, and the reader is informed, that the deceased did good works, died in the Lord, and is surely blessed. As I read this popular epitaphic Scripture, I do not hear smugness, but rather an encouraging message to the reader to strive for so satisfactory a parting message for themselves.

In Palmer Center Cemetery, a very different text was chosen (Figure 20):

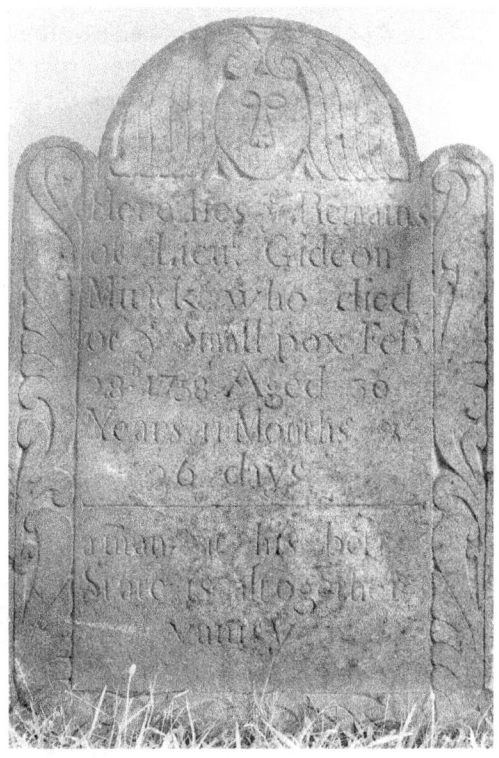

Here lies y^e Remains
of Lieu^t. Gideon
Mirick who died
of y^e Small pox Feb
28th 1758 Aged 30
Years 11 Months &
26 days

*a man at his best
State is altogether
vanity.*

To our modern ears this is not a particularly consoling message, but to Gideon Mirick's survivors I believe it represented an appropriately pious reminder of the vanity of earthly concerns when measured against the awesome prospect of eternity. Any contemporary reader would have recognized the source immediately, Psalm 39:5: "Behold, thou hast made my days as an handbreadth; and mine age is as nothing before thee: verily every man at his best state is altogether vanity. Selah."

Figure 20. Gideon Mirick stone (courtesy of American Antiquarian Society).

In Amherst West Cemetery, the grave of Mrs. Mary Dickinson (1763, age 63) has a similar message of respectful resignation from Job 9:12:

*Behold he taketh away
Who can hinder him
Who will say unto him
What dost thou*

The theme of taking away occurs again even more forcefully in Longmeadow Cemetery:

> In Memory of
> Mrs. ABIGAIL
> wife of
> Mr. THOMAS HALE
> who died
> March 28th 1773;
> in the 64. year
> of her age.
>
> *Lover and friend hast*
> *thou put far from me,*
> *and mine acquaintance*
> *into darkness.*

This is a direct quotation of Psalm 88, a song of grievous supplication. This sounds like a very personal choice of verse by the bereaved widower Thomas.

On a more comforting note, Proverbs 10:7 appears many times in many locations; this example from Northampton can stand for dozens of others:

> In Memory of
> Captⁿ Roger Clap
> who died Jan 9
> Anno Dom 1762
>
> *The Memory of the Just is blessed*

Like the choice of Revelation 14:13, this short line informs the reader that the late Captain Clap was among the Just, expresses his survivors' warm memories as well as their confidence that he is blessed, and gently encourages the reader (all of us) to live among the just, that we too might die among the blessed.

In Ludlow Center Cemetery, Proverbs 27:1 was chosen for the grave of a young wife:

> In memory of
> Mrs. Anna ye wife
> of Mr. John Sikes
> who died June 9
> 1772 in ye 23rd Year of her Age
>
> *Bost not thyself*
> *of tomorrow for*
> *thou knowest not*
> *what a day may*
> *bring forth.*

This is an entirely different and less comforting message for the reader. The warning not to boast of, or put one's faith in, living to see tomorrow recurs often among these stones. Recall that we also heard the same verse on the Elisha Parks stone. Over and over, these stones record the contemporaneous contrasts in attitudes towards life and the afterlife—contentment, resignation, or fear.

In Old Hadley Cemetery there is a sumptuously-carved memorial with an affectionate testimonial to a woman twice married to ministers, capped by a highly appropriate verse from Proverbs (Figure 21):

Here rests SARAH, wife of y^e
Rev:^{d} S. HOPKINS. & relict of y^e
Rev:^{d} C. WILLIAMS; an Exem=
plary Christian, pleasant &
lovely in her Life, & lament=
ed in her Death. She left {to
go & be with CHRIST,} a sorrow=
ful Husband & 14 Children
Feb^r. 5th AD 1774. AE 48.

*Favour is deceitful, & Beauty is
vain: but a Woman that feareth
the Lord, she shall be praised.*

This is a direct quotation from Proverbs 31:30 and expresses the Reverend Hopkins's professional devotion and, I think, his admiration and respect for his late wife. For our part, we can only commend her exemplary life, and marvel at her fortitude in producing fourteen surviving children in her forty-eight years.

In Lancaster's Old Settlers Burial Ground we find a verse from Job that appears several times in these graveyards:

Figure 21. Sarah Hopkins stone (courtesy of American Antiquarian Society).

Here lies interred
the Body of Mrs.
LUCY FAIRBANK,
ye wife of Deacn.
CYRUS FAIRBANK
who died Sept. ye 16th.
1776, Aged 36
Years & 8 Days.
Likewise Ephraim, Son of the
Deceas'd, still born, Sept. ye 1st, 1776
The Small and Great are here.

Let us pause and consider this brief epitaph carefully. The text is from Job 3, the harrowing Scripture passage in which Job curses the day he was born. For context, let me quote at moderate length:

13. Why died I not from the womb? why did I not give up the ghost when I came out of the belly?
14. Why did the knees prevent me? or why the breasts that I should suck?
15. For now should I have lain still and been quiet, I should have slept: then had I been at rest,
16. With kings and counselors of the earth, which built desolate places for themselves;
17. Or with princes that had gold, who filled their houses with silver:
18. Or as an hidden untimely birth I had not been; as infants which never saw light.
19. There the wicked cease from troubling; and there the weary be at rest.
20. There the prisoners rest together; they hear not the voice of the oppressor.
21. **The small and great are there**; and the servant is free from his master.

22. Wherefore is light given to him that is in misery, and life unto the bitter in soul;
23. Which long for death, but it cometh not; and dig for it more than for hid treasures;
24. Which rejoice exceedingly, and are glad, when they can find the grave?

Given the circumstances of Lucy Fairbanks's death, this is an exquisitely meaningful choice of epitaph. This six-word memorial is a play on words: Job is talking about Death leveling the mighty (or great) and the ordinary (or small),* but here the phrase also links the small (stillborn infant) and the large (adult mother), buried together. And reflect that we hear Job wishing he had been stillborn himself—even as we stand over the grave of a stillborn child and the mother who must have suffered terribly for two weeks. Something of real drama is invoked here.

Another memorial in Longmeadow conveys a different and very challenging sentiment from Job 17:14:

In Memory of
Lieu^t. WILLIAM
STEBBINS
Who died Oc^t. 30,th
1776
In the 84th year
of his age.

I have said to Corruption, thou art
my Father: to the worm, thou art
my Mother, and my sister.

This is one of the more challenging chapters in Job. Earlier, the text tells us: "I cannot find one wise man among you. My days are past, my purposes are broken off.... If I wait, the grave is mine house: I have made my bed in the darkness." And the next verse asks: "And where is now mine hope? as for my hope, who shall see it?" This choice of epitaph suggests an octogenarian's deliberate pulling away from friends and the pleasures of this life, in determined preparation for death.

A verse from Job 7 was chosen in several towns, including Deerfield (John Hawks, died 1778), Colrain (Esther Bell, died 1782), and Springfield:

In Memory of
Capt. SAMUEL BURT
who was born September 25, 1724.
& Departed this Life
May 2d 1786 in ye 62d
Year of his Age.

Job VII Chap. 8 & 10, verses
The Eye of him that
hath seen me
Shall see me no more;
thine Eyes are upon me.
and I am Not.
He shall Return no
more to his House,
Neither shall his place
Know him any more.

---

* This is a conceit we will encounter again among the Graveyard Poets.

Someone felt strongly about choosing this particular text for Captain Burt's memorial. The carved citation is precise, the Scripture is reproduced with no changes, and sense of loss is palpable in the language of departure and disappearance.

The Beatitudes (Matthew 5:8 and 5:9) were chosen for the gravestones of a husband and wife in Lancaster's Old Settlers Burial Ground:

> MRS KATHARINE SPRAGUE,
> the amiable Consort of ye
> Honble JOHN SPRAGUE, Esqr.
> And a daughter of the late
> RICHARD FOSTER, Esqr,
> Died May 5th AD. 1787.
> in the 49th. year of her age,
> And is here interred.
>
> *Blessed are the pure in Heart,*
> *for they shall see God.*
>
> The Remains
> of the
> Hon'ble John Sprague, Esqr.
> Chief Justice of the Court
> of Common Pleas for the
> County or Worcester,
> who deceased Sept. 28, AD. 1800,
> AEtatis 61,
> are here deposited.
>
> *Blessed are the peace-makers, for they*
> *shall be called the children of God.*

These two examples can stand for dozens of other quotations from the Beatitudes. There is the same sense of comforting (but not arrogant) confidence that the deceased were worthy, and are blessed, that we heard in the early selection from Revelation, and a similar gentle reminder of how we ought to live.

A grave in Wilbraham's Adams Cemetery has this lovely verse from Proverbs:

> IN Memory of
> Mrs. Elisabeth wife
> of Mr. Abel BLISS
> who died March 8th
> AD: 1788. in the 44th
> year of her age.
>
> *Prov. 31, 26. she*
> *openeth her mouth*
> *with wisdom;*
> *and in her tongue*
> *is the law of*
> *kindness.*

Note that here the source is specifically cited as part of the epitaph text. This is uncommon, but you see it from time to time. I like to think Abel Bliss selected this verse himself; I have no evidence, of course, but the choice conveys a personal sense of affection and admiration.

In Sheffield's Bow Wow Cemetery there stands a beautiful white marble double-head stone with a short bleak verse from Genesis 47:9 (Figure 22):

> In memory of Roger
> Ashley. who died Dec^r.
> 10 1795 in the 21 year
> of his age.
>
> In memory of Samuel
> Ashley who died April
> 17. 1790 in the 12 year
> of his age.
>
> *Few and evil were our days.*

Figure 22. Ashley brothers stone (author's collection).

This is the only grave I have found that uses this verse, or any other from Genesis. The Biblical context sheds an interesting light on the choice of epitaph. Joseph, as Governor of Egypt, presents his father Jacob to Pharaoh. Pharaoh asks Jacob his age, and the old man replies: "The days of the years of my pilgrimage *are* one hundred and thirty years; **few and evil have been the days** of the years of my life…." It is strange to read the lifespans of a young man and a boy compared to an old man of one hundred and thirty years. Yet even old Jacob reckons his days have been few and evil compared to the length of his pilgrimage, and perhaps to eternity.

This striking epitaph in Worthington Center Cemetery combines an apparently bespoke description of a fatal accident with a profoundly resonant passage from Matthew (24:44), in which Jesus admonishes His disciples—and all of us—to be prepared at any hour for His judgment:

> Sacred
> To the memory of
> GAIUS ROWE,
> who departed this life,
> Octr 17th 1820,
> in the 32nd year of his age.
>
> *Blooming in health until the*
> *tub it fell, & ended his days*
> *within the fatal well.*
>
> *Be ye also ready, for in such an*
> *hour, as ye think not, the Son of*
> *man cometh.*

Given the suddenness of Rowe's death (struck on the head and drowned in a well) this could be evidence of a collaboration between a minister or stone carver who had an apt lesson from the Gospels at his fingertips appropriate for this unexpected tragedy, and a bereaved friend or family member capable of composing a simple verse for the occasion.

The most extended Bible verse I have found is in South Lee Cemetery, a combination of John 14 and John 11:

> MRS MERIBAH BROWN,
> wife of Mr. Horatio Brown,
> died July 18, 1822 in
> the 42 year of her age.
>
> *Jesus said unto her, I am the*
> *resurrection and the life; he*
> *that believeth in me, though*
> *he were dead, yet shall he live*
> *And whosoever liveth, and*
> *believeth in me, shall never*
> *die. Believest thou this? she*
> *saieth unto him, yea, Lord: I*
> *believe, And when she had*
> *so said: she went her way*

This is a lot of carving for a verse that most readers would have recognized from just the first line or two. The combining of verses from two different chapters suggests a discrete "editor" who knew his Scripture and set himself the task of composing a personalized message—the surviving husband, perhaps? He must have deeply admired his late wife's faith, and was willing and able to pay for a substantial amount of stonework.

And sure enough, seven years later we find Meribah's widower's epitaph also using a passage from John. It is surely possible that Horatio Brown composed his wife's memorial text, and also had his own ready when needed:

> IN
> Memory of
> HORATIO BROWN,
> who died
> May 10, 1829,
> AE. 49 Y's.
>
> *Jesus saieth unto him I am the way*
> *the truth, & the life; he that believeth*
> *my works, & believeth on him that sent*
> *me hath eternal life; then Jesus turned*
> *& saw him following him, &, saith whom*
> *seek ye? he saith unto him rabbi, which is*
> *to say master, where dwellest thou.*

Not surprisingly, Matthew 19:14 is a commonly-used text for children, as here in Lee:

> ISAAC G.
> son of widow
> Clarria Anderson
> DIED
> Nov. 20 1841:
> aged 8 years
> 1 mon & 21 d's.

*Suffer little children,
to come unto me, and
forbid them not, for
of such is the kingdom
of Heaven.*

Also in Lee Center Cemetery we find this singular Bible verse:

> ELIJAH
> son of
> Silas & Sophia
> Garfield,
> DIED
> Nov. 29, 1842,
> AE 20½ Y's.
>
> *Is it nothing to you, all ye that pass by?*

The full text is Lamentations 1:12. The short text would presumably have called to the minds of contemporary readers this expression of terrible grief:

> Is it nothing to you, all ye that pass by? Behold, and see if there be any sorrow like unto my sorrow, which is done unto me, wherewith the Lord hath afflicted me in the day of his fierce anger.

Why this bleak, almost plaintive message? And again, who selected this text? I find it hard to imagine a minister recommending this message, especially in 1842, by which time epitaphs typically tended to more sentimental assurances of rest and resurrection. It strikes me this is the choice of a profoundly bereaved, indeed angry, parent.

All these epitaphs quote more or less directly from Scripture, but others are the work of writers comfortable adapting a Bible verse and turning it into an original composition. Here is an example in Longmeadow Cemetery:

> In Memory of
> Mr.
> THOMAS HALE
> who died May 9th
> 1750 In His
> 78th year.
>
> *The Age of Man
> Is but A Span
> His days on Earth A few
> At Death he must
> Embrace the dust
> And bid this World Adieu*

Whoever composed it apparently had a few Bible verses in mind, including Psalm 39:5 which we have already encountered ("Behold, thou hast made my days as an handbreadth") and Job 14:5 ("Seeing his days are determined, the number of his months are with thee, thou hast appointed his bounds that he cannot pass"). There may be yet another source of inspiration for this verse, a line by Francis Bacon (1561–1626) from his poem *The Life of Man*: "The world's a bubble, and the life of man less than a span."

On initial reading, the regular scansion and meter of the verse sound nicely "polished," more like something composed for a "collection of original epitaphs" than the work of a local writer. But I discovered the identical verse in Enfield, Connecticut, on the gravestone of Samuel Hale (d. 1774, aged 76). Father and son, perhaps? The ages would be about right. Or at least relatives? And if so, it is plausible that Thomas's epitaph was composed locally, and that Samuel knew it and liked it well enough to use it twenty-four years later. All in the family, I suppose. Whatever the case, these little instances that combine genealogy with the creation, distribution, and carving of texts are among the constant delights of my work.

Here is a combination of Bible verses that recurs often in Lancaster, but I have not found elsewhere—evidently a local favorite text:

> Here lies interred ye
> Body of Mr.
> JOSIAH LOCKE,
> who died May ye 16
> A.D. 1769, AEtats. 33.
>
> *Every man at his best*
> *State; is altogether Vanity*
> *Cease ye from Man, whose*
> *Breath is in his Nostrils; and*
> *trust in ye EVER LIVING GOD*

The identical verse was used for John Carter in 1766, Ephraim Wilder in 1770, and Josiah Wilder in 1788, all in Lancaster. Some unknown hand stitched it together from two or three scripture verses. The first two lines are, yet again, Psalm 39:5. It is probable that a contemporary reader, more deeply versed in Scripture than most people are today, would recall verse 4 of the same Psalm, highly appropriate in a graveyard: "LORD, make me to know mine end, and the measure of my days, what it is; that I may know how frail I am." The next phrase is from Isaiah 2:22: "Cease ye from man, whose breath is in his nostrils: for wherein is he to be accounted of?." The final call to trust in God could come from any number of Scriptures, including I Timothy 4:10: "For therefore we both labour and suffer reproach, because we trust in the living God, who is the Saviour of all men, specially of those that believe." Clearly this is the creative hand of a local writer well-read in the Scriptures, and not afraid to improvise with (not to say improve upon) them.

A short, arresting text based on Exodus is found several times, first in Hatfield's Hill Cemetery, on a stone with intricate geometric designs (Figure 23):

> In Memory of Capt.
> Seth Dwight, who died
> June 9th 1774, in the 6^{-th}
> year of his age.
>
> *Decaying mortals here's the place*
> *The house destin'd for Adams race*
> *Be ready then to meet the Lamb*
> *of God, the Judge, the Great I AM*

The identical text was chosen over the hills in Lanesborough several times. The verse evokes—but does not directly quote—Exodus 3:14: "And God said unto Moses, I Am That I Am: and he said, Thus shalt thou say unto the children of Israel, I Am hath sent me unto you." I admire how the author also incorporated a reference to the Lamb, a rather sophisticated integration of Old and New Testaments. The presence of this verse in Hatfield and Lanesborough proves it was published and distributed in some form, now lost.

This grave in New Marlborough's Old Center Cemetery features a Psalm with a slight but noteworthy variation:

Figure 23. Seth Dwight stone (courtesy of American Antiquarian Society).

> Sacred to the Memory
> of Mr. Joseph Strong
> late of New Marlborough
> deceased, who departed
> this life Dec. 9 AD. 1786;
> in the 35,
> year of his age.
>
> *Man cometh forth like a*
> *flower, in the morning he*
> *groweth up and flourisheth;*
> *at noon he is cut down*
> *& withered.*

This text is based on Psalm 90, quite a popular choice in these graveyards:

3. Thou turnest man to destruction; and sayest, Return, ye children of men.
4. For a thousand years in thy sight are but as yesterday when it is past, and as a watch in the night.
5. Thou carriest them away as with a flood; they are as a sleep: **in the morning they are like grass which groweth up.**
6. **In the morning it flourisheth, and groweth up; in the evening it is cut down, and withereth.**
7. For we are consumed by thine anger, and by thy wrath are we troubled.
8. thou hast set our iniquities before thee, our secret sins in the light of thy countenance.

See how the language has been re-worked to emphasize that Joseph Strong died in what should have been the noon of his life—not the evening. It is also worth noting again that contemporary readers would have been expected to know the whole Psalm; carving these few lines was enough to provide a perpetual reminder that death doesn't just happen, it is the result of God's righteous wrath at our iniquities.

Here is another adaptation of the same Psalm that recurs widely, in this case in Lancaster's Old Settlers Burial Ground:

> ERECTED
> In Memory of
> Mr John Prescott,
> who departed this life,
> April 1st: 1791:
> In the 79th: year
> of his age.

*Death like an overflowing flood,
Doth sweep us all away:
The young, the old, the middle aged
To death becomes a prey.*

This is another example of someone taking creative license with the word of God and modifying it to fashion a personalized expression of mourning. At some point an anonymous author penned this version and published it in a volume that was accessible to people choosing epitaph verses all across Colonial and Federal New England.

The Book of Common Prayer was the source for an epitaph in the Norton or Old East graveyard in Otis. I must say a word about the site, which is noteworthy in every regard. Picture a hillside clearing of maybe an acre, off a dirt road, cut into a forest, with mossy turf underfoot and tall pines growing up among (and in some cases out of) the graves, the whole belted around with an old stone wall in excellent repair. I have never seen so many foot-stones still in place, aligned with their headstones. In most other graveyards, the footstones have long since been buried or broken or carted away by caretakers looking to ease the task of mowing. Footstones were clearly a pronounced community preference out here, for several generations, and their state of preservation is amazing. There are also a couple dozen stumps of old stones scattered around like so many rotten teeth, their inscriptions long gone. Some of the graveyard enclosure is entirely empty; I assume many stones have vanished altogether, leaving scores of early graves un-marked, and the departed settlers whose dust lies in them entirely forgotten.

Here is an impressive white marble monument, its two inscriptions, for wife and husband, still perfectly clear after two and a quarter centuries (except the last word of the last line; Figure 24):

In Memory
of Mrs. Sarah Lawton
consort of Mr. Joshua Lawton
who departed this life
April 17th 1785
AE 31

*Though the cold grave is my place
To the sinner fain would I speak
And warn him of his woful case
Unless his sins he doth forsake*

Also in memory of said Joshua who died on his passage from N. orleans to N. York July 6th 1795 AE 48.

*When earth & sea give up their dead
In Christ the Lord we hope to* [wed?]

What an interesting memorial. Sarah's epitaph is a fascinating variant of The Classic. It may well be an original composition; the meter is very forced, especially in the first two lines (try reading them aloud—they are clunky). The syntax is complicated;

Figure 24. Sarah & Joshua Lawton stone (author's collection).

the verse purports to be her voice telling us, the reader, that she would gladly warn a sinner of his (not "your," thank you very much) need for repentance. Or perhaps the author just means to catch the eye of any passing reader who happens to be a sinner—of which, no doubt, there have been many over the years.

Looking at the stone, it is hard to judge if it was erected before Joshua died or after. He may have had it inscribed for his wife while leaving room enough (but only just) for his own memorial someday. Or his survivors may have economized by not buying a second stone, and instead having his name and epitaph squeezed into the space left on hers. Regardless, the few lines tell a dramatic story. What business, do you suppose, took Joshua from the uplands of the Berkshires to New York, then on to New Orleans and back in 1795?

Joshua's epitaph is from the service for the burial of the dead in *The Book of Common Prayer*. Given the unfortunate circumstances of his death he would not have selected it himself; I suspect it was the local minister:

> Forasmuch as it hath pleased Almighty God, in his wise providence, to take out of this world the soul of our deceased brother, we therefore commit his body to the ground; earth to earth, ashes to ashes, dust to dust; looking for the general Resurrection in the last day, and the life of the world to come, through our Lord Jesus Christ; at whose second coming in glorious majesty to judge the world, **the earth and the sea shall give up their dead**; and the corruptible bodies of those who sleep in him shall be changed, and made like unto his own glorious body; according to the mighty working whereby he is able to subdue all things unto himself.

I will close this section with an epitaph in Sheffield's Barnard Cemetery that bears an interesting provenance. It is not quite Scripture, but it is deeply Scriptural in tone and intent:

> Sacred to
> the Memory of
> Mrs. Hannah Ashley
> Consort of
> Col. John Ashley Esq.
> who died June 19
> AD 1790
> in the 78 year
> of her age.
>
> *As Death leaves you*
> *so Judgment will find you.*

Though not a Bible verse, it is deeply rooted in the religious teaching of the time. The earliest use of the phrase on Hannah Ashley's gravestone I have found is in *THREE DECADES OF SERMONS lately preached to the University in Oxford* (1660) by the Rev. Henry Wilkinson. In Sermon 10, "The Dignity of the Soul," Wilkinson warned his congregation:

> Consider, as death leaves thee, so judgment will find thee. As the tree falls, so it lies. If thy soule be filthy and guilty, and unwasht by the blood of Christ, when separated from thy body, it will ever so remain in that condition.

Henry Wilkinson (1616–1690) was a Yorkshire native who studied at Magdalen College, Oxford. He became a noted scholar and preacher. During the Civil War he was a staunch Parliamentarian and returned to Oxford as part of the parliamentary purge of preachers and teachers, later being appointed Principal of Magdalen Hall. He was ejected after the Restoration and eventually ended his days as a Presbyterian in Suffolk.

I cannot say for certain that Wilkinson coined the phrase "as death leaves thee, so judgment will find thee," but I find no earlier usage. There is an echo of it in *The New England Primer*, in one of that book's many instructive lessons for children:

> ... [T]hou wilt leave this World and all behind
> To be with Worms, in some Church yard confind,
> And as from all thy friends grim death shall take thee
> So God will find thee when [illegible but I assume the rhyme is "He wakes thee"]

The phrase recurs often in sermons throughout the eighteenth and nineteenth centuries, so it must have struck a happy chord in many ecclesiastical ears. Intriguingly, I found it used in western Massachusetts twenty years before Hannah Ashley's death, in sermon preached on the occasion of a murderer's execution. The Rev. Moses Baldwin wrote:

> By the ungodly then, we may understand a sinner under the guilt and power of sin; disobedient and rebellions against the sovereign authority and righteous law of a holy God, and unrighteous towards man. This is the man, who, among others, must die and come to judgment. Being a sinner, death must be his inevitable portion; and as death leaves him, so judgment will find him!*

It is likely that either the Reverend Baldwin's sermon, or the Reverend Wilkinson's original, was read and made an impression upon Colonel Ashley or his minister—though one hopes in the case of Hannah, the intended message is that she lived and died virtuously, and Judgment found her so!

~~~

All these verses (and many more not included here) show that the Bible was an essential text for survivors seeking to express their feelings on the death of a loved one—as certainly it remains to this day. But as we will see, it was by no means the only source these people drew upon.

---

* Moses Baldwin, *The ungodly condemned in judgment. A sermon preached at Springfield, December 13 1770. On the occasion of the execution of William Shaw, for murder.*

Psalms and Hymns

As described in Part I, psalms and hymns are the third common and un-surprising source of epitaph texts. By far the most popular hymnodist I have encountered in these graveyards is Isaac Watts—the examples I include here are just a small sample of all the Watts verses I have collected. Watts (1674–1748) was an English minister, hymn writer, and theologian. He has been called the "Father of English Hymnody," credited with some 750 hymns and psalms. Whether read or sung in church, memorized for recitation, or studied in private devotional reading, Watts's work was absolutely integral to the literary and religious experience of rural New Englanders. Quotations from his hymns, psalms, and poetry are found in most of these graveyards, and in contemporary commonplace books and samplers. His books were in lending libraries, ministers' bookshelves, and private collections. I am fortunate to own a lovely edition of Watt's *Psalms, Hymns, and Holy Songs*, printed in tiny font, just the right size for tucking into a waistcoat pocket or lady's bag when heading out to church. Watts was also an innovative marketer; he recommended that parents give copies of his *Divine Songs for Children* as gifts to well-behaved girls and boys. Prolific, popular, and often anthologized, Watts was one of the most widely read (not just sung) writers of his time.

In Old Hampden Cemetery, we find a selection from Watts with an uncommonly specific attribution (Figure 25):

> In memory of Lt. Paul
> Langdon who died
> Decr 3rd 1761 in y^e 69th
> Year of his Age
>
> *My flesh shall slumber in
> the Ground Till the last
> Trumpets joyful Sound
> Then burst the Chains
> with sweet Surprize
> And in my Savour's
> Image rise. Psalm 17th
> D^r. Watts Version*

Figure 25. Paul Langdon stone (courtesy of American Antiquarian Society).

Psalms and Hymns

This is one of Watts's *Psalms of David*—in which Watts specifically set out to "Christianize" the Old Testament Book of Psalms by adding New Testament imagery and context.* The identical text was chosen later over in Washington's Town Hall Cemetery (Dr. Joseph Chaplin, 1776), in New Marlborough Center Cemetery (Azubah Wheeler, 1790), and forty-five years on in Great Barrington's Mahaiwe Cemetery (Elizabeth Hamelin, 1807), though these do not include the inscribed attribution. Here is the full text of *Psalm XVII*:

> Lord I am thine; but thou wilt prove
> My faith, my patience, and my love;
> When men of spite against me join,
> They are the sword, the hand is thine.
>
> Their hope and portion lie below:
> 'Tis all the happiness they know;
> 'Tis all they seek; they take their shares,
> And leave the rest among their heirs.
>
> What sinners value, I resign;
> Lord, 'tis enough that thou art mine;
> I shall behold they blissful face,
> And stand complete in righteousness.
>
> This life's a vain and empty show;
> But the bright world to which I go
> Hath joys substantial and sincere;
> When shall I wake and find me there?
>
> O glorious hour! O blest abode!
> I shall be near and like my God!
> And flesh and sin no more control
> The sacred pleasures of the soul.
>
> **My flesh shall slumber in the ground,**
> **Till the last trumpet's joyful sound;**
> **Then burst the chains with sweet surprise,**
> **And in my Saviours's image rise.**

"What sinners value, I resign" is a wonderful line. Like so much of Watts, it is effortlessly mellifluous and says more in five words than many religious tracts say in fifty pages. And "O glorious hour! O blest abode!"—what a joyous, uplifting expression of confidence in salvation. The delightfully alliterative phrase "sweet surprise" was used by many other epitaph versifiers.

Someone in Northfield selected a very different verse from the same *Psalm* for a 96-year-old frontier woman (Figure 26):

> ***Memento Mori***
> Mrs. HANNAH, Relict
> Of Ens^n NATHANIEL
> MATTOON died April
> 16 1797 in the 96 y^r
> of her age

---

* Watts's *Hymns*, in contrast, are original songs based more or less loosely on a Bible verse.

72   Part II—Categories of Epitaphs

This life is a vain and empty show
But the bright world to which I go
Hath joys substantial and sincere
When shall I wake and find me there

Here again we must pause over the recurring question of who selected the epitaph. Did Hannah choose this hymn herself, having lived too long amidst the vain and empty show? In her old age, had she grown impatient for the bright next world? Or is some surviving relative putting these words, as it were, in her mouth, to make their own point? Whoever made the choice, I am left with the impression that old Hannah must have been a stern and righteous character in old Northfield.

A splendid verse from Watts was chosen for a young girl's grave in Longmeadow:

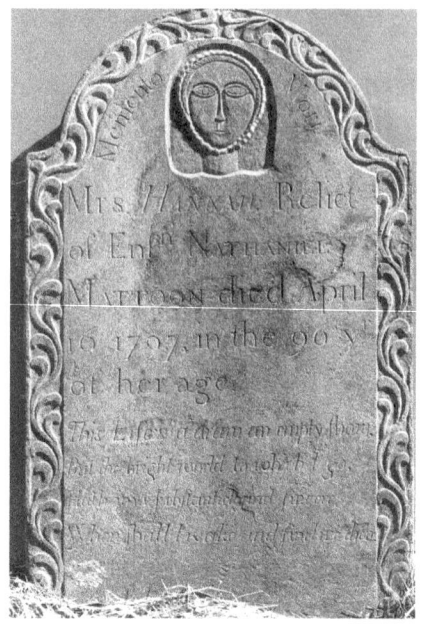

Figure 26. Hannah Mattoon stone (courtesy of American Antiquarian Society).

In Memory of
Mrs. ESTHER
Daughter of
Mr. HEZEKIAH &
Mrs. CHARITY COOLEY
Who died
April 7th 1777
in Her 6th [?] Year.

Amazing Grace
That kept my Breath
Nor did my Soul remove
Till I had Learn'd
My Saviour's Death
And well Insur'd his love.

When I first read this I thought "Eureka! I have finally found John Newton's famous hymn *Amazing Grace* among these gravestones!" But in fact this is the last verse of a Watts hymn popularly known as "The Dying Sinner."* The full text of the hymn is worth reading. In it, Watts gives us the first-person voice of a sinner lying in terror upon his death-bed who is saved at his last breath by a return to religion and the grace of Christ. Pietistic writers like William Dodd, James Hervey, and George Wright (whom we shall meet in due course) often made an example of the dying sinner—without the dramatic last-minute salvation:

---

* We will encounter John Newton as a poet on another gravestone. Newton's enduringly popular hymn was published decades after the death of Isaac Watts. Newton would have grown up with Watts hymns, and it is possible that the phrase stuck in his head and inspired the later work.

Psalms and Hymns

My thoughts on awful subjects roll,
Damnation and the dead;
What horrors seize the guilty soul
Upon a dying bed!

Lingering about these mortal shores
She makes a long delay,
Till like a flood, with rapid force,
Death sweeps the wretch away.

Then swift and dreadful she descends
Down to the fiery coast,
Amongst abominable fiends,
Herself a frightful ghost.

There endless crowds of sinners lie,
And darkness makes their chains;
Tortur'd with keen despair they cry,
Yet wait for fiercer pains.

Not all their anguish and their blood
For their old guilt atones;
Nor the compassion of a God
Shall hearken to their groans.

Amazing grace, that kept my breath,
Nor bid my soul remove,
Till I had learn'd my Saviour's death,
And well insur'd his love!

In Northampton's Bridge Street Cemetery there is an epitaph that combines two different Watts hymns. The deceased was a Minister, who would have heard these words all his working life, especially when officiating at the funerals of his parishioners. I like to think he picked them himself in advance, to convey his own religious convictions and sentiments when the occasion finally arose:

Sacred to the Memory
of
Dr. SAMUEL MATHER
who died
April 29th 1779
In the 74th year
Of his age

Corruption, earth and worms,
Shall but refine this flesh
Till my triumphant spirit comes,
To put i[t] on afresh.
Hark from the tombs
A doleful sound,
Mine ears attend the cry,
Ye living men come view the ground
Where you must shortly lie.

The first four lines are from Watt's "And must this body die?":

And must this body die?
This mortal frame decay?

And must these active limbs of mine
Lie mould'ring in the clay?

Corruption, earth, and worms
Shall but refine this flesh,
Till my triumphant spirit comes
To put it on afresh.

God my Redeemer lives,
And often from the skies
Looks down, and watches all my dust,
Till He shall bid it rise.

Arrayed in glorious grace
Shall these vile bodies shine,
And every shape, and every face,
Look heav'nly and divine.
…
Dear Lord, accept the praise
Of these our humble songs,
Till tunes of nobler sound we raise
With our immortal tongues.

Notice how Watts shows us the swift, dramatic transition from corruption, earth, and worms to God in the skies. I also appreciate the confidence of the last verse, in which he places the congregation securely in Heaven.

The last five lines of Dr. Mather's epitaph are from a different Watts hymn, *Hark from the tombs*, which I have found quoted often, up and down the Connecticut River:

Hark from the tombs a doleful sound,
Mine ears attend the cry,
Ye living men come view the ground
Where you must shortly lie.

Princes! This clay must be your bed,
In spite of all your towers—
The tall, the wise, the reverend head
Must lie as low as ours.

Great God! Is this our certain doom,
Must we too slumber there?
Are we fast hastening to the tomb,
And yet no more prepare?

O, grant us heavenly power afresh,
To fit our souls to fly;
Then, when we drop this dying flesh,
We'll rise above the sky!

The theme of the grave as the common destination of princes, the mighty, the reverend, and the rest of us is one we will encounter often among the Graveyard Poets.

Another Watts Psalm was chosen for a young woman buried in Belchertown's South Cemetery:

IN Memory of
Mrs CHARITY
Daut^r of the Rev^d
Julius & Mrs.

Psalms and Hymns

> VIOLET FORWARD
> who died April
> 17th 1782 in the 18th
> Year of her Age
>
> *Dear jesus thou*
> *Hast power to save;*
> *In thee I trust*
> *While in the grave:*
> *My flesh in dust*
> *Shall be thy care*
> *And thou wilt raise*
> *Me strong & fair.*

This is the last verse of Watts's *Psalm 71–Part 3*, which Watts subtitled "The aged Christian's Prayer and Song." The Psalm is written in the voice of one whose long experience has taught enduring lessons in faith and devotion; whoever chose this text for the epitaph of a young woman thus introduces a gentle irony:

> God of my childhood, and my youth,
> The guide of all my days,
> I have declar'd thy heav'nly truth,
> And told thy wond'rous ways.
>
> Wilt thou forsake my hoary hairs,
> And leave my fainting heart?
> Who shall sustain my sinking years,
> If God my strength depart?
>
> Let me thy pow'r and truth proclaim
> To the rising age,
> And leave a savour of thy name
> When I shall quit the stage.
>
> The land of silence and of death
> Attends my next remove;
> Oh may these poor remains of breath
> Teach the wide world thy love!
> …
> Oft have I heard thy threat'nings roar,
> And oft endur'd the grief;
> But when thy hand has prest me sore,
> Thy grace was my relief.
>
> **By long experience I have known**
> **Thy sov'reign pow'r to save;**
> **At Thy command I venture down**
> **Securely to the grave.**
>
> **When I lie buried deep in dust,**
> **My flesh shall be thy care;**
> **These wither'd limbs with thee I trust**
> **To raise them strong and fair.**

Compare the Watts lines carefully to Charity Forward's epitaph. Here is yet another instance of a local hand re-purposing a text to fit their own circumstances. Inspired by the words of a hoary-haired old Christian, the unknown writer here ascribes the same sentiments to an eighteen-year-old young woman: the hope that her brief life will be a testament to God's power and love for those who remain behind, and confidence that the God of her childhood will keep her safe and secure in the grave, though she is scarcely out of childhood. Watts's words showed the way for someone who loved Charity Forward to create an original expression of devotion and hope in the face of death.

In Lenox's Church on the Hill Cemetery stands a substantial double-headed stone with a popular Watts verse that also provides an interesting and hymnodic expression of a theme we will meet again later on, the recurring-but-unattributed "Death is a debt to Nature due." Here the emphasis is on the delights of life as something we borrow:

> Henry, died March 5,
> 1785, aged 5 months;
> Betsey died Jan 29 1794
> in the 4 year of her age.
>
> Children of Doct. Thaddeus and
> Mrs. Betsey Thompson
>
> *The dear delights we here enjoy*
> *and fondly call our own*
> *Are but short favors borrowed now*
> *to be repaid anon.*

Notice that this inscription reveals much about the question of timing that we discussed in Part I. Henry died at five months, then his sister died almost eleven years later. Presumably the double-headed stone was only commissioned after young Betsey's death, and who knows how long after? I wonder if Henry had any sort of memorial in the meantime.

The verse itself if a popular selection—I have also found it in Hadley (Martha Nash, 1788, age 42), East Otis (James Nutt, 1794), and Springfield (Arabilla Chapin, 1798, age 2). The source is a Watts hymn based on Job 1:21, *Naked as From the Earth we Came*, which eloquently teaches respectful resignation to God's will:

> Naked as from the earth we came,
> And crept to life at first,
> We to the earth return again,
> And mingle with our dust.
>
> **The dear delights we here enjoy**
> **And fondly call our own**
> **Are but short favours borrowed now**
> **To be repaid anon.**
>
> 'Tis God that lifts our comforts high,
> Or sinks 'em in the grave.
> He gives, and (blessed be his Name)
> He takes but what he gave.
>
> Peace, all our angry passions then!
> Let each rebellious sigh
> Be silent at his sovereign will,
> And every murmur die.
>
> If smiling mercy crown our lives,
> Its praises shall be spread;
> And we'll adore the justice too
> That strikes our comforts dead.

Psalms and Hymns

In Hardwick's Old Cemetery on the Common there is a memorial that quotes one of Watts's most enduring works, *Psalm 90 Part 1*:

> In Memory of
> Mrs. Ruth Hathaway
> Relict to Mr. Ebene-
> zer Hathaway she
> died May 31st
> 1789 In the 69th
> year of her age.
>
> *Thy word commands our flesh to dust*
> *Return, ye sons of men*
> *All nations rose from earth at first*
> *And turn to earth again.*
>
> By D DW*

Taken in its full context, this is certainly an appropriate text for an epitaph. It forcefully acknowledges God's power and authority over the busy tribes of flesh and blood, while also confidently asserting that he is a source of shelter, defense, and rebirth. If anything, I am surprised I have not encountered it more often. The complete text, which will be familiar to many hymn-singers even to this day, is:

> Our God, our help in ages past,
> Our hope for years to come,
> Our shelter from the stormy blast,
> And our eternal home:
>
> Under the shadow of thy throne
> Thy saints have dwelt secure;
> Sufficient is thine arm alone,
> And our defense is sure.
>
> Before the hills in order stood
> Or earth received her frame,
> From everlasting thou art God,
> To endless years the same.
>
> **Thy word commands our flesh to dust,**
> **"Return, ye sons of men";**
> **All nations rose from earth at first,**
> **And turn to earth again.**
>
> A thousand ages in thy sight
> Are like an evening gone;
> Short as the watch that ends the night
> Before the rising sun.
>
> The busy tribes of flesh and blood,
> With all their lives and cares,
> Are carried downwards by thy flood,
> And lost in following years.

---

* I assume that D DW is a reference to Doctor Watts, or Watts DD, though I am not certain. The initials do not belong to the carver because the Farber Collection attributes the Hathaway stone to the carver Jonas Stewart.

> Time, like an ever-rolling stream,
> Bears all its sons away;
> They fly forgotten, as a dream
> Dies at the opening day.
>
> Like flowery fields the nations stand,
> Pleased with the morning light;
> The flowers beneath the mower's hand
> Lie withering e'er 'tis night.
>
> Our God, our help in ages past,
> Our hope for years to come,
> Be thou our guard while troubles last,
> And our eternal home.

The reader will recall having encountered the images of Psalm 90 in the Scripture section: the flood that bears us all away, the grass that stands tall in the morning but is cut down before evening. Admire here how Watts conveys the same essential message, but with more melodious language and more homely, accessible similes (an evening gone, a dream that dies at sunrise, the flowers beneath the mower's hand). No wonder he was so popular, not just in church but at home, in closet devotional reading.

A host of Watts hymns appear in the Northfield Center Cemetery. Apparently the minister and congregation of Northfield responded especially strongly to the message of Watts hymns over many years. Note the familiar Classic warning to prepare for death in the eulogistic text (with its eccentric line-breaks):

> Mr. Hezekiah Stra
> tton Died Jany 3
> 1800 In the 76 year
> of his age His Last counsels and ad
> vice to His Children and
> Friends was to prepare
> for death reminding them
> of Christ's words "ye must be born again"
>
> *Life is the time to serve the Lord,*
> *The time t' ensure the Great Reward;*
> *And while the Lamp holds out to burn,*
> *The vilest sinner may return*

This is from the hymn *Life is the time to serve the Lord*, a choice that perfectly reinforces the Classic warning to turn away from vain sublunary things and prepare your soul for Heaven, and, because life is short, to be ceaselessly devoted to that task—but in warmer, more poetic language:

> **Life is the time to serve the Lord,**
> **The time to ensure the great reward;**
> **And while the lamp holds out to burn,**
> **The vilest sinner may return.**
>
> Life is the hour that God has given
> To 'scape from hell and fly to Heav'n;
> The day of grace, and mortals may
> Secure the blessings of the day.

Psalms and Hymns

> The living know that they must die,
> But all the dead forgotten lie;
> Their memory and their sense is gone,
> Alike unknowing and unknown.
>
> Their hatred and their love is lost,
> Their envy is buried in the dust;
> They have no share in all that's done
> Beneath the circuit of the sun.
>
> Then what my thoughts design to do,
> My hands, with all your might pursue;
> Since no device nor work is found,
> Nor faith, nor hope, beneath the ground.
>
> There are no acts of pardon passed
> In the cold grave, to which we haste;
> But darkness, death, and long despair,
> Reign in eternal silence there.

"There are no acts of pardon passed / In the cold grave, to which we haste": a strict Calvinist minister could not have said it better—though he would have had more to say about sin and pain. The same sentiment is pithily expressed in another epitaph: "There is no repentance in the grave."

Watts hymns remained relevant for these people well into the nineteenth century. I read this verse from New Marlborough's Old Center Cemetery in several books about the Berkshires, always described as "quaint" or "curious" but never sourced (Figure 27):

> SACRED
> to the Memory
> of M^{rs}. ELIZABETH
> SHELDON wife of M^{r}.
> ERASTUS SHELDON
> who departed this
> life Jan. 5 1809
> AE^{t}. 24
>
> *Oh may you scorn these cloths of flesh*
> *These fetters and this load*
> *And long for evening to undress*
> *That you may rest with God.*

I can understand how a casual reader would find this an odd turn of phrase to find on a gravestone. And even we, though familiar with the carefully-constructed cadences and spiritually uplifting imagery of Watts hymns, might be a bit startled by the sensual language of clothing and undressing. Read in context, the lines become less suggestive; *Hymn 61* is a marvelously sustained meditation on the vast contrast between the clay and fetters and

Figure 27. Elizabeth Sheldon stone (author's collection).

worms of this life and our unknown but glorious home to come. Watts wonders how we could ever prefer the former to the latter:

> My soul, come, meditate the day,
> And think how near it stands,
> When thou must quit this house of clay,
> And fly to unknown lands.
>
> And you, mine eyes, look down and view
> The hollow gaping tomb;
> This gloomy prison waits for you,
> Whene'er the summons come.
>
> Oh! Could we die with those that die,
> And place us in their stead;
> Then would our spirits learn to fly,
> And converse with the dead.
>
> Then should we see the saints above
> In their own glorious forms,
> And wonder why our souls shall love
> To dwell with mortal worms.
>
> **How we should scorn these clothes of flesh,**
> **These fetters, and this load;**
> **And long for ev'ning, to undress,**
> **That we may rest with God.**
>
> We should almost forsake our clay
> Before the summons come,
> And pray and wish our souls away
> To their eternal home.*

In addition to his *Psalms and Hymns*, Watts also published several books of very fine poetry. I read this example on a fading stone in Tyringham Village Cemetery:

> In Memory of
> GILES SLATER
> who departed this life Feb.
> [Illegible] 1814 in the 65th year
> of his age
>
> *Vain world, farewell to you;*
> *Heaven is my native air;*
> *I bid my friends a short adieu,*
> *Impatient to be there.*

This passage is taken from "Looking Upward," a poem in Watts's *Horae Lyricae* or "Sacred Songs" (1706) that was later turned into a hymn:

> The heavens invite mine eye,
> The stars salute me round;
> Father, I blush, I mourn to lie
> Thus groveling on the ground.

---

* In Northampton, the epitaph of William Hunt (d. 1795, age 17), using lines from the second verse, warns the reader:

> This gloomy prison waits for you,
> Whene'er the summons come.

Psalms and Hymns

My warmer spirits move,
And make attempts to fly;
I wish aloud for wings of love
To raise me swift and high

Beyond those crystal vaults,
And all their sparkling balls;
They're but the porches to thy courts,
And paintings on thy walls.

Vain world, farewell to you;
Heaven is my native air;
I bid my friends a short adieu,
Impatient to be there.

I feel my powers released
From their old fleshy clod;
Fair guardian, bear me up in haste,
And set me near my God.

Horae Lyricae is a collection of lyric poems that was popular for private devotional reading. Its words appear often in these graveyards. This is a fine choice for a gravestone—the survivors, though mourning, must pick themselves up off the ground, look up into the night sky, stop worrying about their fleshly clods and think instead of what lies beyond the stars. I expect the images of crystal vaults and sparkling balls must have fired the imaginations of Giles Slater's friends and neighbors—such things were scarce in Tyringham in the early 1800s.

Here is another charming epitaph based on a poem in *Horae Lyricae* entitled "On The Sudden Death of Mrs. Mary Peacock." I have found many slightly different choices of lines from this work, across more than sixty years and many miles, from Williamstown to Lanesborough to Palmer to Alford to Agawam; this is from Northfield Center Cemetery:

> In memory of
> Mrs. SARAH wife to
> Mr OLIVER SMITH
> who Died Augst 4th 1784
> In ye 35th year of her Age
>
> *Bright Soul farewell a short farewell*
> *Till we shall meet Again Above*
> *In Groves of bliss where pleasure Dwells*
> *And trees of Life bear fruits of love*
> *While the dear dust she leaves behind*
> *Sleeps in thy bosom sacred tomb*
> *Soft be Her bed Her slumbers Kind*
> *And all Her dreams of joy to come*

Here is the source text:

> **Hark! She bids all her friends adieu;**
> **Some angel calls her to the spheres;**
> **Our eyes the radiant saint pursue**
> **Through liquid telescopes of tears.**
>
> **Farewell, bright soul, a short farewell,**
> **Till we shall meet again above,**

**In the sweet groves where pleasures dwell,
And trees of life bear fruits of love:**

There glory sits on every face;
There friendship smiles in every eye;
There shall our tongues relate the grace
That led us homeward to the sky.

O'er all the names of Christ, our King,
Shall our harmonious voices rove;
Our hearts shall sound, from every string,
The wonders of his bleeding love.

Come, sovereign Lord, dear Savior, come,
Remove these separating days;
Send thy bright wheels to fetch us home;
That golden hour, how long it stays!

How long must we lie ling'ring here,
While saints around us take their flight:
Smiling they quit this dusky sphere,
And mount the hills of heavenly light.

Sweet soul, we leave thee to thy rest;
Enjoy thy Jesus and thy God,
Till we, from bands of clay released,
Spring out and climb the shining road.

**While the dear dust she leaves behind
Sleeps in thy bosom, sacred tomb!
Soft be her bed, her slumbers kind,
And all her dreams of joy to come!**

What a joyous, consoling message, and what comfort for the faithful survivors. Don't you love the image of the liquid telescopes of tears? This may strike some readers as a bit too obviously crafted, or straining a little too hard for an effect. But consider that in this era telescopes (and microscopes, and lenses in general) were cutting-edge technology, revealing every day new secrets about the workings of the universe and man's place in it. I read this as Watts taking a piece of current vocabulary and placing it in an unexpected context, combining the two different images (celestial exploration, tearful mourning) into an entirely original metaphor.

A verse from *Horae Lyricae* was chosen, and somewhat edited, for an epitaph that appears in Lenox's Church on the Hill Cemetery:

In Memory of
M^{RS} LOIS wife of M^R
SAMUEL DUNBAR
who died Nov^{br} 17th 1787
Aged 61 Years

*We mourn but not as wretches do
When vicious lives all hope destroy
A falling tear is natures due
While faith looks up to joys on high.*

This is from a composition in the *Horae* entitled "At the Death of that excellent Man Sir Thomas Abney, A soliloquy, or Mourning Meditation." Part I verse X reads:

> We mourn; but not as wretches do,
> Where vicious lives all hope in death destroy:
> A falling tear is nature's due,
> But hope climbs high, and borders on celestial joy.

I find the epitaph to be a bit dilutive of the power of Watts's verse. The second line is cut short, and the critical image of vicious lives destroying hope *in death*—unprepared, too late for any opportunity to repent—is lost. The last line also loses its action (climbing, not just looking) and sense of the sublime (bordering on—but not quite attaining—celestial joy). The abridgements do Watts no service. I hope they were not driven merely by economy, a need to pay for fewer words on the stone.

Still another passage from *Horae Lyricae* was chosen from a grave in the Bernardston Old Cemetery. This memorial appears in several of those irritating anthologies of "quaint and interesting" epitaphs:

> TO the memory
> of Doctor
> POLYCARPUS
> CUSHMAN
> who died 15th December
> AD 1797. Aetate 47.
>
> *Vain censorius beings little know*
> *What they must soon experience below,*
> *Your lives are short, eternity is long;*
> *O think of death, prepare & then be gone*
> *Thus art & Nature's powers and charms*
> *And drugs & receipts and forms*
> *Yield all, at last, to greedy worms,*
> *A despicable prey.*
>
> *Mors absque morbo vorax*
> *Mortalium rapuit nedicum*

The first quatrain appears to be bespoke, made up of a series of borrowed lines and commonplace images. The trope of "life how short, eternity how long" appears often in these graveyards and was thus readily at hand for someone to weave into this verse. So too The Classic's reminder that we must think of death and prepare. The whole composition sounds a little angry, don't you think? Those words "& then be gone" strike me as harsh and dismissive: "After you prepare, go die." It is a command, not just a prediction or reminder of the inevitable. Did Dr. Cushman have to suffer carping criticism from his fellow-citizens?

The phrase "vain censorious" can also be found elsewhere, though later. In Mrs. Francis O'Neill's *Poetical Essays* (1802) a poem called *To Mr. Kelly* reads:

> The modest Muse such horrid vice detests,
> At once despising both thy grins and jests;
> 'Tis mine to curb, thou vain censorious fool,
> To curb the fictious tongue of ridicule

A passage from 1820 *Sunday Class Book, or Elements of Christian Knowledge* uses the same phrase: "Was I dull, careless, thoughtless, absent; vain, censorious, inclined to scoff at all Religion, and to caval [sic] at the difficult passages of the Scriptures...?" One Charles Bucke, in his 1837 *Book of Human Character,* observes: "Men, who practise easy virtues, are, nevertheless, far more vain, censorious, and presumptuous, than those who practise difficult ones." Funny how catch-phrases embed themselves in everyday usage, then as now. I hope someday to find the original coinage of this one.

Next, the anonymous author reworked a passage from Watts's *To Thomas Gibson*, subtitled *The Life of Souls* (1704). The imagery of Watts's first stanza—lending, borrowing, and paying interest—appears often in these graveyards in the form of the recurring but unsourced epitaph "Death is a debt to Nature due / Which I have paid and so must you." The second stanza reads like a critical documentary on medical practice in the late seventeenth century:

> Swift as the sun revolves the day
> We hasten to the dead,
> Slaves to the wind we puff away,
> And to the ground we tread
> 'Tis air that lends us life, when first
> The vital bellows heave:
> Our flesh we borrow of the dust;
> And when a mother's care has nurst
> The babe to manly size, we must
> With usury pay the grave.
>
> Rich juleps drawn from precious ore
> Still tend the dying flame;
> And plants and roots of barbarous name,
> Torn from the Indian shore.
> Thus we support our tottering flesh;
> Our cheeks resume the rose afresh,
> When bark and steel play well their game
> To save our sinking breath,
> And Gibson, with his awful power,
> Rescues the poor precarious hour
> From the demands of death.
>
> **But art and nature, powers and charms,**
> **And drugs, and recipes, and forms,**
> **Yield us, at last, to greedy worms**
> **A despicable prey.**
> I'd have a life to call my own,
> That shall depend on heaven alone;
> Nor air, nor earth, nor sea,
> Mix their base essences with mine,
> Nor claim dominion so divine
> To give me leave to be.
>
> Sure there's a mind within, that reigns
> O'er the dull current of my veins;
> I feel the inward pulse beat high
> With vigorous immortality.
> Let earth resume the flesh it gave,
> And breath dissolve amongst the winds;
> Gibson, the things that fear a grave,
> That I can lose, or you can save,
> Are not akin to minds.

> We claim acquaintance with the skies,
> Upward our spirits hourly rise,
> And there our thoughts employ:
> When heaven shall sign our grand release,
> We are no strangers to the place,
> The business, or the joy.

Aren't the rich juleps and Asian plants and roots wonderful? So too the idea that each day we are hastening to join the ranks of the dead despite all the best efforts of doctors to forestall the inevitable. The poem is perhaps one that Dr. Johnson had in mind when he said of Watts's poetry: "[H]is diction, though perhaps not always pure, has such copiousness and splendor, as shews that he was but a very little distance from excellence." Very little distance, indeed.

Finally, a rough translation of the concluding Latin epigram would be: "Voracious death, without disease, has snatched the healer of mortals." Mrs. Lucy Kellogg, in her 1902 *History of the Town of Bernardston*, attributes the phrase to Dr. Gideon Ryther, a pupil of Dr. Cushman's. Perhaps Dr. Ryther is the unnamed author of the entire epitaph.

Forgive the long exegesis, but this is the sort of textual exploration that for me adds depth and richness to otherwise merely "notable" epitaphs, and brings us a little closer to once-living people whose reading and learning informed the creation of these verses.

A beautiful selection from "The Welcome Messenger," a poem in Watts's *Horae Lyricae*, was chosen for the grave of a venerable old citizen (though in the original, the speaker is a mere stripling of seventy years) in Becket Center Cemetery, a lovely burial ground on a hillside sloping gently down behind the stately old Meeting House and venerable carriage sheds:

> In memory of Mr. William
> Watson who died July 20th
> 1779 in the 93d year
> of his age.
>
> *I'd leap at once my ninety years*
> *I'd rush into his arms*
> *And lose my breath & all my cares*
> *Amidst those heavenly charms*
> *Joyful I'd lay this body down*
> *And leave the lifeless clay*
> *Without a sigh, without a groan*
> *And stretch & soar away.*

Becket's graveyard provides a joyful chorus of Watts hymns and poems; this is one of many examples. "The Welcome Messenger" is an extraordinary little poem, ecstatic, almost erotic in its depiction of the feelings of the narrator towards the Angel of Death, for whose embrace he yearns impatiently, chiding him for his laziness. Here is the epitaph in the context of the two stanzas that precede it:

> Oh! if my threatening sins were gone,
> And death had lost his sting,
> I could invite the angel on,
> And chide his lazy wing.

> Away these interposing days,
> and let the lovers meet;
> The angel has a cold embrace,
> But kind, and soft, and sweet.
>
> **I'd leap at once my seventy years**
> **I'd rush into his arms,**
> **And lose my breath, and all my cares,**
> **Amidst those heav'nly charms.**
>
> **Joyful I'd lay this body down**
> **And leave this lifeless clay,**
> **Without a sigh, without a groan,**
> **And stretch and soar away.**

I treasure that concluding image of the soul, new-born, stretching its wings before soaring to Paradise. "The Welcome Messenger" also appears in *Elegant Extracts*, among other contemporary anthologies.

Another passage from *Horae Lyricae* appears twice, across considerable time and distance. First, in Williamstown's South Lawn Cemetery, in one of the few instances I have observed of the epitaph verse starting in the same line as the biographic text (Figure 28):

> Here lies inter'd the Body of
> Mr Barnabas Woodcock who was
> born in Dedham the 25th of Septemb^r
> 1710
> and departed this Life march the 14th 1786
> being seventy six years five months &
> eight days
> old *tier'd with the sorrows & the cares*
> *A tiresome train of almost fourscore years*
> *the prisoner smil'd to be releast*
> *He felt his fetters loose & mounted to his*
> *rest.*

Then one hundred miles away, and several decades later, in Palmer Center Cemetery:

> This stone is erected to perpetuate the
> memory of
> Rev. Moses Baldwin,
> who died Nov. 2, A.D. 1813, ae. 81.
>
> *Tired with the sorrows and the cares,*
> *A tedious train of four score years,*
> *The prisoner smiled to be released*
> *He felt his fetters loose and mounted to*
> *his rest.*

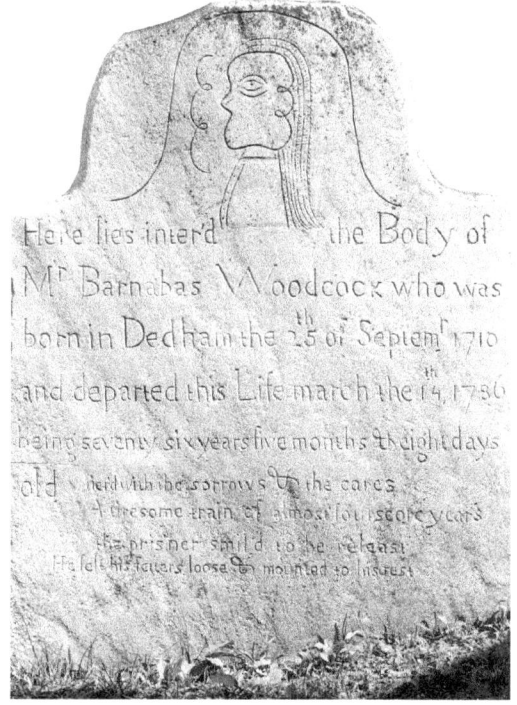

Figure 28. Barnabas Woodcock stone (courtesy of American Antiquarian Society).

Also in 1813, the identical verse was chosen for a stone in Washington's Town Hall Cemetery (Maryan Millikan, age 81). Note how the punctuation has become more normalized over time. There is something satisfyingly tactile in the image of the oppressed or enslaved breaking fetters and ascending to paradise—it brings to mind the old Gospel hymn *I'll Fly Away*:

> Oh how glad and happy when we meet
> I'll fly away
> No more cold iron shackles on my feet
> I'll fly away

The source is the second verse of a poem Watts wrote *On the Death of an Aged and Honour'd Relative, Mrs. M.W. July 13 1693* (in fact, his grandmother):

> Tir'd with the Sorrows and the Cares,
> A tedious Train of fourscore Years,
> The Pris'ner smil'd to be releast,
> She felt her Fetters loose, and mounted to her rest.

How did it get to Williamstown, Washington, and Palmer? These are the only places I have found this verse, and I have not read it in any anthologies. Incidentally, this is a second appearance for *Horae Lyricae* in Williamstown and Palmer. Clearly they are the work of different carvers. Perhaps a single person with a single copy of the book had a connection to all three of these memorials—I don't suppose I will ever know.

To conclude with Watts, here is an epitaph from Old Hadley Cemetery that chose a verse found in another collection of his poetry:

> In Memory of
> Mr. Nathaniel
> Montague
> who died Nov.
> 14 1784, aged
> 35 Years
>
> *Unveil thy bosom faithful tomb*
> *Take this new treasure to thy trust*
> *And give these pretious relicts room*
> *To slumber in thy silent dust.*

At first glance we are struck by the finality of this statement. The tomb opens to admit the dead, not to release the soul. The mortal relics are interred, without any idea of the empty tomb, or promise of resurrection and afterlife in Heaven. But in fact this is just the first verse; if you know the whole hymn you are assured that after a rest, Nathaniel Montague will indeed ascend to meet his Lord.

> **Unveil thy bosom, faithful tomb,**
> **Take this new treasure to thy trust,**
> **And give these sacred relics room**
> **To seek a slumber in the dust.**
>
> Nor pain, nor grief, nor anxious fear
> Invades thy bounds, no mortal woes,
> Can reach the lovely sleeper here,
> And angels watch her soft repose.
>
> So Jesus slept; God's dying Son
> Passed through the grave, and blessed the bed:
> Rest here, fair saint, till from His throne
> The morning break and pierce the shade.

> Break from His throne, illustrious morn!
> Attend, O earth! His sovereign Word:
> Restore thy trust: a glorious form
> She must ascend to meet her Lord!

What a splendid, uplifting composition this turns out to be. The poem begins with the earth opening to receive the dead, then there is a middle phase of peaceful repose, climaxing with a triumphant ascent to meet the Saviour. I have found the same hymn used often in these graveyards, from the Berkshires to the Connecticut River valley. I am not surprised; who would not be consoled to read these words on the grave of a loved one? This is a Watts poem that was later turned into a hymn. "A Funeral Ode at the Interment of the Body, supposed to be sung by the Mourners" was published in his *Reliquiae Juveniles* (1734) and subsequently passed into several hymn-books in Great Britain and America. As the title indicates, this is a collection of Watt's youthful writings. It is a testament to the widespread demand for his works that, in his 60th year, Watts's publishers would compile such a volume.

Notwithstanding the evident popularity of Watts's hymns among the deceased, their survivors, and their ministers, not all the hymns used in these epitaphs were his. For example, in the Stockbridge Cemetery there is an epitaph with an entirely different meter and rhythm than Watts, livelier and more flowing (Figure 29):

> In Memory of
> Capt JOSIAH JONES
> Who died April 22^d
> AD 1795 in the 70th
> Year of his Age
>
> *How blest is the Man who bereft*
> *Of all that could burden the Mind*
> *How easy the Soul that hath left*
> *The wearisome Body behind.*

Some quarter century later, another verse from the same hymn appears in a tiny family plot in Hancock known as the Townsend Cemetery, entirely overgrown with trees:

> In memory of
> REUBEN ELY
> who died July 18th
> 182*
> in his 74th (?) year
>
> *His earth is afflicted no more*
> *With sickness or shaken with pain*
> *The war in the members is o'er*
> *And never shall vex him again*

Figure 29. Josiah Jones stone (author's collection).

You may recall we read this verse in Part I. The source text is a hymn from John Wesley's *Funeral Hymns* (1746) with the startling opening line "Ah lovely appearance of death":

Ah! lovely appearance of death,
No sight upon earth is so fair;
Not all the gay pageants that breathe,
Can with a dead body compare.

With solemn delight I survey
The corpse, when the spirit is fled,
In love with the beautiful Clay,
And longing to lie in his stead.

How blest is our brother, bereft
Of all that could burden his mind?
How easy the soul, that hath left
This wearisome body behind!

Of evil incapable thou,
Whose relics with envy I see;
No longer in misery now,
No longer a sinner like me.

This earth is affected no more,
With sickness, or shaken with pain;
The war in the members is o'er,
And never shall vex him again.

No anger henceforward, or shame,
Shall redden this innocent clay;
Extinct is the animal flame,
And passion is vanished away.

This languishing head is at rest,
Its thinking and aching are o'er;
This quiet immovable breast
Is heaved by affliction no more.

This heart is no longer the seat
Of trouble and torturing pain;
It ceases to flutter and beat,
I never shall flutter again.

The lids he so seldom could close,
By sorrow forbidden to sleep,
Sealed up in eternal repose,
Have strangely forgotten to weep.

The fountains can yield no supplies,
These hollows from waters are free!
The tears are all wiped from these eyes,
And evil they never shall see.

To mourn and to suffer is mine,
While bound in a prison I breathe;
And still for deliverance pine,
And press to the issues of death.

What now with my tears I bedew,
O might I this moment become,
My spirit created anew,
My flesh be consigned to the tomb.

I quote the entire hymn in an effort to bring us a little closer to Reuben Ely and Josiah Jones and the world in which they lived, worshipped, and died. It is hard to imagine a congregation singing all twelve verses at a funeral. And to modern ears the first two verses would be challenging for a bereaved family to get through. The very sentiments seem alien to us. Who, today, attending a funeral, finds the appearance of death delightful, or longs to take the deceased's place and lie down in the clay? But then we hear Wesley's optimistic message: Death is not a terrible imminent threat, and life is no longer a gaudy distraction from which our attention needs to be recalled. Now, death is a welcome release from the sufferings of life—a state positively to be preferred. We might or might not, today, raise up our voices in the last stanza to proclaim our tearful desire to die instantly, but it is edifying to contemplate the spirit of the people that did so.

Wesley (1703–1791) was an English cleric, theologian and evangelist who was a leader of a revival movement within the Church of England known as Methodism. The societies he founded became the dominant form of the independent Methodist movement that continues to the present day. I look forward to finding more of Wesley's work. Compared to Watts, he is found less often in these graveyards. Wesley argued against the Calvinist doctrine of predestination, and I expect this reflects the relative prevalence of Methodism and Congregationalism in rural Massachusetts in the 1820s.*

Other hymn writers appear as well. For example, the work of one Joseph Hart appears in the Chestnut Hill Cemetery in Monterey, a secluded and disused little burial ground on a rocky little hillside:

> Sacred to the memory
> of the Revnd Joshua
> Morse who died July
> 26th 179(?) in the 70th year
> of his age ---- of his ministry
>
> *Deep interred in earth's dark womb*
> *The mouldering body lies*
> *But the Christian from the tomb*
> *Shall soon triumphant rise.*

Hart (1712–1768) led an interesting if now-forgotten life. He showed youthful precocity with his translations of Herodian and Phycolides, then went through a phase as a defiantly atheistic libertine during which he published a long attack on religion in general and Wesley in particular. Then at the age of about forty-five, Hart had a religious conversion and became a Calvinist minister and popular hymnodist. What interesting lives lie hidden behind these old stones, awaiting their own recognition and resurrection! This verse is from *Hart's Hymns*, a much-loved hymnal amongst evangelical Christians for over 200 years:

---

* I have a fine old edition of Wesley's hymns (London, 1813), complete with brass buckles for keeping the book closed. It features a charming sequence of prior owner's inscriptions, starting on the fly-leaf: "William Tanner Frampton Man[?] Glos Shire 1819." Continued on next page: "Elizabeth Tanner [illeg] Glostershire July 8th 1820" and on the next page, in a much clearer script: "William Tanner His book July 18th 1819 Stale not this Book / For fear of Shame / For hear you see / the owners Name." And on yet another following page, in faint pencil and a shaky and possibly much older hand, " Elizabeth Tanner her Book." Apparently William and Elizabeth either shared, or contested, this book!

> Christians view this solemn scene,
> Nor pensive be, nor sad;
> Look beyond the cloud between,
> And let your hearts be glad;
>
> Never from your memory lose,
> The resurrection of the just;
> Death's a blessing now for those,
> Who in the Saviour trust.
>
> **Deep interred in earth's dark womb,**
> **The mouldering body lies;**
> **But the Christian from the tomb**
> **Shall soon triumphant rise,**
>
> Jesus Christ the Righteous Judge,
> For all his people's sins was slain:
> Give the Saviour without grudge,
> The purchase of his pain.
>
> Now the grave's a downy bed,
> Embroidered round with blood:
> Say not the believer's dead,
> He only rests with God;
>
> Lord we long to be at home,
> Lay down our head, and sleep in thee:
> Come, Lord Jesus, quickly come,
> And set thy prisoners free.

Hart has the manner of Watts, if not the same level of inspired invention nor smoothness of rhythm and flow. Pause over the image of the grave as "a downy bed / embroidered round with blood"; it may stay with you for a while.

Williamstown's South Lawn Cemetery is a singularly quiet spot, set well back from the highway in a rural corner of town, surrounded still by a dairy farm's fields. In it, one cloudless summer day, I read this a fine verse from a hymn by Anne Steele:

> In memory of Mrs.
> BETSY BULKELEY
> wife of Capt. Charles
> Bulkeley, who departed this
> life March 19th AD 1797, in
> the 45th year of her age.
>
> *Lord I commit my soul to thee*
> *Accept this sacred trust*
> *Receive this nobler part of me*
> *And watch my sleeping dust*

Anne Steele (1717–1778) is one of the writers I discovered for the first time in these graveyards, and I would like to know her better. She was born at Broughton, Hampshire. Her father was a timber merchant and a Baptist lay pastor. She had a sad childhood: Her mother died when she was three, as a teenager she became an invalid after injuring her hip, and at twenty-one her fiancé drowned on the day of their wedding.[*] For most of her life, she exhibited symptoms of malaria, but despite her sufferings,

---

[*] Full disclosure: this part of her story may be apocryphal but it is too gripping not to include here.

her religious faith enabled her to maintain a cheerful attitude. She published a book of *Poems on subjects chiefly devotional* in 1760 under the pseudonym "Theodosia." Her remaining works were published after her death, including some 144 hymns and 34 metrical psalms. This particular hymn was widely used as an epitaph; an on-line search found it as far away as the South Park Street Burial Ground in Calcutta in 1824 (George Minor, age 28, erected by his afflicted widow).

> **Lord, I commit my soul to thee;**
> **Accept the sacred trust;**
> **Receive this nobler part of me,**
> **And watch my sleeping dust;** —
>
> Till that illustrious morning come,
> When all they saints shall rise,
> And clothed in immortal bloom,
> Attend thee to the skies.
>
> When thy triumphant armies sing
> The honors of thy name,
> And heaven's eternal arches ring
> With glory to the Lamb; —
>
> O let me join the raptured lays,
> And with the blissful throng
> Resound salvation, power, and praise,
> In everlasting song.

This is another example, as we have seen often, where the single verse of the inscription does not include the assurance of resurrection—but the reader would have recognized the hymn and known it had a joyous conclusion.

In Lanesborough's Center Cemetery a verse was chosen from a hymn that was popular with Revivalists throughout the nineteenth century:

> Widow Jerusha Hildreth, died March 12, 1817, in her 35th year.
> She was taken with a fit and expired within four hours.
>
> *Farewell vain world, I bid adieu,*
> *Your glories I despise,*
> *Your friendships I no more pursue,*
> *Your flateries are but lies*

This is the work of by Thomas Sheperd (1665–1739). Sheperd began his career as an Anglican minister but seceded from the Church in 1694 and became an Independent pastor. His publications consisted chiefly of sermons and a book of *Penitential Cries* (1693), some of which are still in use today including "My God, my God, my Light, my Love" and "When wilt Thou come unto me, Lord." The full text is:

> **Farewell vain world, I bid adieu,**
> **Your glories I despise;**
> **Your friendship I no more pursue,**
> **Your flatteries are but lies.**
>
> You promise happiness in vain,
> Nor can you satisfy;
> Your highest pleasures turn to pain,
> And all your treasures die.

> Had I the Indies, East and West,
> And riches of the sea;
> Without my God I could not rest,
> For he is all to me.
>
> Then let me soul rise far above,
> By faith I'll take my wing
> To the eternal realms of love,
> Where saints and angels sing.
>
> There's love and joy that will not waste,
> There's treasures that endure;
> There's pleasure that will always last,
> When time shall be no more.

Here there is no admonishment to the reader, no urgent call to think upon Death. Rather, we hear a celebration of the departed's certain passage from the labyrinths of amusement and dissipation to the eternal realms of love.

This is another occasion to reflect upon the question of who selected the verse. Clearly not the widow Jerusha Hildreth, as she was taken with a fit and died within four hours (though it might have been known to be her favorite hymn). More likely the minister or a bereaved survivor who wants to see her enjoy "the pleasures that will always last / When time shall be no more," selected this verse from a familiar hymnal. Who might that survivor might have been? Jerusha was already a widow, so not her grieving husband. And as she was thirty-five, her orphaned children (if any) would probably not have been old enough to select a hymn for their mother's epitaph. I wonder, but I won't ever know.

Parenthetically, I have found another text that appears to draw from the same source. David Brainerd (1718–1747) was a missionary among the Delaware Indians of New Jersey. His short and difficult life became a source of inspiration and encouragement to many Christians, including Second Great Awakening missionaries and evangelists. He died at Jonathan Edwards's house in Northampton, Massachusetts. On April 25, 1742, David Brainerd wrote in his diary that he composed two poems:

> "Farewell, vain world; my soul can bid Adieu;
> My Saviour's taught me to abandon you.
> Your charms may gratify a sensual mind;
> Not please a soul wholly for God design'd.
> Forbear to entice, cease then my soul to call;
> 'Tis fix'd through grace; my God shall be my ALL.
> While He thus lets me heavenly glories view,
> Your beauties fade, my heart's no room for you."
>
> "Lord, I'm a stranger here alone;
> Earth no true comforts can afford;
> Yet, absent from my dearest One,
> My soul delights to cry, My Lord!
> Jesus, my Lord, my only love,
> Possess my soul, nor thence depart;
> Grant me kind visits, heavenly Dove;
> My God shall then have all my heart."

Was Brainerd familiar with Sheperd's *Penitential Cries*, and consciously or unconsciously echoing them here? And might his writings have been known in

Lanesborough? It is plausible but unprovable. I only observe that what appears to initially to be a bit of commonplace versification turns out to reveal a complicated web of religious texts and ideas available to the deceased and their families.

A stone in Conway's Howland Cemetery bears this noteworthy verse (Figure 30):

Mrs.
Clarissa Wife of
Doct. Washington Hamilton
Died 28 Feb.
1826.
AEt. 36 years.

Think o ye who fondly languish
Oer the grave of those you love,
While your bosoms throb with anguish
They are warbling hymns above.

We could not be any farther from the language of Jonathan Edwards and The Classic. Here the lesson for the reader is not a warning to prepare, but a comforting reminder to let our throbs of anguish be consoled by the happy warbling of the deceased, who is assuredly in paradise. The rest of the hymn continues in much the same vein. The hymnodist provides ecstatic descriptions of the soul's experience in Heaven, and makes no mention of any sinners suffering eternal punishment:

Figure 30. Clarissa Hamilton stone (courtesy of Bob Drinkwater).

Think, O ye who fondly languish
O'er the grave of those you love,
While your bosoms throb with anguish,
They are warbling hymns above:
While your silent steps are straying,
Lonely through night's deepening shade,
Glory's brightest beams are playing
Round the happy Christian's head.

There the sun's inferior lustre,
Never sheds a feeble ray;
There no envious shadows cluster,
Blotting out the cheerful day:

Night the face of nature veiling,
Rears her sable throne no more
'Mid those spirits pure, inhaling
Life from him whom they adore.

Light and peace at once deriving
From the hand of God most high;
In his glorious presence living,
They shall never, never die!

> Endless pleasure pain excluding,
> Sickness there no more can come;
> There no fear of woe intruding,
> Sheds o'er heaven a moment's gloom.
>
> From their eyes celestial swelling,
> Drops of sorrow ne'er shall roll;
> God himself has fix'd his dwelling
> In the temple of the soul:
>
> Cease then, mourner, cease to languish,
> O'er the grave of those you love;
> Pain, and death, and night, and anguish,
> Enter not the world above.

This is from *Hymns, Partly Collected and Partly Original, Designed as a Supplement to Dr. Watt's Psalms and Hymns* (ca. 1812), by William Bengo Collyer. Collyer (1782–1854) was an English minister and hymn-writer. In 1822 he published a magazine article attacking the works of Byron and Shelley as "Licentious Publications in High Life" (and received a reply "Canting Slander: To the Reverend William Bengo Collyer" written by William Hazlitt). He was accused, in an anonymous poem, of immoral behavior in the Addington Bathhouse. Surely this is a life well worth a biography. Collyer is one of the minor literary figures I delight in encountering throughout these researches. There is no greater pleasure than coming across an unusually interesting or suggestive inscription, then later identifying it as the work of a previously unknown (to me) author. I can add a new profile to the roll of writers who were appreciated by these early New Englanders, and my appreciation for the richness of their vocabulary for expressing emotions about death and the afterlife grows deeper.

Collyer also appears in Monterey just a few years later. The Corashire Cemetery was founded in 1813, so most of its gravestones are too recent to be included in my collecting. But among its earliest stones, on a hillside with breathtaking views west across the Berkshire Hills to the Taconic range, is a small weathered double-tympanum stone[*]:

> IN memory of Lucinda & Laura
> daughters of Asa and Lovinia Fowler.
> Laura died March 29 AEt 15: Lucinda
> Died June 8th, Aet. 19. 1829
>
> *Receive, O earth, these faded forms*
> *In thy cold bosom let them lie:*
> *Safe let them rest from evry storm*
> *Soon must they rise no more to die.*

We must pause and consider the family tragedy described here, with two teen-age sisters dying three months apart. I hope the grieving parents found comfort in the assurance that although the grave is a cold place, it is safe and restful compared to the travails of life; and that the resurrection is confidently expected. The epitaph is taken from a widely-published Collyer hymn, *The Dying Christian*:

---

[*] Today the stone is so sunk so deep that the epitaph is barely legible. Cynthia Tryon Hoogs, a tremendously diligent transcriber of Berkshire gravestones, was able to record the full epitaph before it disappeared into the ground. Without her efforts, I could never have made this identification.

> From his low bed of mortal dust,
> Escap'd the prison of his clay,
> The new inhabitant of bliss
> To heav'n directs his wond'rous way.
>
> Ye fields, that witness'd once his tears,
> Ye winds, that wafted oft his sighs,
> Ye mountains, where he breath'd his pray'rs,
> When sorrow's shadows veil'd his eyes;
>
> No more the weary pilgrim mourns,
> No more affliction wrings his heart;
> Th' unfetter'd soul of God returns—
> Forever he and anguish part!
>
> **Receive, O earth, his faded form**
> **In thy cold bosom let it lie;**
> **Safe let it rest from ev'ry storm—**
> **Soon must it rise, no more to die!**

The same passage recurs all over New England in the late 1700s and early 1800s. I can understand why this hymn was popular in rural towns like Monterey, with its evocation of fields and mountains and winds.

Also in Monterey, in the Chestnut Hill Cemetery, is a hymn with the intimation of a lost but potentially compelling back-story:

> DIED
> Dcr 14th 1843
> ALBERT FARGO
>
> *His brightest Visions just appear*
> *Then Vanish and no more are found*
> *The statelist pile his pride could rear*
> *A breath did level with the ground*

This is from a much-anthologized hymn by William Enfield (1741–1797) on the folly of pride and vanity. Enfield was a British Unitarian minister, who published a bestselling book on elocution entitled *The Speaker* (1774). Enfield's full text reads:

> Wherefore should man, frail child of clay,
> Who, from the cradle to the shroud,
> Lives but the insect of a day,
> O why should mortal man be proud?
>
> **His brightest visions just appear,**
> **Then vanish, and no more are found;**
> **The stateliest pile his pride can rear,**
> **A breath may level with the ground.**

Notice the slight but suggestive differences between the source hymn and the epitaph as carved. Enfield warns that the edifices our pride build up *may* be brought to ruin by a breath. It seems that in the case of Alfred Fargo, his pile *was* leveled. I discern a hint of ambiguity in this choice. Did Fargo display worldly pride in his lifetime, and the reader is being warned not to do the same? Or is this simply an expression of sincere regret that despite Fargo's accomplishments, everything was leveled in a single breath.

Finally, a short epitaph in the Tyringham Village Cemetery provides a truly astonishing example of just a few short lines in stone leading to a complicated, far-reaching string of source texts:

> In Memory of
> HULDAH
> Wife of Capt. Riley Sweet
> O.B. April 1, 1822
> AE. 20 yrs 9 mos
>
> *Leaving two small children and*
> *a Husband whose feelings*
> *cannot be written*
>
> *Where immortal spirits reign*
> *There may we all meet again*

First, take a moment to reflect on the actual situation memorialized here, the death (likely in childbirth) of a 20-year-old mother of two. The first lines are an unexpectedly direct and heartfelt statement by her widowed husband, or by someone who loved them both. The ensuing couplet sounds like a snatch of hymnody; in fact it turns out to have a surprisingly complex origin.

In the *New England Farmer* magazine, dated October 20 1826, tucked in amongst a story about the Rhode Island Cattle Show, advertisements from various plant nurseries, and a paper on "Raising Fish in Freshwater Ponds," these lines appear in *A Parting Hymn, composed by three Indian friends, (who graduated at Dartmouth College) at a favourite Bower*. The magazine is probably too late to have been the source of Huldah's epitaph—though it could take several years to commission, carve, and pay for a stone, so it is not out of the question. Regardless, the publication of the poem in a farmers' magazine provide a tantalizing clue to how texts like this reached the hands, and hearts, of the residents of these remote towns.

The same verse then starts to appear in mid- to late-nineteenth-century hymnals, as early as 1839, as either *Indian's Farewell* by Wm. Walker or *When Shall we all Meet Again?* by E.E. Hewitt. It continued to be highly popular in the Civil War era, as it provided a welcome message that the dead are not really gone, but only separated from bereaved loved ones by a thin veil, soon to be seen again:

> When shall we all meet again?
> When shall we all meet again?
> Oft shall glowing hope expire,
> Oft shall wearied love retire,
> Oft shall death and sorrow reign,
> Ere we all shall meet again.
>
> Though in distant lands we sigh,
> Parched beneath a hostile sky,
> Though the deep between us rolls
> Friendship shall unite our souls,
> And in fancy's wide domain,
> Oft shall we all meet again.
>
> When our burnished locks are gray,
> Thinned by many a toil spent day,
> When around the youthful pine
> Moss shall creep and ivy twine;

> Long may the loved bower remain,
> Ere we all shall meet again.
>
> When the dreams of life are fled,
> When its wasted lamps are dead,
> When in cold oblivion's shade,
> Beauty, fame, and wealth are laid,
> **Where immortal spirits reign,**
> **There may we all meet again.**

Pulling further on this thread led me to a learned article in Stedman and Hutchinson's *Library of American Literature: An Anthology in Eleven Volumes. 1891. Vols. IX–XI: Literature of the Republic, Part IV., 1861–1889* (New York, 1889). There Helen Kendrick Johnson (1844–1917) has an essay on "When Shall We Three Meet Again?" I will quote from it here at length:

> There is a thrice familiar and yet half-forgotten song which illustrates in an odd way the power of association against that of language, if not of melody. It is "When Shall We Three Meet Again?" It is known that Samuel Webbe, a celebrated composer, born in London in 1740, wrote the music; but the words have been claimed for our country through two college traditions. One attributes them to a member of the first company of young men who devoted themselves to foreign missions, and so links them with the famous hay-stack of Williams College. Another speaks of them confidently as the work of an Indian, an early graduate of Dartmouth. In proof of the latter theory the following stanza is quoted:
>
>> When around this youthful pine
>> Moss shall creep and ivy twine;
>> When these burnished locks are gray,
>> Thinned by many a toil-spent day;
>> May this long-loved bower remain,
>> Here may we three meet again.
>
> The apparent allusion to the old pine at Dartmouth, and the word "burnished," so descriptive of an Indian's hair, constitute an argument. An old resident of New Hampshire told me that his sister and he learned the song from hearing it sung in his mother's house by an Indian graduate of the class of 1840. In an old English collection, the lyric appears without the quoted stanza. It is there attributed to "a lady." I judge it to be English, perhaps written by the wife of a missionary. It was so appropriately sung by the first foreign missionaries in this country that it might easily be attributed to one of them. That was about 1810, when Dartmouth College was still known as Moor's Indian School. An Indian graduate, I conjecture, wrote for the graduating exercises, perhaps the tree-planting of his class, the stanza given above, which, although good for an Indian, is as much out of place in the lyric as a bit of wampum would be in a pearl necklace. I like to recall the beautiful original verses without the poor stanza:
>
>> When shall we three meet again?
>> When shall we three meet again?
>> Oft shall glowing hope expire,
>> Oft shall wearied love retire,
>> Oft shall death and sorrow reign,
>> Ere we three shall meet again.
>
>> Though in distant lands we sigh,
>> Parched beneath the burning sky;
>> Though the deep between us rolls,
>> Friendship shall unite our souls.

Psalms and Hymns

> Still in fancy's rich domain
> Oft shall we three meet again.
>
> When the dreams of life are fled,
> When its wasted lamp is dead;
> When in cold oblivion's shade
> Beauty, wealth, and power are laid;
> Where immortal spirits reign,
> There shall we three meet again.

If words could keep a song upon the lip, would not this one be often heard? If association were not as powerful as melody, would not the Indian stanza have been rejected?

Thank you for that context, Helen Kendrick Johnson! But wait, the more we search, the more we find. Here is a posting from a blog relating to Dartmouth[*]:

> Dartmouth's graduating seniors still hold their annual Class Day event in the Bema and at the Old Pine, in College Park, as they have done since the 1850s or even the 1830s. Although students do not sing it today, for a number of decades beginning by the late nineteenth century the students sang a well-known hymn called "When Shall We Three Meet Again?" at Class Day or at other events, such as Dartmouth Night. The lyrics involve three people parting around a "youthful pine" and vowing to meet again there in the future, so it must have seemed appropriate.
>
> Around the time it was first sung at a Dartmouth event, or probably before then, the song appears to have become associated with Dartmouth in the popular mind. Most accounts acknowledged that the connection was legendary, but the idea was that three eighteenth-century Indian graduates wrote the song as they parted ways around a memorial pine tree, perhaps the Old Pine itself.
>
> The Kashmir Connection: The earliest publications found are from Boston and London, both dating to 1807. Both publications attribute the hymn to "a Casmerian Indian." U.S. publications continued to attribute the hymn to "a Cashmerian Indian" into the 1820s. The reference to a Casmerian (i.e., Kashmiri) Indian appears to place this particular air within the broader genre of the "Hindoostanee air."

A Hindoostanee air was a European (especially British or Anglo-Indian) transcription of a traditional Indian song that was sung by dancers in houses or court festivals in India during the late eighteenth and early nineteenth centuries. While those transcribing the music were often British women, the lyrics were typically translated by local translators, often with an eye to authenticity. Hindoostanee airs became part of British popular culture, and Byron wrote a poem called "Stanzas to a Hindoo Air" in 1822.

So that's it: Dartmouth's old-time farewell hymn might have been written on the Indian Subcontinent centuries ago and translated for English ears in the early nineteenth century, its "Indian" authorship giving rise to confusion soon after its publication in the U.S.

Who knows where the trail of this much-travelled text might lead next? In the meantime, we can only speculate about how this text traveled from Kashmir to Dartmouth to Tyringham, to be carved on a simple gravestone in or after 1822. I go back to the idea that the lines appeared in a magazine or almanac that fell before Riley Sweet's eye one long-ago day.

---

[*] www.Dartmo.com, *The Indian Origins of "When Shall We Three Meet Again?"* posted 16.01.2011

English and American Poetry

As mentioned in Part I, I have been consistently surprised and delighted by the range of poetry chosen for these epitaphs. Let us start with some of the more famous names, as in this verse from the Westfield Old Burying Ground (Figure 31):

> In Memory of
> M^{rs}. RUTH Relict
> of ye REVEREND
> Mr. EDWARD
> TAYLOR Died
> January ye 27th
> 1730 in ye 70th yr.
> of her age.
>
> *Hope humbly then,*
> *With Trembling*
> *Pinions soar,*
> *Wait the Gret*
> *Teacher Death,*
> *& God Adore.*

The identical verse was also chosen almost fifty years later in nearby Agawam. The author is Alexander Pope (1688–1744), the Catholic poet and satirist best known today for *The Rape of the Lock*, *The Dunciad*, and his translations of Homer. Pope wrote his distinctive "heroic couplets" with an elegant meter and superbly polished diction. Recite a few lines of Pope out loud and you will be delighted by how easily and melodiously they roll off the tongue. I sometimes think he went through the day speaking in these brilliantly rhyming pairs of lines. They are so finely crafted that Pope makes it look easy, but try composing a few dozen lines and you'll see how hard it is.

This passage is taken from Pope's *Essay on Man* (1733–34), Epistle I. In this work, Pope argues that man should accept his place in the great Chain of Being, entirely subject to the righteous rule of God. The Taylor epitaph in context is:

> **Hope humbly then; with trembling pinions soar;**
> **Wait the great teacher Death; and God adore!**
> What future bliss, he gives not thee to know,
> But gives that hope to be thy blessing now.
> Hope springs eternal in the human breast:
> Man never is, but always to be blest:

Figure 31. Ruth Taylor stone (courtesy of American Antiquarian Society).

> The soul, uneasy and confin'd from home,
> Rests and expatiates in a life to come.*

Notice that Ruth Taylor died three years *before* the poem was published. This illustrates the time lag that could occur between a death and having the gravestone commissioned and carved. By the way, Ruth's husband, the Rev. Edward Taylor (1642–1729), was a strict Congregationalist who wrote religious poetry of his own, including *Preparatory Meditations* (1682–1725) and *God's Determinations Touching His Elect and the Elects Combat in Their Conversion and Coming up to God in Christ: Together with the Comfortable Effects Thereof* (c. 1680). It is noteworthy that the widow of so pious a Congregationalist quotes a Catholic poet on her gravestone. This suggests a certain ecumenicism on the Reverend Taylor's part where pious and devotional literature is concerned. One can abhor Popery yet still quote Pope.†

---

* The last couplet of Epistle I of the *Essay on Man* expresses a sentiment that runs through many of these epitaphs: It is not for us to question God's will, and "spite of pride, in erring reason's spite / One truth is clear, Whatever is, is right."

† As I have mentioned, not the least of the pleasures of my reading of these epitaphs are the unexpected authors and texts that I stumble across. In this case, researching Pope's *Essay on Man* led me tangentially to John Wilkes's ribald parody of it, *An Essay on Woman,* dedicated to a famous courtesan of the day. Wilkes (1725–1797) was a radical politician, infamous libertine, and a member of the legendary Hellfire Club. He was an antagonist of Samuel Johnson, though after Boswell arranged an introduction they became friends. Wilkes is remembered for a famous witticism. When the Earl of Sandwich once told Wilkes "Sir, I do not know whether you will die on the gallows or of the pox," legend has it that Wilkes replied, "That depends, my lord, on whether I embrace your lordship's principles or your mistress." Wilkes also wrote scurrilous pornographic poems. I cannot quote *An Essay on Woman* here, but can recommend it to the unabashed reader as a fine example of eighteenth-century low parody of high literature. But I digress.

Parenthetically, decades later an interesting verse that also uses the image of flying on pinions was chosen for a grave in Lee's Center Cemetery:

> In
> Memory of
> Lemuel Barlow,
> who died
> March 10, 1813 in
> the 55 year of his
> Age
>
> *Now clos'd in death beneath the dust he lies,*
> *Silent his voice, forever clos'd his eyes,*
> *The immortal part has on swift pinions flown*
> *To take its sentence in the world unknown.*

This text also appears in *A sermon, occasioned by the death of Gen. George Washington, late president of the United States of America: delivered at Lebanon, in the town of Canaan. February 22d, 1800*. The sermon was preached by Silas Churchill, A.M., Pastor of the First Presbyterian Church in Canaan, New York. This was a Masonic ceremony, and includes a passage that contains the same lines:

> "Since WASHINGTON is dead, let us reflect on our own mortality. Death knocks equally at the doors of palaces and cottages. Others die around us: Soon it will be our turn. Yes, each of us in this assembly must soon lie in solemn silence beneath the dust.—In respect to us,
>
> Soon some acquaintance, mournfully will say,
> Here sleeps my friend, once active, young & gay,
> **Now cold in death; beneath the dust he lies**
> **Silent his voice, forever clos'd his eyes**
> **The immortal part, has on swift pinions flown**
> **To take its sentence, in the world unknown.**"

The Lemuel Barlow carving could be based on the Washington sermon, which was given just over the New York state line. Perhaps there is a Masonic connection among them? I am still not clear if the Revered Silas Churchill quoted or coined it, though I suspect he is quoting from some to-be-discovered source.

Now, back to Alexander Pope. An epitaph in Monterey's Woods Cemetery quotes from another Pope poem:

> In memory of
> Mrs. Sarah Dix died
> Feb. 11th, 1768, in the 39
> year of her age.
>
> *Hark the --- my spirit away*
> *--- what is this which is quite --- my*
> *senses but my spirit draws my*
> *soul, can this be Death.*

Though only partially legible, there is enough text to identify the source: Pope's *The Dying Christian to his Soul*:

> Vital spark of heav'nly flame!
> Quit, O quit this mortal frame:
> Trembling, hoping, ling'ring, flying,

O the pain, the bliss of dying!
Cease, fond Nature, cease thy strife,
And let me languish into life.

**Hark! they whisper; angels say,
Sister Spirit, come away!
What is this absorbs me quite?
Steals my senses, shuts my sight,
Drowns my spirits, draws my breath?
Tell me, my soul, can this be death?**

The world recedes; it disappears!
Heav'n opens on my eyes! my ears
With sounds seraphic ring!
Lend, lend your wings! I mount! I fly!
O Grave! where is thy victory?
O Death! where is thy sting?

The first verse of the same work was chosen not far away in Richmond, some thirty years later (Jane Sherril, died 1798). This ode was written in 1712, at the request of Richard Steele. I read a version of it appended to a ca. 1799 chapbook account of a "poor half-witted man" who was deeply moved by a sermon he heard one day preached on I Timothy 1:15 ("...Jesus Christ came into the world to save sinners, of whom I am the chief") and came to realize he was equal to all other men in the eyes of Christ. While too late to be a source for Sarah Dix's memorial, this provides another glimpse into the rich flow of printed devotional material available to readers at the time.

There is a vitality and genius to Pope's poetry that I did not appreciate as a younger reader. What a marvelous emotional intensity is distilled into just one couplet: "Trembling, hoping, ling'ring, flying, / O the pain, the bliss of dying!" And the next two lines express in a compressed way a profound religious concept, that what appears to be a slow death can be understood to be languishing into (eternal) life.

I come across the lines "O Grave, where is thy victory? / O Death, where is thy sting?" frequently in these graveyards—they are from I Corinthians 15:55. Considering the relevance of the overall composition and the popularity of Pope, I am surprised I haven't seen more lines from *The Dying Christian* used on these stones.*

This unexpected verse from Pope commands our attention in the Stockbridge Cemetery:

In Memory of Mr.
Silas Bingham Who
Died Jan. the 6th 1781, in
the 49th Year of his Age.

*But all is calm in this eternal sleep
Here Grief forgets to groan and Love to Weep
Evn superstition loses every fear
For God, not man, absolves our frailties here.*

This is from the epistolary poem *Eloisa to Abelard* (1717), Pope's re-telling of a medieval tale of illicit, doomed romance between the beautiful young Eloisa (or Heloise) and her much older tutor, Abelard. Here is the passage in its context:

---

* John Wilkes also parodied this one, in *A Dying Lover to His Prick*. But enough of Wilkes.

> See in her cell sad Eloisa spread,
> Propp'd on some tomb, a neighbour of the dead.
> In each low wind methinks a spirit calls,
> And more than echoes talk along the walls.
> Here, as I watch'd the dying lamps around,
> From yonder shrine I heard a hollow sound.
> "Come, sister, come!" (it said, or seem'd to say)
> "Thy place is here, sad sister, come away!
> Once like thyself, I trembled, wept, and pray'd,
> Love's victim then, though now a sainted maid:
> But **all is calm in this eternal sleep;**
> **Here grief forgets to groan, and love to weep,**
> **Ev'n superstition loses ev'ry fear:**
> **For God, not man, absolves our frailties here."**
>
> I come, I come! prepare your roseate bow'rs,
> Celestial palms, and ever-blooming flow'rs.
> Thither, where sinners may have rest, I go,
> Where flames refin'd in breasts seraphic glow:
> Thou, Abelard! the last sad office pay,
> And smooth my passage to the realms of day;
> See my lips tremble, and my eye-balls roll,
> Suck my last breath, and catch my flying soul!

These doomed lovers are not obvious role models for a deceased Congregationalist. Still, whoever chose this verse as an epitaph found a calming devotional message in that spectral voice urging Eloisa to lay down the tribulations of life and resign herself to God's absolution. A good friend commented: "'For God, not man, absolves our frailties here' is a line of real Popean genius that makes this selection an elegant tribute and reminder of the Christian rewards for a good life…. The line has a tone of a commonplace, which the meter emphasizes, but the breathtaking propriety of the theological assertion is wonderful, both pithy and full of hope." I can add nothing further without diluting the insight.

Another deeply moving verse by Pope can be found several times, first in the Gilead Cemetery in Hebron, Connecticut:

> In Memory of Mrs.
> Hannah relict of Capt.
> Abijay Rowlee who died
> Oct 18th 1810, Aged 83
> Years.
> Also of Capt. Abijah Rowlee
> who left his native land
> for the defence of his country
> and died at Shoram st. (?) Ver-
> mont Sep. 18th 1776. Aged
> 46 years.
>
> *By foreign hands his diing eyes were clos'd*
> *By foreign hands his decent limbs compos'd*
> *By foreign hands his humble grave adorn'd*
> *By strangers honour'd, and by strangers mourn'd.*

This is an apt choice of memorial verse for a Revolutionary volunteer killed far from his home (Shoreham was the jumping-off point for the Green Mountain Boys attacking Fort Ticonderoga in 1776). The source is Pope's *Elegy to the Memory of an Unfortunate Lady* (ca. 1715–1717):

> **By foreign hands thy dying eyes were closed,**
> **By foreign hands thy decent limbs composed,**
> **By foreign hands thy humble grave adorn'd,**
> **By strangers honour'd, and by strangers mourn'd!**

The same verse was chosen for grave in Lee's Center Cemetery that must have a captivating back-story, now long lost:

> In memory of
> FREDERICK CASEY Esq.
> An English Resident of
> St. Thomas, W.I. who died
> in this town, March 14,
> 1826, aged 34 years.
>
> *By Strangers honour'd, and*
> *by Strangers mourn'd.*

I would love to know how this fellow got from the West Indies to Lee, and why. Shopping for limestone or specialty paper, perhaps? It seems a highly unlikely itinerary.

A third version of the same verse appears in Lanesborough's Talcott Cemetery, where I transcribed it on one of my boyhood collecting expeditions. I went in search of it recently but could not find it again. Forty years of weather and neglect have either rendered the carving entirely illegible or the stone itself is toppled:

> Bernard McGinty died April 10, 1832. Age 26 years.
>
> *By stranger hands his dying eyes were closed,*
> *By stranger hands his decent limbs composed,*
> *By stranger hands the funeral rites performed,*
> *By strangers honored and by strangers mourned.*
>
> *Erected by his fellow craftsmen -------? ----------? Stone cutters.*

The solemn rhythms of this verse stayed with me through the years, as did the image of a young quarry worker dying in Lanesborough, far from his unnamed home (perhaps in Ireland?), among strangers. Not only strangers, but Protestant strangers, burying a surely Catholic young man from away. There is no other McGinty buried in Lanesborough cemeteries, so he truly had no family to bury him.

This use of this *Elegy* across miles and decades implies the existence of that anthology of "Appropriate Epitaphs for Varied Occasions" or "Verses Suitable for Use as Epitaphs" I mentioned in Part I—in this case for an out-of-towner, and with "stranger" replacing "foreign." I find it hard to believe individuals in three different communities each had access to Pope's *Elegy* and independently had the same idea of using it as an epitaph for a deceased stranger in their midst. In addition to these memorials, by the way, the same verse was widely quoted in nineteenth-century letters, obituaries, and Civil War memoirs as a "go-to" text for mourning one who died far from home.

In Lancaster's Old Settlers Burial Ground another verse from *Elegy to the Memory of an Unfortunate Lady* was chosen:

ERECTED
To the Memory of
WILLIAM DUNSMOOR Esqr.
who departed this Life
May ye 20th, 1784:
in the 51st year
of his age.

Life how short, Eternity how long.

How lov'd, how valu'd, once avales thee not,
To whom related or by whom begot;
A heap of dust alone remains of thee,
Tis all thou art, & all that die shall be.

This quatrain is quoted by James Hervey in his *Meditations Among the Tombs in a Letter to a Lady.* William Dunsmoor's infant son is buried next to him, with a verse from Matthew Prior (the Dunsmoors apparently had a taste for poetry, and were willing to pay to have it carved on their family gravestones). The verse also appears across Massachusetts at roughly the same time, including the John Gordon stone in Chester (d. 1799), which also features a finely rendered hourglass which has run itself out (Figure 32). I have found it used as late as 1808 in the Norton Cemetery in Otis (Timothy Whitney, age 73). The verse appears in Murray's *English Reader*, which may explain its appearance in different places at different times. "Eloisa to Abelard" and "Elegy to the Memory of an Unfortunate Lady" also appear in the first edition of Pope's *Collected Poetry.*

Pope's *On Elijah Fenton*, mentioned in Part I, appears again up in Northfield Center Cemetery, along with yet another Pope verse:

Deacon
Samuel Smith
Died Decemr the 21st
1799
Aged 95

Reader deny it if you can
Here lies interred an honest man
By Pope denominated rightly
The noblest work of the Almighty

The reference in the second couplet is to Pope's *Essay on Man*, Epistle IV line 247:

A wit's a feather, and a chief a rod;
An honest man's the noblest work of God.

The tone and composition of the Northfield verse seem distinctive. It is perhaps not a great work of versification, but it is

Figure 32. John Gordon stone (courtesy of Bob Drinkwater).

witty, almost snappy. The author has confidence in his ability to work with Pope's texts and customize them. Until I find it elsewhere in the same form, I will argue this is the work of a well-read local Pope enthusiast, who knew and admired Deacon Smith and composed this verse specifically for his memorial.*

We find another great poet, John Milton, chosen for an epitaph in Westfield's Old Burying Ground:

> SACRED
> To the Memory of Mrs
> Margaret Consort of D^r
> David Shepard of Cheste^r
> who died Feb. 10. AD 1769.
> In the 20 year of her age.
>
> *Many are the shapes of Death. &*
> *many are the ways that leads to his*
> *grim Cave: all dreadfull. But*
> *Virtue alone assures that Peace,*
> *Which age nor death can ne'er destroy*
> *Affords the Mind a lasting Ease,*
> *And fills it with immortal Joy*
> E.S.

Note the initials added to the end of the inscription—this is the carver Elijah Sikes, who also signed his work in Belchertown (among several other towns). John Milton (1608–1674) was a poet, man of letters, and civil servant under Oliver Cromwell. He wrote at a time of religious flux and political upheaval—aptly parallel to the controversies roiling New England Congregationalism and the spirit of Revolution that characterize the era of these epitaphs. The first lines are from Book XI of Milton's masterpiece *Paradise Lost*, though with some changes. The Archangel Michael is speaking to Adam and Eve as he prepares them for expulsion from Eden:

> Death thou hast seen
> In his first shape on Man; **but many shapes**
> **Of Death, and many are the ways that lead**
> **To his grim cave, all dismal**; yet to sense
> More terrible at the entrance, than within.

The rhyming quatrain appended to the Milton verse in Mrs. Shepard's epitaph is unique, though it sounds like an echo of a couplet from Pope's *Essay on Man* (1733–34): "Know then this truth (enough for man to know), / Virtue alone is happiness below.'" There are many other examples of this "splicing" of texts, revealing some local hand participating in the memorializing process—but without disclosing his or her identify.

Examples like this, and we find many of them, provide a vivid window into this specific event, the death and remembrance of one young woman, two centuries ago and more. Someone in Westfield knew Milton, or was inspired by this passage in an anthology, then added a personal testimony in their own words to Margaret's virtue, then commissioned a relatively expensive custom carving job. It amounts to quite a literary endeavor, when you stop to think about it, out there in the foothills of the Berkshires.

---

* I found the complete couplet used on the grave of Benjamin Goodridge in Lunenberg (d. 1773).

Another passage from Book XI of *Paradise Lost* was chosen for a grave in Amherst's West Cemetery (Figure 33):

IN
memory of
Mrs. Eunice Parsons
Consort of the Rev.
David Parsons,
who died Sept. 20th
1796 in ye 74th yr
of her age.

Let me
Interpret for him, Me his advocate
And Propitiation, all his works on me
Good or not good, ingraft my merit those
Shall perfect & for these my death shall pay.

Here, the speaker is the Son of God, interceding with the Father on behalf of Adam and Eve as they humbly seek forgiveness for their great sin. This is a marvelous text for an epitaph, invoking Christ's intervention for the soul of Mrs. Parsons. Here is the passage in context:

Figure 33. Eunice Parsons stone (courtesy of Bob Drinkwater).

See Father, what first-fruits on earth are sprung
From thy implanted grace in Man; these sighs
And prayers, which in this golden censer mixed
With incense, I thy priest before thee bring;
Fruits of more pleasing savour, from thy seed
Sown with contrition in his heart, than those
Which, his own hand manuring, all the trees
Of Paradise could have produced, ere fallen
From innocence. Now therefore, bend thine ear
To supplication; hear his sighs, though mute;
Unskilful with what words to pray, **let me**
Interpret for him; me, his advocate
And propitiation; all his works on me,
Good, or not good, ingraft; my merit those
Shall perfect, and for these my death shall pay.
Accept me; and, in me, from these receive
The smell of peace toward mankind: let him live
Before thee reconciled, at least his days
Numbered, though sad; till death, his doom, (which I
To mitigate thus plead, not to reverse,)
To better life shall yield him: where with me
All my redeemed may dwell in joy and bliss;
Made one with me, as I with thee am one.

I sometimes respect Milton more than I enjoy him, frankly, but isn't this noble, deeply moving language? The idea that Adam's and Eve's fall contains the seed of redemption, that their sighs and prayers have a "more pleasing savour" than if they had never sinned because they are contrite, is theologically rich and merits the admiration of contemplative readers.

In Lancaster's Old Settlers Burial Ground we find a moving epitaph (briefly discussed in Part I), that concludes with a verse by Robert Burns:

> DEO PATRIAE AMICIS
> In Memory of Mr.
> WILLIAM HARRIS
> who fled from ye destruction
> of Charlestown, A.D. 1775,
> where he was Public School
> Master 11 Years: and came
> to this town, where he died,
> Octr 30th, 1778, aged 34
> Years & 3 months: he left
> behind a Wife & 4 children,
> who raised this stone to perpe
> tuate ye memory of a man
> justly beloved.
>
> *O ye whose cheek ye tear of pity stains*
> *Draw near with pious reverence & attend;*
> *Here lie ye loving Husband's dear remains,*
> *The tender Father, & the generous Friend;*
> *The pitying heart that felt for human woe;*
> *The dauntless heart oppos'd to human pride;*
> *The friend of man to vice alone a foe,*
> *"For e'en his failings lean'd to virtue's side."*

This is an almost word-for-word rendition of *On My Ever-Honored Father*, which Burns composed on the occasion of his father's death in 1784:

> O ye whose cheek the tear of pity stains,
> Draw near with pious rev'rence, and attend!
> Here lie the loving husband's dear remains,
> The tender father, and the gen'rous friend;
> The pitying heart that felt for human woe,
> The dauntless heart that fear'd no human pride;
> The friend of man-to vice alone a foe;
> For ev'n his failings lean'd to virtue's side.

How appropriate these sentiments are for a worthy minister, and how fortunate that the widow Harris somehow had access to these words as a perpetual monument to her late husband.

I have found William Shakespeare chosen only once, in Old Bennington Cemetery in Vermont, on a minister's richly-carved stone which also features this respectful eulogy:

> In Memory of the Revd. Mr.
> JEDIDIAH DEWEY First Pastor of the
> Church in Bennington. Who after
> a Laborious Life In the Gospel
> Ministry, Resignd his Office in

> Gods Temple For the Sublime
> Employment of Immortality.
> Decembr. 21st 1778
> In the 65th year of his Age.
>
> *Of Comfort no Man Speak:*
> *Let's talk of Graves, and worms,*
> *and Epitaphs, Make dust our*
> *Paper, and with Rainy Eyes,*
> *Write sorrow on the bosom*
> *of the Earth.*

This is from *Richard II* (III.2), a haunting, melancholy passage in which the deposed King meditates upon his surely impending death. Richard's speech also includes the famous lines: "For God's sake, let us sit upon the ground / And tell sad stories of the death of kings…." It is surely noteworthy to find this secular verse on a distinguished minister's grave. I cannot help but think the Reverend Dewey enjoyed reading Shakespeare, and found comforts there that were not available in his more orthodox devotional books. The lines originated in the worldly context of the theater, the very last place you might expect a proper Congregationalist to look for inspiration, yet they evoke a fitting reflection on how all mortals, even Kings, must end:

> Let's choose executors and talk of wills:
> And yet not so, for what can we bequeath
> Save our deposed bodies to the ground?
> … nothing can we call our own but death
> And that small model of the barren earth
> Which serves as paste and cover to our bones.

The poet William Cowper (1731–1800) was chosen for the impressive monument in Stockbridge Cemetery that we saw in Part I:

> Erected to the Memory
> Of SOLOMON GLEZEN
> Who, made Prisoner by the
> Insurgents, fell at the Bat
> tle in Sheffield Feb. 27th
> 1786 in the 26th year of
> his age.
>
> *Oh for a lodge in some vast Wilderness*
> *Some boundless contiguity of Shade*
> *Where rumor of oppression & deceit*
> *Of unsuccessful or successful War,*
> *Might never reach us more.*

This is from Cowper's extended blank verse masterpiece *The Task* (1785), specifically the opening lines of Book II (*The Time-Piece*). Certainly it is a fitting choice of words for a young man killed on the last day of a nasty little civil war, Shay's Rebellion. "Boundless contiguity of shade" may be a mouthful, but the desire to rest beyond the reach of rumors of war, whether triumphant or defeated, is achingly fitting. Here is the passage in context:

> **Oh for a lodge in some vast wilderness,**
> **Some boundless contiguity of shade,**

> **Where rumour of oppression and deceit,**
> **Of unsuccessful or successful war,**
> **Might never reach me more.** My ear is pain'd,
> My soul is sick, with ev'ry day's report
> Of wrong and outrage with which earth is fill'd.

Cowper's verse can be ponderous (my ear is pain'd, indeed), yet he endures as an early innovator in what we now consider Romantic poetry, expressing great truths about God's creation and the human condition through close observation of everyday life. Cowper was a staunch abolitionist, and campaigned against slavery with his friend John Newton, a poet we shall encounter shortly. He was a devout evangelical hymn-writer; in one he coined the phrase "God moves in a mysterious way / His wonders to perform." He also suffered from periodic bouts of insanity. He was recovering from one such episode when he assigned himself the task of describing poetically the room in which he was recovering, starting with the sofa. This effort expanded into his great work, *The Task*.

Cowper's *The Task* appears again almost twenty years later, in Northampton's Bridge Street Cemetery:

> In Memory of
> MRS. Phebe Strong
> the Relict of Mr.
> Caleb Strong who
> died Jan 5 An Dom
> 1802 in the 85 year
> of her age.
>
> *We loved but not enough the gentle hand that reared us,*
> *Gladly would we now read [heed?] that softest Friend, a Mother,*
> *Whose mild converse and faithful council we in vain regret.*

This is an elegant re-working of a passage from Book VI, *The Winter Walk at Noon*:

> **We loved, but not enough, the gentle hand,**
> **That reared us**. At a thoughtless age allured
> By every gilded folly, we renounced
> His sheltering side, and wilfully forewent
> **That converse, which we now in vain regret**.
> How gladly would the man recall to life
> The boy's neglected sire! **A mother too,**
> **That softer friend**, perhaps more gladly still,
> Might he demand them at the gates of death.

I find this melancholy, rueful passage is even more moving as rendered on this gravestone than in its original context. The epitaph is complex and suggestive, combining paraphrase with some original imagery to turn the text into a highly personalized expression of loss and regret. I see the hand of someone in Northampton familiar with his or her Cowper and comfortable enough to compose this poem for their mother. By the way, we will come across Phebe Strong's late husband's epitaph soon, from another eighteenth-century poet.

This lovely and apposite verse was chosen for an epitaph in Wrentham Center Cemetery (a bit outside usual my geographic focus, but too good an example to pass up):

In memory of
Mr. EBENEZER HAWES
who departed this life
April 19th, 1812,
In the 91st Year
Of his age

Of no distemper, of no blast he dy'd,
But fell like autumn fruit, that mellow'd long;
E'en wondered at, why he no sooner dropt.
Fate seemed to wind him up for fourscore years,
Yet restless ran he on, ten winters more,
Till like a clock worn out with eating time,
The wheels of weary life at last stood still.

I love the simile of death as a clock worn out from *eating* time (not just *counting* time). The image of fate seeming to "wind him up for fourscore years" is felicitous among these epitaphs. Many refer to the "three score and ten" years that mankind is granted in Psalm 90:10, "The days of our years are threescore years and ten; and if by reason of strength they be fourscore years, yet is their strength labour and sorrow; for it is soon cut off, and we fly away." Here, the speaker begins with a sorrowful lot of fourscore, then adds another ten winters the more to impress on the reader the great age of the subject. In the case of Ebenezer Hawes, he had ninety-*one* winters to his name when the wheels of his weary life at last came to a stop.

Ebenezer Hawes's epitaph is a verbatim excerpt from John Dryden's *Oedipus* (1678), a text that somehow found its way to southeastern Massachusetts in the early nineteenth century. Dryden (1631–1700) was one of the great figures of Restoration literature, revered by Pope and Samuel Johnson for creating an elegant, formal English poetic style to succeed the complex metaphysics of John Donne. He is perhaps best known for the heroic satires *Absalom and Achitophel* (1681) and *Mac Flecknoe* (1682). *Oedipus* was a collaboration with Nathaniel Lee, a contemporary dramatist. Dryden had a fascinating and mutable political career. He wrote an early Royalist elegy in honor of Charles I, yet later took a job with one of Oliver Cromwell's ministers, John Thurloe. He composed a notable poetic eulogy when Cromwell died, but after the Restoration he successfully re-invented himself by writing panegyrics to Charles II and ultimately became Poet Laureate.

The context for the Hawes epitaph verse is complicated. We are in Act IV, and Oedipus is relieved to learn that his presumed father King Polybus is dead. Dryden portrays Oedipus fervently hoping to hear that Polybus was killed by someone else, and that the Oracle's dreadful prophecy has been thwarted. Instead, he hears of this gentle and natural passing. An unlikely Classical backstory for a good Christian's memorial.

Dr. Johnson, the great man of eighteenth-century letters, was chosen for a gravestone in Lanesborough Center Cemetery:

In Memory
of
CATHERINE C. WASHBURN
who died June 18, 1817. Age 43 years.
This stone erected
by
Luther Washburn

> Her bereaved husband, as a
> testimonial of his esteem and
> affection for her while living.
>
> *New sorrow rises as the day returns,*
> *A partner sickens, and a partner dies,*
> *Till pitying nature signs a last release,*
> *And bids afflicted worth retire in peace.*

Samuel Johnson (1709–1784) was an essayist, poet, editor, biographer, lexicographer, and center of an extensive circle of novelists, playwrights, poets, and actors. He is probably most widely known today for his *Dictionary* (1755) and as the subject of James Boswell's *Life of Johnson*. He was also a devout Anglican whose writings were often intended to be morally instructive. Catherine Washburn's epitaph is a close adaptation of a passage from Johnson's *Vanity of Human Wishes* (1749):

> **New Sorrow rises as the Day returns,**
> **A Sister sickens, or a Daughter mourns.**
> Now Kindred Merit fills the sable Bier,
> Now lacerated Friendship claims a Tear.
> Year chases Year, Decay pursues Decay,
> Still drops some Joy from with'ring Life away;
> New Forms arise, and diff'rent Views engage,
> Superfluous lags the Vet'ran on the Stage,
> **Till pitying Nature signs the last Release,**
> **And bids afflicted Worth retire to Peace.**

Johnson's great poem was widely popular and well-known long before the early 1800s. Its overarching theme of the futility of worldly achievements without Christian grace makes it an apt text for a funerary memorial. It is not just a theological work; who does not respond with emotion to the images of "lacerated friendship" and "year chasing year"? This epitaph strikes me as the handiwork of a literate person, comfortable shaping the words of Johnson to express his particular situation and feelings.

Note that there is a clear attribution of the individual who chose the text—the widowed husband. This is rare on these stones. Luther (or an acquaintance) apparently knew his Johnson, out there in the fields and hills of Lanesborough. I also think Luther must have held Catherine in particularly high regard. First, he paid to have the carver memorialize his "esteem and affection for her." And notice how "Sister" in the original becomes "partner" on the grave; not a wife or consort but a full partner. Good for him, and may all husbands take note.

Samuel Taylor Coleridge (1772–1834) is quoted or alluded to in several of these graveyards. Here are two from Northampton' Bridge Street Cemetery:

> In Memory of
> JULIA AUGUSTA STRONG,
> youngest daughter of Theodore and Martha Strong,
> Born March 30, 1822, died Nov. 10, 1827,
> aged 5 year and 7 months.
>
> *Ere sin could blight, or sorrow fade,*
> *Death came with friendly care,*
> *The opening bud to heaven conveyed,*
> *And bade it blossom there*

> ELIZABETH W.,
> Daur of F.W. and L.B. Clarke,
> died Sept. 28, 1848, aged 8 years.
>
> *Death came with friendly care,*
> *The opening bud to heaven conveyed,*
> *And bade it blossom there.*

This is from Coleridge's *Epitaph on an Infant* (1794). But how did this one come to be used in Northampton, twice across 20 years? Perhaps one or two households in town owned an edition of Coleridge's poetry. But this is more likely to be evidence of my hypothesized anthology of epitaphs, in this case from a section entitled "Appropriate for an Infant."

One text, used in several different versions across time and distance, can be found in just such an collection. *A Cypress Wreath for an Infant's Grave* by the Rev. John Bruce (1820) was created for specifically mothers who had lost infants. Bruce attributes the lyric to Coleridge, but I cannot identify the original poem. First, in West Stockbridge's South Cemetery:

> Memory of
> CHARLES WINCHELL
> [son?] of
> Mr [Illegible] Winchel
> who died August 28th, 1818
> in the 2 Year of his age
>
> *This lovely bud so young and fair*
> *called hence by early doom*
> *Just came to show how sweet a flower*
> *In paradise would bloom.*

I have found many more recurrences, the last one in Lee:

> HARIET D.
> daught. of
> Curtis & Mary
> WOODWARD,
> died
> Aug. 3, 1850,
> AE 1½ Y's
>
> *This lovely babe so young and fair*
> *Called hence by early doom,*
> *To see how beautiful a flower*
> *In Paradise could bloom.*

This hopeful, sentimental little quatrain evidently had a run of popularity over fourteen years across several adjacent towns. Of course I cannot be sure *A Cypress Wreath* was the source used when choosing epitaphs for these memorials. The same verse is found in *The Oxford Entertaining Miscellany* (1824), a compendium of humorous anecdotes, scientific essays, poetry, and epitaphs. It may be that a copy of the *Oxford Miscellany*—or another volume like it—made its way to the Berkshires. Or perhaps, as in Northampton, someone in these towns just really liked Coleridge.

Texts by other poets, far less read today than Pope, Milton, Burns, Cowper, Dryden, Johnson, or Coleridge, were also chosen for use in these graveyards. As you read these works by long-neglected but evidently once-popular writers, I hope you appreciate the sheer range of literature they comprise, and the volume of related activity they imply—printing, distribution, and above all reading—in these remote little villages.

Let us begin with this stone in Belchertown's South Cemetery (Figure 34), which quotes a popular source; the same lines are in Falmouth (1775), Salem (1794), and Granby (1789)[*]:

> In memory of M^r.
> Joseph Bardwell.
> who died June 1. 1791.
> In the 78. year of his
> age.
>
> *His virtues wou'd a*
> *monument supply,*
> *But underneath this stone*
> *his ashes lie.*

Figure 34. Joseph Bardwell stone (courtesy of American Antiquarian Society).

It has a bit of an Alexander Pope ring to it, but whereas Pope was an eighteenth-century Catholic, this verse has its roots firmly in seventeenth-century Calvinism. The source is the epitaph of one John Flavel, as it appears in a collected edition of his works. The epitaph reads in its entirety:

> Happy in his studies; an acute disputant;
> A seraphic preacher; an elegant writer;
> In all full of learning, and very famous;
> Exact in his sentiments, and excellent in his morals;
> An unwearied patron of Christian truth, piety and charity;
> An utter enemy to all kinds of vice and error:
> The glory of the church and the city he belong to
> Where he had worn himself quite out in praying,
> And watching for the good of God's people,
> Peacefully fell asleep in JESUS
> ON JUNE 26, 1691; AGED 61
>
> ***His virtues would a monument supply,***
> ***But underneath this stone his ashes lie.***
> *Could grace or learning from the grave set free,*
> *FLAVEL thou hadst not seen mortality.*

---

[*] Another case of recurrence which I think must be accounted for by the elusive ur-anthology of "Appropriate Epitaphs."

Tho' here thy dusty part death's victim lies,
Thou by thy works thyself doth eternize,
Which death nor rust of time shall overthrow;
Whilst thou does reign above these live below.

John Flavel (1627–1691) was an eminent minister and popular writer who sought to convey Christian Revelation in terms easily understood by ordinary people. His two most famous works are *Husbandry Spiritualized*, which takes its language and metaphors from the world of the farmer, and *Navigation Spiritualized*, which does the same from the experience of sailors. I have in my collection the hefty seventh edition of *The Whole Works of the Reverend Mr. John Flavel*, (Edinburgh, 1762), measuring 9½ × 15½ inches. In it, *Husbandry* and *Navigation* include carefully folded over-size pages, the text concerning elements of theology displayed in a circular arrangement of spokes or rays. Upon seeing these pages unfolded, a good friend and letter-press printer commented admiringly: "Now *that* took a lot of work." Flavel's works, though theologically dense, have a vigorous diction and strong evangelical thrust, and have been published more or less continuously for five hundred years. His *Token for Mourners* was a particularly popular reading for bereaved parents.

The first section of the epitaph, which borders on the panegyric, was originally composed in Latin and is of unknown origin.[*] Joseph Martin, the publisher of a collection of Flavel's works (Richmond, 1826) in his preface credits Richard Baxter with the verse section. Baxter (1615–1691) was also a Puritan preacher and a staggeringly prolific theologian, writing hundreds of books and, apparently, this elegy to Flavel.

Baxter appears again in Peterborough, New Hampshire, on a handsome stone with a distinctive architectural design (Figure 35):

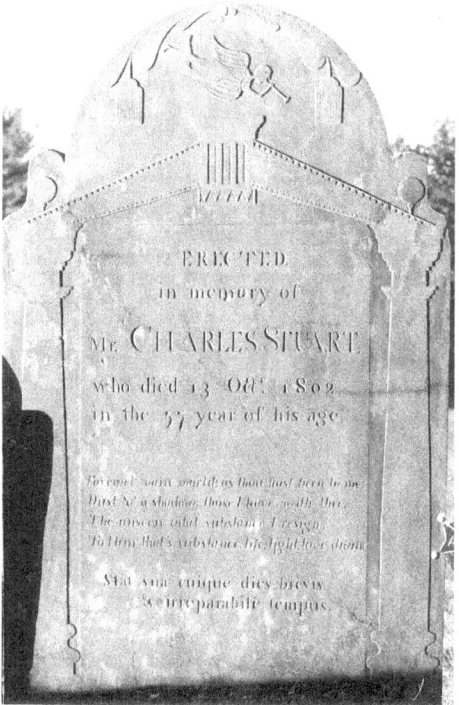

ERECTED
in memory of
Mr. CHARLES STUART
who died 13 Octr 1802
In the 57 year of his age.

Farewell vain world: as thou has been to me,
Dust & a shadow; those I leave with thee,
The unseen vital substance I resign,
To Him that's substance, life, light, love divine.
Stat sua cuique dies; brevis
& irreparabilie tempus.

The same quatrain is used in New Haven, Connecticut (Samuel Hall, died 1755) and Chadkirk in England (the Rev. Charles Shepley, died 1769). It is a slight variation of an

Figure 35. Charles Stuart stone (courtesy of American Antiquarian Society).

---

[*] I envy him the epithet "seraphic preacher and elegant writer."

unattributed epigram found at the beginning of Baxter's *The Reasons of the Christian Religion*:

> **Farewell vain World! As thou hast been to me**
> **Dust & a Shadow; those I leave with thee:**
> **The unseen Vitall Substance I committ**
> **To him that's Substance, Light & Life to it.**
> The Leaves & Fruit here dropt are holy seed,
> Heaven's heirs to generate; to heale & feed:
> Them also thou wilt flatter & molest
> But shalt not keep from Everlasting Rest.

The provenance is enforced in an 1831 sermon preached by one Benjamin Luckock in the Barbados; Luckock attributes the lines to Baxter, calling them "unctional" and "homely." The imagery is perhaps a little commonplace; Baxter is not the first or last writer who bids this alluring existence farewell and resigns his soul to light and life with God. Personally I find the second half of the poem more interesting, with the metaphor of the dead body as leaves and fruit that will nurture souls to come, and the dismissive image of a world that flatters and molests us.

The Latin text is a fitting quotation for Virgil's *Aeneid* (X 467): "The last day is fixed for everyone; brief and unrecoverable is the time [of life]." This is another of the infrequent, but always fascinating, uses of Latin in these graveyards. This juxtaposition of Baxter's Christian rejection of worldly pleasures and distractions while actively moving on to everlasting peace, with Virgil's pagan reflection on the finality of death, is striking.

This epitaph raises the tangential subject of Classical literature as a source for these stones. Consider, for example, this gravestone in Sheffield's Barnard Cemetery, which contains an eighteenth-century translation of Horace:

> Erected
> to the memory of
> Ballantine Ashley
> who died March
> 7 1799 aged 29
>
> *Life's span forbids us*
> *to extend our cares*
> *Or stretch our hopes*
> *beyond our years.*

In *The Spectator* No. 289 (January 31, 1712) Joseph Addison wrote a sustained essay on Death in which he urges every reader to

> consider, that he is in this Life nothing more than a Passenger, and that he is not to set up his Rest here, but to keep an attentive Eye upon that State of Being to which he approaches every Moment, and which will be for ever fixed and permanent. This single Consideration would be sufficient to extinguish the Bitterness of Hatred, the Thirst of Avarice, and the Cruelty of Ambition.

The edition begins with the epigram "Vitæ summa brevis spem nos vetat inchoare longam.—Hor." Addison's corresponding footnote reads:

> *Translation of motto:*
> *HOR. 1 Od. iv. 15.*

> *"Life's span forbids us to extend our cares,*
> *And stretch our hopes beyond our years."*
> (Creech).

Thomas Creech (1659–1700) was an English translator of Lucretius, Manilius, Horace, and Theocritus, among others. His early work was favorably compared to Dryden's Virgil and Pope's Homer, but posterity has not been as kind. Creech's *The Odes, Satyrs, and Epistles of Horace. Done into English* was published in 1684 and went through multiple reprintings well into the eighteenth-century (long after his death, by suicide over disappointment in love). We cannot know if Ballantine Ashely (or whoever chose this epitaph) knew the full Ode, but it is wonderfully apt. Horace describes the coming of spring and the re-emergence of life after a hard winter—then reminds his friend Sestius that Death is amongst us all the time, choosing which house to visit next. I could not hazard a guess as to whether his work found its way to rural western Massachusetts via *The Spectator*; a copy of *The Odes, Satyrs, and Epistles*; or some anthology of quotations.

I read another translation of Horace, chosen for the grave of an amiable woman in Enfield, Connecticut (Figure 36):

> Sacred to the Memory of
> M^{rs}. HANNAH ALDEN
> the amiable consort of
> Maj^r. AMOS ALDEN
> who was born Septr 14th 1744
> and died Octr. 10th 1801.
>
> *Day presses on the heels of day,*
> *And moons increase to their decay;*
> *But you with thoughtless pride elate*
> *Unconscious of impending fate,*
> *Command the pillar'd dome to rise.*
> *When lo, the tomb forgotten lies.*

This is a translation of a Horace ode (Book 2 Ode xviii) by Philip Francis D.D., published in 1743. Francis (1708–1773) was born in Dublin and became something of a literary celebrity in his day, known for his various Classical translations. I like the vivid imagery of each day pressing on the heels of the day before, and the contrast between the palaces we try to raise on high and the yawning grave beneath our feet. This ode is on the subject of the pointlessness of greed for material riches given the certainty of death which takes the rich and poor alike—a message in harmony with contemporary hymns and devotional

Figure 36. Hannah Alden stone (courtesy of American Antiquarian Society).

poetry. Again, we cannot know if this verse was known to Hannah Alden's bereaved survivors via a copy of Dr. Francis's verses, or an anthology. Horace's original text is:

> Traditur dies die
> Novaeque pergunt interire Lunae:
> Tu secanda marmora
> Locas sub ipsum funus; et sepulcri
> Immemor, struis domos.

Isn't it a fine sentiment for a grave, in either language?

I came across another epitaph from the Classics, and an intriguing one, in the Orleans Old Burying Ground, on the memorial of Dr. Joseph Seabury (1801):

> *Alas the meanest flowers which gardens yield*
> *The vilest weeds that flourish in the field*
> *Which dead in wintry sepulchres appear*
> *Revive in spring and bloom another year*
> *but we the great the brave the larned the wise*
> *Soon as the hand of death has closd our eyes*
> *In tombs forgotten lie no suns restore*
> *We sleep forever sleep to wake no more.*

This is surely not a particularly Christian choice of memorial. There is no promise of resurrection; on the contrary the message is clearly that once we die we never wake again, while even vile weeds come back to life each spring. As it turns out, the epitaph is a line-for-line quotation from an eighteenth-century translation of a work by the Classical Greek poet Moschus (ca. 150 BC), found in *The Works of Anacreon, Sappho, Bion, Moschus, and Musaeus Translated from the original Greek* by Francis Fawkes (1760). "Larned" here is a mis-carving of "learned" in the original.

Fawkes (1720–1777) was an English poet and Classical translator of some renown. Perhaps his most enduring work is a humorous poem, *The Brown Jug*. A good friend who is a Classics professor assures me that the phrase "minor poet" might have been coined expressly with Moschus in mind. He is read today, to the extent he is read at all, for a short narrative poem or idyllium on the myth of Europa. Dr. Seabury's epitaph is from another idyllium, *On the Death of Bion*. The choice and source of text beg the question of how skeptical the Doctor was in his faith, and also how this somewhat obscure text found its way to Cape Cod.

The fact is that Classical literature is not often found in these graveyards. Contemporary ministers learned their Latin and Greek at Yale and Harvard, and many of their gravestones bear elaborate encomia in carefully-composed New Latin. These carved eulogies, however, tended to be written for the learned, by the learned; apparently Latin did not serve well to express the emotions of their rural congregations. The phrase "Memento Mori" or "Tempus Fugit" is sometimes carved at the top of the stone, and Aet. or Aetatis is used frequently. But beyond that, Latin (let alone Greek) is rare, especially out in the hinterlands. The two others instances I have found are the motto NASCENTES MORIMUR* on a stone for three young siblings in Lee Center Cemetery and this in Granby, Connecticut, Cemetery:

---

* This can be translated as "As we are born we begin to die" or "We are born only to die"—all too literally true of Jerusha (7 months), John (5 months), and William (5 weeks) Foot, whose three solemn faces are movingly carved on the tympanum of the stone. See p. 193.

> In Memory of
> Sarah Pelleireau ye
> Daughr of Rev.d
> Joseph & Mrs. Jane
> Strong who died
> Septr. 24th [176?]4
> aged 2 years 13 days.
>
> *Omnes cadunt morte*

Which I translate as: All fall in death. It is noteworthy that the Reverend Strong used Latin used on his child's gravestone and not a Bible verse or a passage from the New England Primer.

Now, back to the subject of lesser-known poets. Matthew Prior was chosen for the stone of a baby boy in Lancaster's Old Settlers Burial Ground:

> John Dunsmoor, Son of
> William Dunsmoor Esqr,
> & Mrs Hannah his wife;
> who died Oct. 29th,
> 1756: Aged 1 Year
> & 8 Months.
>
> *Happy the babe, who preveleg'd by fate,*
> *To shorter labour, and a lighter weight,*
> *Receiv'd but yesterday the Gift of breath,*
> *Order'd to-morrow to return to death.*

Prior (1664–1721) was an English poet, diplomat, and essayist. Based on his reputation as a satirist, his noble patron secured him ambassadorial roles in The Hague and Paris.* Later, Prior was imprisoned for two years when he wound up in the wrong political camp after the death of Queen Anne. This epitaph chooses a passage from Book III of his *Solomon on the Vanity of the World*:

> Happy the mortal man, who now at last
> Has through this doleful vale of misery past,
> Who to his destin'd stage has carry'd on
> The tedious load, and laid his burthen down;
> Whom the cut brass, or wounded marble, shows
> Victor o'er Life, and all her train of woes.
> **He, happier yet, who, privileg'd by Fate**
> **To short labour and lighter weight,**
> **Receiv'd but yesterday the gift of breath,**
> **Order'd tomorrow to return to death.**

Solomon was one of Prior's most ambitious though perhaps least successful efforts; he is known in English literature for his many occasional poems, which display a lighter epigrammatic wit. Still, *Solomon*'s admirers included Thackeray and Dr. Johnson, who said: "[T]he work is far from deserving to be neglected. He that shall peruse it will be able to mark many passages, to which he may recur for instruction or delight; many from which the poet may learn to write, and the philosopher

---

* Evidently the transition from entertainer to politician is not a uniquely recent phenomenon.

to reason."* I do not disagree; Prior's couplets lack Pope's brilliant polish but as seen here, he could achieve eloquent expression of the familiar theme of the vanity of worldly things.

With that said, it commands our attention to see such a sentiment chosen for the grave of a toddler. I am challenged to imagine that the heartbroken parents consoled themselves with the thought that little John was happier dead than alive.† Still, I find the same passage chosen at about the same time in Sheffield, Bradford, Fairfield and Groton in Connecticut, and the Carolinas—so it was evidently relevant to the parents of deceased children (and broadly distributed). I also observe that this is longer, and therefore a more expensive commission, than is typical for a baby's gravestone. So it must have delivered emotional value for money.

Another example of a meaningful epitaph from a now-obscure source is this, in Longmeadow Cemetery:

> In Memory of
> Miss DINAH
> Daughter of
> M^r. THOMAS & M^{rs}.
> DEBORAH COLTON
> who died
> March 9th 1784
> In Her 30 year.
>
> *My peaceful grave shall keep*
> *My bones, 'till that sweet day,*
> *I wake from my long sleep,*
> *And leave my bed of clay.*

There is something lovely and comforting about most of this text. The grave is peaceful and indeed protective, and beloved Dinah is not dead, just sleeping to awake some sweet day. The last line jars my ear a bit, pulling the reader back to the grimmer reality of the bed of clay. The source is *Hope in Death*, a poem by Samuel Crossman (1624–1683). According to *A Library of Religious Poetry* (Schaff and Gilman, New York, 1881), Crossman "was prebendary of Bristol and a writer of considerable prose. His poetry is not generally of a high order. His piece on Heaven is considered the best he wrote." The poem was put to music and became a popular hymn beginning "My life's a shade, my days / Apace to death decline."

Gentle reader, you may judge for yourself if it is fair to judge his poetry as not of a high order:

> My life's a shade, my days
> Apace to death decline ;
> My Lord is Life,
> He'll raise My dust again, ev'n mine.
> Sweet truth to me !
> I shall arise,

---

* On the other hand, Johnson also said of Prior "Tradition represents him as willing to descend from the dignity of the poet and statesman to the low delights of mean company… [T]he woman with whom he cohabited was a despicable drab of the lowest species. One of his wenches … while he was absent from his house, stole his plate, and ran away…" Such have ever been the vicissitudes of the artist's life.

† Recall that William Dunsmoor, the father, had an epitaph with verse by Alexander Pope.

And with these eyes
My Saviour see.

**My peaceful grave shall keep
My bones till that sweet day :
I wake from my long sleep
And leave my bed of clay.**
Sweet truth to me !
I shall arise,
And with these eyes
My Saviour see.

My Lord His angels shall
Their golden trumpets sound,
At whose most welcome call
My grave shall be unbound.
Sweet truth to me !
I shall arise,
And with these eyes
My Saviour see.

Perhaps not a surpassing piece of work—you would certainly not confuse this for the eloquence of Isaac Watts. Still, I admire the sincere conviction in the short assertion "sweet truth to me!"

Another grave in Longmeadow from the same year, a great impressive table tomb, uses a verse from a poet who should be much more widely read than she is today:

Sacred to the Memory of
Mr. SAMUEL COLTON
Merchant
who departed this life
Nov. 5, 1784 in the 57th year
of his age.

*The Sun's too quick revolving beams
Apace dissolves the humane dreams
And brings the appointed hour.
Too late we catch his parting ray
And mourn the idly wasted day
No longer in our power.
then happiest he whose lengthened sight
Pursues by virtue's constant light
A hope beyond the skies
Where frowning Winter ne'er shall come
But rosy Spring forever bloom
And suns eternal rise*

This is a commendable bit of writing. The rhyme scheme is clever (AAB, CCB), and those short every-third lines have real punch: "appointed hour / no longer in our power," "hope beyond skies / suns eternal rise."

The source is *Ode to Spring* by Elizabeth Carter (1717–1806). Carter was an English poet, classicist, writer, musician, linguist, and polymath. She won renown for completing the first English translation of the *Discourses* of Epictetus, the 2nd-century CE Stoic philosopher. She was a prominent member of the Bluestockings, an informal women's social movement that emphasized education and mutual co-operation, and also published poems and translations from French and Italian. I read somewhere with interest that Mrs. Carter was a life-long user of snuff. She was a friend of Dr. Johnson, and helped edit some issues of *The Rambler*. This poem is also anthologized the *Pleasing Instructor or Entertaining Moralist*, a compendium of items from contemporary newspapers, magazines, and other anthologies of literature (London, 1770, ed. Anne Fisher).

This is a good example of the era's taste for finely-crafted verse in which the observation of nature (the setting sun, the rosy Spring) serves to provide moral instruction (do not waste your time, live virtuously, keep your mind on eternal things). It is representative of her work, which is always skillfully written and morally improving, but perhaps lacking the spark of true genius. Mrs. Carter's work was chosen again a few years later in Sheffield's Barnard Cemetery (Figure 37):

Here lies
until the resurrection
the body
of Mrs. Mary Hickok.
Consort of
Col. Jere^h. Hicok
who died
Nov. 22 AD 1791
AEt. 42

In Earth's soft bosom sooth to rest
She sleeps by smiling dreams caresd
That gently whisper peace:
Till the last morn's fair opening ray
Enfolds the bright eternal Day
Of active life and Bliss

This is from her *Ode to Melancholy*. In Carter's *Ode*, the first line reads "In Death's soft slumber lulled to rest"—a version with "Earth's Soft Bosom" appears in *The Gentleman's Magazine* as early as November 1739, and the *Ode* is also anthologized in Knox's *Elegant Extracts*.

Figure 37. Mary Hickok stone (author's collection).

Here is the poem in its entirety. To our ears it may sound more didactic than moving, but respect must be paid to the fact that it was popular enough to be widely distributed, and proved meaningful to the mourners of Mary Hickok:

COME, Melancholy! silent pow'r,
Companion of my lonely hour,
To sober thought confin'd:
Thou sweetly-sad ideal guest,
In all thy soothing charms confest,
Indulge my pensive mind.

No longer wildly hurried thro'
The tides of mirth, that ebb and flow,

In folly's noisy stream:
I from the busy croud retire,
To court the objects that inspire
Thy philosophic dream.

Thro' yon dark grove of mournful yews
With solitary steps I muse,
By thy direction led:
Here, cold to pleasure's tempting forms,
Consociate with my sister-worms,
And mingle with the dead.

Ye midnight horrors! awful gloom!
Ye silent regions of the tomb,
My future peaceful bed:
Here shall my weary eyes be clos'd,
And ev'ry sorrow lie repos'd
In death's refreshing shade.

Ye pale inhabitants of night,
Before my intellectual sight
In solemn pomp ascend:
O tell how trifling now appears
The train of idle hopes and fears
That varying life attend.

Ye faithless idols of our sense,
Here own how vain your fond pretence,
Ye empty names of joy!
Your transient forms like shadows pass,
Frail offspring of the magic glass,
Before the mental eye.

The dazzling colours, falsely bright,
Attract the gazing vulgar sight
With superficial state:
Thro' reason's clearer optics view'd,
How stript of all its pomp, how rude
Appears the painted cheat!

Can wild ambition's tyrant pow'r,
Or ill-got wealth's superfluous store,
The dread of death controul?
Can pleasure's more bewitching charms
Avert, or sooth the dire alarms
That shake the parting soul?

RELIGION! ere the hand of fate
Shall make reflexion plead too late,
My erring senses teach,
Amidst the flatt'ring hopes of youth,
To meditate the solemn truth,
These awful relics preach.

Thy penetrating beams disperse
The mist of error, whence our fears
Derive their fatal spring:
'Tis thine the trembling heart to warm,

And soften to an angel form
The pale terrific king.

When sunk by guilt in sad despair,
Repentance breathes her humble pray'r,
And owns thy threat'nings just:
THY voice the shudd'ring suppliant chears,
With MERCY calms her tort'ring fears,
And lifts her from the dust.

Sublim'd by thee, the soul aspires
Beyond the range of low desires,
In nobler views elate:
Unmov'd her destin'd change surveys,
And, arm'd by faith, intrepid pays
The universal debt.

In death's soft slumber lull'd to rest,
She sleeps, by smiling visions blest,
That gently whisper peace:
'Till the last morn's fair op'ning ray
Unfolds the bright eternal day
Of active life and bliss.

There is style and skill in many of these lines. The shortened meter of each stanza's third and sixth lines provide a firm, almost solemn cadence to some of the most significant images of the poem: led/dead, bed/shade, superficial state/painted cheat. Here Mrs. Carter uses many of the tropes and images of the Graveyard School of poets, whom we shall meet shortly. Note finally the sibilant alliteration of the last stanza, with its soft slumber, sleep, whispered peace, and bliss; easing us off to the quiet of the tomb.

John Pomfret (1667–1702) was an English poet and clergyman whom I encountered for the first time in these graveyards, starting with this stone in Lanesborough:

Sacred to the Memory
of Mrs. Rebekah,
Consort of
Mr. Nat. Hickox;
who died Nov. 11,
1787 in the 34.
year of her age.

All that was noble, beautify^d her mind,
Bles^{sd} was her temper with good reason join^d
In health and sickness, calm her passions were,
And for a future state shew^d proper care.

The first two lines are from Pomfret's *A Pastoral Essay on the Death of Queen Mary* (1694), a somewhat mannered panegyric in which the shepherd Strephon and the dairy-maid Cosmelia together mourn the untimely death of Caelestia, "the brightest Nymph, the Princess of the Plain / by an untimely Dart, untimely slain." The style of the poem tends to the artificial and over-wrought, but the lines chosen pay a lovely compliment to Mrs. Hickox. I have not been able to source the second two lines—they strike me as a perfect epigrammatic summary of Congregationalist virtues.

Pomfret was chosen again almost twenty-five years later, in Norfolk Connecticut:

Mr. PITT BLISS
died
Sept. 4th 1810
aged 50
If to the seats of happiness I go,
There end all possible returns of woe.
and when to these blest mansions I arrive,
With pity I'll behold those who survive.

To say "if" I go to the blessed mansions, not "now that I have gone" to them, seems an interesting choice in this context. The source for the verse is even more interesting: Pomfret's *Cruelty and Lust: An Epislatory Essay*. This long, dramatic poem "was occasioned by the barbarity of Kirke, a commander in the western rebellion, 1685, who debauched a young lady with a promise to save her husband's life, but hanged him the next morning." Like *Eloisa and Abelard*, not an obvious source for an epitaph. The lines on Pitt Bliss's stone are spoken by Charion, the unfortunate husband, as he pleads with his wife to abandon him and flee the evil Neronior's lust:

> Beyond the grave stupendous regions lie,
> The boundless realms of vast eternity;
> Where minds, remov'd from earthly bodies, dwell;
> But who their government or laws can tell?
> …I can submit to my Creator's will;
> Let him recall the breath from him I drew,
> When he thinks fit, and when he pleases too.
> The way of dying is my least concern;
> That will give no disturbance to my urn.
> **If to the seats of happiness I go,**
> **There end all possible returns of woe:**
> **And when to those blest mansions I arrive,**
> **With pity I'll behold those that survive.**
> Once more I beg, you'd from these tents retreat,
> And leave me to my innocence and my fate.

Pomfret is best known today for his occasional poem *The Choice*, a charming and eminently readable idealization of a gentleman's life: sufficient income, a pleasant but not ostentatious house in the country not too far from London, lots of good books, eating and drinking (in moderation) with a couple of sympathetic friends, and a "witty nymph" at hand. Pomfret muses "[t]o this fair creature I'd sometimes retire / Her conversation would new joys inspire / Give life an edge so keen…." This nymph had dire consequences, as Dr. Johnson relates in his short and guardedly complimentary chapter on Pomfret ("he pleases many, and he who pleases many must have some species of merit") in his *Lives of the English Poets*:

> [Pomfret] was rector of Malden in Bedfordshire, and might have risen in the Church; but that, when he applied … for institution to a living of considerable value … he found a troublesome obstruction raised by a malicious interpretation of some passage in his *Choice*; from which it was inferred, that he considered happiness as more likely to be found in the company of a mistress than of a wife…. The malice of his enemies had … a very fatal consequence: the delay constrained his attendance in London, where he caught the small-pox, and died….

So many back-stories out in these graveyards!

This stone from the Westfield Old Burying Ground is a wonderful example of how one epitaph may incorporate allusions to and echoes of multiple poetic sources (including the ubiquitous Isaac Watts):

> In Memory of
> Mrs. MARGARET
> ASHLEY. who
> died 25th July
> 1791. in the 77th
> Year of her Age.
>
> *Life is a bubble*
> *quickly broke:*
> *A tale forgot*
> *as soon as smoke*
> *A shadow changing*
> *with the* [moon? morn?]
> *Which spreads itself*
> *& then is Gone.*

The bursting bubble as a metaphor for the fragility of life appears in many contemporary texts that could have been available to a reader in Westfield. Here's an example from *The Life of Man*, a poem by the widely respected seventeenth-century scientist, philosopher, and devotional writer Francis Bacon:

> **The World's a bubble, and the life of man**
> **less than a span;**
> In his conception wretched, from the womb
> so to the tomb:
> Curst from the cradle, and brought up to years
> with cares and fears.
> Who then to frail mortality shall trust,
> But limns the water, or but writes in dust.
>
> Yet since with sorrow here we live opprest,
> what life is best?
> Courts are but only superficial schools
> to dandle fools.
> The rural parts are turned into a den
> of savage men.
> And where's the city from all vice so free,
> But may be termed the worst of all the three?
>
> Domestic cares afflict the husband's bed,
> or pains his head.
> Those that live single take it for a curse,
> or do things worse.
> Some would have children; those that have them moan,
> or wish them gone.
> What is it then to have or have no wife,
> But single thraldom, or a double strife?
>
> Our own affections still at home to please
> is a disease:
> To cross the seas to any foreign soil
> perils and toil.

> Wars with their noise affright us: when they cease,
> we are worse in peace.
> What then remains, but that we still should cry
> Not to be born, or being born to die.

Alexander Pope uses the same image in *An Essay on Man* (I.87), adjacent to a passage we have already encountered:

> Who sees with equal eye, as God of all,
> A hero perish or a sparrow fall,
> Atoms or systems into ruin hurl'd,
> And **now a bubble burst, and now a world.**
> Hope humbly then; with trembling pinions soar;
> Wait the great teacher Death, and God adore!

Isaac Watts uses the same metaphor in one of his hymns, and he also includes the smoke:

> God of my life, look gently down,
> Behold the pains I feel;
> But I am dumb before Thy throne,
> Nor dare dispute Thy will.
>
> Diseases are Thy servants, Lord,
> They come at Thy command;
> I'll not attempt a murmuring word
> Against Thy chastening hand.
>
> Yet may I plead with humble cries,
> Remove Thy sharp rebukes;
> My strength consumes, my spirit dies,
> Through Thy repeated strokes.
>
> Crushed as a moth beneath Thy hand,
> We molder to the dust;
> Our feeble powers can ne'er withstand
> And all our beauty's lost.
>
> This mortal life decays apace,
> **How soon the bubble's broke!**
> **Adam and all his numerous race**
> **Are vanity and smoke.**
>
> I'm but a sojourner below,
> As all my fathers were;
> May I be well prepared to go,
> When I the summons here!
>
> But if my life be spared a while,
> Before my last remove,
> Thy praise shall be my business still,
> And I'll declare Thy love.

Recall that Margaret Ashley lived to the ripe old age of seventy-seven when the bubble of her life broke. Her lesson is that life is always precarious, even when it is not short. We may never know whether her epitaph was locally composed or copied from some as-yet-undiscovered emblem book or anthology. Nor can we be certain if these texts, or others like them, provided direct inspiration to the anonymous writer. But we can see that the metaphors of bubble and smoke were current in the literary and spiritual culture of the age.

In Westfield's Old Burying Ground this remarkable stone includes a text from a writer better known for his novels than his poetry:

> While this Stone shall last,
> Let it commemorate
> PAUL WHITNEY, A.M. & M.D.
> A Dea^n of the Church in this place
> who, on Mar^h 9th 1795, aged 42,
> departed this life—a man of ho
> nest and noble heart; and, tho' with
> out office, was capable, in any
> office, of doing honour to
> his country.
>
> *Column & urn but vainly show*
> *A scene of decorated woe,*
> *The friend, who faithful & sincere,*
> *Will need to art to urge the tear.*
> *Regardless of the labour'd verse*
> *It flows spontaneous o'er his hearse*

I admire the humility and sense of awareness in those unique opening lines, which acknowledge that no funeral marker will endure forever. Also, doesn't the list of virtues sound genuinely warm, the words of a true friend of Paul Whitney's? The source is *Epitaph on a Lady*, a charming and well-crafted little poem by Laurence Sterne. The friend who composed the eulogistic lines also took creative license with Sterne's verse, which reads in the original:

> **Columns and labour'd urns but vainly show**
> **An idle scene of decorated woe.**
> **The sweet companion, and the friend sincere,**
> **Need no mechanic help to force a tear.**
> In heart-felt numbers, never meant to shine;
> 'Twill flow eternal o'er a hearse like thine;
> 'Twill flow whilst gentle goodness has one friend,
> Or kindred tempers have a tear to lend.

Sterne (1713–1768) was an Anglo-Irish writer best known for his two innovative novels, *Tristram Shandy* and *A Sentimental Journey*. He was also a minister and published many sermons, letters, and occasional verse—including this *Epitaph*.

In Sheffield's Barnard Cemetery this gentle, comforting, lyrical verse was chosen (Figure 38):

> IN Memory of
> Mrs. MARY FELLOWS.
> consort of
> General John Fellows;
> who died Decr 7th *1797;*
> in the 58th year of
> her age.
>
> *Each lonely scene shall thee restore;*
> *For thee the tear be duly shed;*

*Belov'd till worth can charm no more,
And mourn'd till pity's self be dead.*
Ely fecit Pittsfield

Note the explicit marketing message from the carver. These advertisements not common, but one sees them from time to time.

I am not sure this verse works all that well as an epitaph. The first two lines serve a purpose, but the sentiment feels pedestrian—I will think of you when I am lonely, and shed an expected tear. And the last two lines seem unhelpfully dense. So let us turn to the source. The epitaph is a close—but slightly edited—paraphrase of a passage from *Dirge in Cymbeline* by William Collins. Born in Sussex and educated at Magdalen College, Oxford, Collins (1721–1759) declined to be a clergyman, then was rejected by the army. He moved to London to become a writer, where he made the acquaintance of Johnson and Garrick. Sadly, he was notorious for producing more ideas than books, his productivity marred by alcohol and, eventually, insanity. Yet over time his reputation grew. His *Odes* were composed explicitly to create a new, more emotive poetry than the formal structures of Pope and the Augustans; they were admired and emulated by the early Romantic poets. Here is the *Dirge* in its entirety:

Figure 38. Mary Fellows stone (author's collection).

> To fair Fidele's grassy tomb
> Soft maids and village hinds shall bring
> Each opening sweet of earliest bloom,
> And rifle all the breathing Spring.
>
> No wailing ghost shall dare appear
> To vex with shrieks this quiet grove;
> But shepherd lads assemble here,
> And melting virgins own their love.
>
> No wither'd witch shall here be seen,
> No goblins lead their nightly crew;
> The female fays shall haunt the green,
> And dress thy grave with pearly dew.
>
> The redbreast oft at evening hours
> Shall kindly lend his little aid,
> With hoary moss, and gather'd flowers,
> To deck the ground where thou art laid.
>
> When howling winds, and beating rain,
> In tempests shake thy sylvan cell;
> Or 'midst the chase, on every plain,
> The tender thought on thee shall dwell;

> **Each lonely scene shall thee restore,**
> **For thee the tear be duly shed;**
> **Beloved, till life can charm no more;**
> **And mourn'd, till Pity's self be dead**.

I mean no offense to lovers and scholars of Collins, but I can assure the common reader that if you have never heard of him, you are not alone. I had not read Collins until I found him on this gravestone. The *Dirge* is an odd piece of work. The wailing ghosts and withered witches feel contrived—I am glad they won't be seen, but did we have any reason to expect them in the first place? Why should we feel relieved that they are absent? Their personalities are out of place in this sylvan scene. I am inclined to agree with Dr. Johnson, who said of Collins the man, "I once delighted to converse, and ... I yet remember with tenderness," but said of Collins the poet: "[H]is diction was often harsh, unskillfully laboured, and injudiciously selected.... As men are often esteemed who cannot be loved, so the poetry of Collins may sometimes extort praise, when it gives little pleasure." "Unskillfully laboured" indeed; I could not have put it better myself.

Here is a notable text from Northampton's Center Cemetery which also turns out to have an author with a decidedly mixed career:

> Sacred to the memory of
> Mr. ELISHA LYMAN
> who departed this life
> August 13th 1798
> Being in the 65th year
> of his age.
>
> *Man departs this early scene,*
> *Ah! Never to return,*
> *No second Spring shall ere revive*
> *The ashes of the urn.*

Note that there not a lot of resurrection here upon first reading. It seems a bleak message for surviving mourners to read. But as with Watts hymns, the single verse carved on the stone does not impart the full message of the poem. The source is *The Complaint of Nature* by John Logan (1748–1788), based on Job 14, itself a popular Scripture source for these gravestones. Logan was a Scottish minister, historian, and poet. He was also depressive drinker and a rake. He fathered an illegitimate son by a servant girl in his Scots parish and fled to London. There, a second pregnant parishioner proved his last straw. Logan resigned his pulpit, and retired on a pension to eke out a living as a hack writer. A captivating rogue, regrettably forgotten today.

I will not quote the complete poem (it goes on at considerable and unrewarding length) but here is enough to give you a feel for the whole:

> Few are thy days and full of woe,
> O man of woman born!
> Thy doom is written, "Dust thou art,
> And shalt to dust return."
>
> ...
>
> Alas! the little day of life
> Is shorter than a span;
> Yet black with thousand hidden ills
> To miserable man.

> Gay is thy morning; flattering hope
> Thy sprightly step attends;
> But soon the tempest howls behind,
> And the dark night descends.
>
> ...
>
> When chill the blast of Winter blows,
> Away with Summer flies;
> The flowers resign their sunny robes,
> And all their beauty dies.
>
> ...
>
> The Winter past, reviving flowers
> Anew shall paint the plain;
> The woods shall hear the voice of Spring,
> And flourish green again:
>
> **But man departs this earthly scene,**
> **Ah, never to return!**
> **No second spring shall e'er revive**
> **The ashes of the urn.**
>
> Th' inexorable gates of death,
> What hand can e'er unfold?
> Who from the cerements of the tomb
> Can raise the human mould?
>
> ...
>
> "Where are our fathers? whither gone
> The mighty men of old?
> The patriarchs, prophets, priests, and kings,
> In sacred books enroll'd?"
>
> ...
>
> Thus Nature pour'd the wail of woe,
> And urged her earnest cry;
> Her voice in agony extreme
> Ascended to the sky.
>
> Th' Almighty heard: then from His throne
> In majesty He rose,
> And from the heaven that open'd wide
> His voice in mercy flows:
>
> "When mortal man resigns his breath,
> And falls a clod of clay,
> The soul, immortal, wings its flight
> To never-setting day.
>
> "Prepared of old for wicked men
> The bed of torment lies;
> The just shall enter into bliss
> Immortal in the skies."

As you see, Logan ultimately assures his reader there *is* a second spring, that God *does* revive the ashes in the urn and raise the human mold. This would have been a welcome and resonant message for the contemporary reader. It also fits the pattern of epitaphs that move beyond the grim implications of The Classic and Job, to the more hopeful conviction that while there is a bed of torment waiting for the wicked, the just may be confident of entering into immortal bliss.

There are some fine passages in this work. The pounding cadence suits the flying days and mighty flood, and the idea that the hour of our death is already on the wing, headed our way, is arresting. But the overall structure lacks tightness, and the meter stumbles into sing-song. So how did this ponderous poem make its way from Grubb Street to the frontier town of Northampton, and onto Elisha Lyman's gravestone? One hint came from friends who collect the work of stone carvers in the Connecticut River valley. They showed me a copy of *An Inventory of the Estate both Real + Personal of the Late Revd Richard S. Storrs* (1819) which contains a volume of Logan's sermons. The Reverend Storrs died in Longmeadow; it is not hard to imagine a fellow-preacher in Northampton having a collection of the fellow's poems.

In the lovely cemetery of the Church on the Hill in Lenox we find this moving statement that reconciles grieving over a death to gratitude for a long life together shared:

> Decmber 2nd
> AD 1802
> died M^{rs}. Eliza-
> beth Consort of
> Col.
> Elijah Northrup
> aged 55.
>
> *Lord She was thine, and not my own,*
> *Thou hast not done me wrong,*
> *I thank thee for that precious loan,*
> *Afforded me so long.*

The source is an elegy written by the Rev. John Newton on the first anniversary of his wife's death. The epitaph is an exact quotation. The same verse was chosen thirty years later in the Center Cemetery at Westhampton, and as far away in Connecticut, Maine, and Pennsylvania at about the same time. Note the rare syntax, with the date of death preceding the name of the deceased.

Newton (1725–1807) was a captain in the slave trade who converted to Christianity, took Holy Orders, and wrote hymns including *Amazing Grace* and *Glorious Things of Thee Are Spoken*. After his wife died in 1790, Newton published *Letters to a Wife* (1793), which includes the lengthy poem from which this epitaph was taken. I have found the same passage used as an epitaph in the United States and England well into the early twentieth century, for both men and women. It enjoyed a much longer life as an inscription than as a poem.

This elegant little verse from the late 1600s was chosen for an epitaph in the early 1800s in the Old Towne Cemetery in Sandwich, on the gravestone of Grace Tobey (d. 1803, aged 67):

> *Circles are prais'd, not that abound*
> *In largeness, but exactly round.*
> *So lives are prais'd not that excell*
> *In length of time, but living well.*

Cape Cod is well east of my usual collecting grounds, but I was struck by both the epitaph and its source. It is a slight variation of a brief epigrammatic poem by Edmund Waller, entitled *The Long and Short Life*:

> Circles are praised, not that abound
> In largeness, but the exactly round:
> So life we praise that does excel
> Not in much time, but acting well.

Waller (1606–1687) was an admired poet in his day who also had a tumultuous political career during and after the English Revolution. He married a London heiress who died young, leaving him in the enviable status as one of England's wealthiest poets. His graceful, polished style marked a transition (akin to Prior) between Donne and the metaphysical poets of the seventeenth century and the beginning of the eighteenth-century Augustan style.*

Doesn't this verse work perfectly as an epitaph? It rewards close reading; observe how each couplet is complete in itself. The first evokes an image of geometry and measuring instruments, praising precision and the expert hand of the draftsman. The second, expanding on the first, makes clear that the length of one's life is less important than how one chooses to live. We must live as well as the draughtsman draws. Of course quality of life or "living well" here is not about material things but about devotion and virtue. There is nothing wrong with living a good long "large" life, but without virtue, without having lived properly, it is not worthy of praise.

I have not seen this poem on other gravestones, but it was extensively anthologized at the time. We can't tell at what point the slight variations in text were introduced, but a version of this poem could easily have made its way in print to a carver, or literate household, at the beginning of the turn of the eighteenth century. To my ears it foreshadows an image we will soon encounter in the work of Edward Young:

> What tho' short thy date?
> Virtue, not rolling suns, the mind matures.
> That life is long, which answer's life's great end.

I wonder if Young had read Waller.

I read an appealing verse chosen in Shelburne, Vermont, Village Cemetery, from the work of another lesser-known writer who should be more widely read today:

> Zeruiah Wife of Mr.
> Oliver Shelpdon died
> June 27th 1805 in the
> 26th year of her age.
>
> *Dear friend adieu,*
> *Go see that quiet shore*

---

* Waller was a Royalist in Parliament after the outbreak of the war, and tried to arrange a reconciliation with Charles I. Caught in conspiracy to force Parliament into a settlement, he abjectly abandoned his confederates, spent more than a year imprisoned in the Tower of London, then bribed his way into exile. From there he managed a reconciliation with Cromwell and returned to England where he wrote panegyrics to the Protector. After the restoration he managed yet another volte face and wrote a congratulatory ode to Charles II after the Restoration. In his *Lives of the Poets*, Samuel Johnson did not mince words regarding Waller's peripatetic loyalties: "[H]e that has flattery ready for all whom the vicissitudes of the world happen to exalt, must be scorned as a prostituted mind, that may retain the glitter of wit, but has lost the dignity of virtue."

Where sin shall vex
And sorrow wound no mor
There share the joy
The words of life impart
The vision promis'd
To the pure in heart.

The source is an epitaph *On Mrs. Blandford* by Hannah More (1745–1833). Like Elizabeth Carter, More was a prominent Bluestocking, an educator, writer, and social reformer. As a playwright and poet she was part of the circle of Edmund Burke, Samuel Johnson and Joshua Reynolds, and was something of a protégée of the brilliant actor David Garrick. By all accounts she was a precocious intellect and an immensely influential teacher. In the course of her long career she became a prolific writer of popular religious tracts, abolitionist and evangelical poetry, and an extensive critique of female educational practices. Her vast output also includes such works as *Sacred Dramas* for the improvement of young readers, *Essays on Various Subjects, Principally designed for Young Ladies* for the improvement of, well, young ladies, and *Thoughts on the Importance of the Manners of the Great to General Society* for the improvement of society's elite. Like Mrs. Carter, Hannah More merits a wider readership. The full text of the poem is:

Meek shade, farewell! go seek that quiet shore
Where sin shall vex, and sorrow wound no more;
Thy lowly worth obtains that final bliss,
Which pride disdains to seek, and wit may miss.
That path thou'st found, which science cannot teach,
But faith and goodness never fail to reach;
Then share the joy the words of life impart,
The Vision promis'd to the pure in heart

In length, meter, and style this is a quintessential example of the literary epitaphs of the age. Read it aloud, and you will see how easily it scans, and how the elegant couplets roll off the tongue. It strikes me as a deft, well-crafted piece of work.

Here is an example of an epitaph by a justifiably neglected poet in Sheffield's Barnard Cemetery:

In Memory of
DELLA ANN GOODRICH
who died Oct. 14th 1809
Aged 1 Year & 9 months

Fair was the blossom, soft the vernal sky,
Elate with hope we deemed no tempest nigh,
When lo a whirlwinds instantanious gust
Left all its beauties withering in the dust.

This is an exact quotation from James Beattie's *Elegy Written in the Year 1758*. Beattie (1735–1803) was a Scottish poet, essayist, and prominent abolitionist. His claim to (limited) fame is his extended poem *The Minstrel* (1771–1774) which ran through many editions and attracted the praise of Samuel Johnson. A representative excerpt of the *Elegy* is:

Ah whither [is Youth] fled!—ye dear illusions stay—
Lo, pale and silent lies the lovely clay.

How are the roses on that cheek decay'd,
Which late the purple light of youth display'd!
Health on her form each sprightly grace bestow'd;
With life and thought each speaking feature glow'd—
Fair was the flower, and soft the vernal sky;
Elate with hope, we deem'd no tempest nigh;
When lo, a whirlwind's instantaneous gust
Left all its beauties withering in the dust.

… O Death, why arm with cruelty thy power,
And spare the idle weed, yet lop the flower!
Why fly thy shafts in lawless error driven!
Is Virtue then no more the care of Heaven! —
But peace, bold thought! be still my bursting heart!
We, not Eliza , felt the fatal dart.
'Scaped the dark dungeon does the slave complain,
Nor bless the hand that broke the galling chain?
… O happy stroke that bursts the bonds of clay,
Darts through the rending gloom the blaze of day,
And wings the soul with boundless flight to soar,
Where dangers threat, and fears alarm no more.

Transporting thought! here let me wipe away
The tear of grief, and wake a bolder lay.

As poetry, this is mediocre stuff. The meter is irregular, and the theme and imagery are far from original, let alone ingenious. But that is not the point. The point is that his words touched the hearts of Della Goodrich's bereaved survivors, wherever they read them, providing a poetic articulation of the lessons their religion taught, that death provides a "happy stroke that bursts the bonds of clay / …And wings the soul with boundless flight to soar / Where dangers threat, and fears alarm no more." Transporting thought, indeed! And if Beattie's *Elegy* brought comfort to these mourners, then who are we to carp about its literary merits and demerits?

In Amherst's West Cemetery the epitaph of Azariah Dickinson (d. 1813 at age 60) uses this lovely passage from one of the truly great women of eighteen-century English letters:

Farewell, conflicting joys & fears,
Where light & shade alternate dwell;
How bright & unchanging morn appears.
Farewell! Inconstant world, farewell!

The source is *The Death of the Virtuous* by Anna Laetitia Barbauld. The complete poem is as follows:

Sweet is the scene when Virtue dies!
When sinks a righteous soul to rest,
How mildly beam the closing eyes,
How gently heaves the' expiring breast!

So fades a summer cloud away;
So sinks the gale when storms are o'er;
So gently shuts the eye of day;
So dies a wave along the shore.

> Triumphant smiles the victor brow,
> Fanned by some angel's purple wing;—
> Where is, O Grave! thy victory now?
> And where, insidious Death! thy sting?
>
> **Farewell, conflicting joys and fears,**
> **Where light and shade alternate dwell;**
> **How bright the' unchanging morn appears!**
> **Farewell, inconstant world, Farewell!**
>
> Its duty done,—as sinks the day,
> Light from its load the spirit flies;
> While heaven and earth combine to say,
> "Sweet is the scene when Virtue dies!"

Note the reference to Pope's *The Dying Christian to his Soul* (or I Corinthians) in the third stanza. Barbauld (1743–1825) was a distinguished literary figure. She was a widely read poet, essayist, and educator. Her *Lessons for Children* and *Hymns in Prose for Children* were extremely popular—so much so that by the Victorian era Barbauld was dismissed as a mere middle-brow writer of pietistic children's verse. She was also a tremendously influential editor. She edited the works of Samuel Richardson and composed the first critical biography of the early novelist. Her *Female Speaker* was a popular anthology of some of the finest poetry of the age, targeted at a specific readership. And her fifty-volume (!) series *The British Novelists* (1810), with introductions to each author, helped cement the legitimacy of the novel as a literary form and established the groundwork for the canon of British fiction. I am embarrassed to have known Johnson's *Lives of the Poets* for years, and never, until I encountered her on Azariah Dickinson's gravestone, to have heard of Anna Laetitia Barbauld. It is encouraging to learn that her work is being read again in academe and her voice has been rediscovered. *The Death of the Virtuous* was set to music and became a popular hymn in the nineteenth century—Dickinson's epitaph could have come from either a collection of her poetry, or a hymnal.[*]

This remarkable, complex poetic text was carved, no doubt at considerable expense, for a gravestone in Lee Center Cemetery:

> CHRISTOPHER E. CHAMPLIN
> DIED
> Nov. 15, 1836
> AE. 31 Y's
>
> *O all in vain! The warning tone*
> *Deepens—"Its word is death!"*
> *I must depart, in youth, alone—*
> *The cherished hope to live hath flown*
> *Like flight of bird on Summer's breath.*
> *Peace must be nigh this weary soul*
> *Which long for life hath striv'n,*
> *Will sink to rest—the "golden bowl"*

---

[*] Barbauld's biography is another of the lives I would never have learned of, but for this project. She married one Rochemont Barbauld, a grandson of French Huguenots with a melancholy disposition that turned to madness later in his life and ultimately his suicide by drowning. The couple apparently could not conceive a child, so she prevailed upon her brother (and literary partner) John Aikin to let them adopt one of his. The son, Charles, became the inspiration for Barbauld's famous children's literature.

> *Be broken—and the spirit, whole,*
> *Will find its home in Heaven!*

The opening verses are from *Arabella Stuart* by Felicia Hemans (1828). Though she died relatively young, Hemans (1793–1845) was arguably the most widely-read woman poet in the nineteenth-century English-speaking world. Her books of poetry were as popular as Scott's novels and the works of Byron, Tennyson, and both Brownings. She was one of the few women to be regarded as "standard" poet and printed in respectable editions as late as the turn of the twentieth century. Two of her poems are still remembered today: *Casabianca* ("The boy stood on the burning deck/ Whence all but he had fled") and *The Stately Homes of England* ("The Stately Homes of England/ How beautiful they stand!") But not many people could name the author, and even these two are, I expect, less read today than a generation ago.

Arabella Stuart is a Romantic meditation about a doomed princess sitting alone in her cell in the Tower of London, separated from her husband, refusing to eat and slowly dying. Towards the end of this long dramatic monologue she cries:

> **Hark! the warning tone**
> **Deepens—its word is Death. Alone, alone,**
> **And sad in youth, but chasten'd, I depart,**
> Bowing to heaven.

I have found the first American edition of her collected poems, published in 1824—evidently in time for her verse to be available to readers and mourners in Lee in the 1830s. Note also the epitaph's Scriptural references, to Ecclesiastes 12:16 "[Remember the Lord] or ever the silver cord be loosed, or the golden bowl be broken, or the pitcher be broken at the fountain, or the wheel broken at the cistern."; and also to Psalm 34: "The LORD is nigh unto them that are of a broken heart; and saveth such as be of a contrite spirit." The rest of the epitaph, however, I cannot identify or find elsewhere. Perhaps they are original? So once again we can only wonder who selected these texts and worked them into this original lyric.

An imposing verse from a now largely-forgotten source evokes a recurring trope of Death as a path that all of us must follow. It appears on a little stone for a little child in the Tyringham Village Cemetery, so small I had to get down on all fours to read it:

> George, son of
> [Isaac?] and Margaret
> Northrop
> died
> Aug. 21 18[illegible]
> Ae 1 Y [?] 36 D
>
> *Where is the passage to the skies*
> *The road through death's dark valley lies.*
> *This path the best of men have trod,*
> *And who'd decline the road to God?*

The source is *Visions in Verse, for the Entertainment and Instruction of Young Minds, Vision IX (Death),* by Nathaniel Cotton (1707–1788). Cotton was a physician who ran an asylum for the care of the mentally ill, including William Cowper. He was also a part-time poet; *Visions in Verse* (1751) is a long book of poems providing young readers with moral instruction on a range of topics including slander, pleasure, health, contentment, happiness, friendship, marriage, life and death. It was his great success, going through more than a dozen editions over the course of a century, before its didactic orotund language went out of style in children's poetry.

Someone may have had a copy of *Visions in Verse* out in Tyringham, but Cotton is also extensively quoted in *Elegant Extracts* and Murray's *English Reader*.

In Becket, I encountered the work of a poet who is not merely obscure, but entirely anonymous. A melancholy family history is recorded on adjacent stones: four children of the town doctor, and the doctor himself, each with fine yet distinctive epitaphs. The first is a double-headed stone of a brother and sister. The carving is a bit disorienting at first glance; it looks like the children's heads are peeking out from under a quilt or duvet. Then you read the inscription and the parents' sorrow becomes palpable (Figure 39):

> In memory of
> Oliver, who died May 6th
> 1784, aged 1 year 23 days
> and of Rubie who died
> Oct 19th 1784, aged 29 days
> Son & dau[tr] of Doct. Oliver
> & Mrs. Jerusha Brewster
>
> *Sickly pleasures all adieu*
> *Pleasure which we never knew*
> *Happy happy from the womb*
> *While we hasten to the tomb.*

The source is a poem titled *Epitaph on an Infant*. It was anthologized in Murray's *English Reader*, in the section called "Promiscuous Pieces," and also in a periodical, the *Universal Magazine* (Volume 58, 1776).[*] The full poem is a fairly complex dramatic dialogue between a dead infant and an anonymous speaker. The babe bemoans its early demise, before it could take any pleasure in life. The speaker in turn assures the late infant that it is better to die at birth than live in this vain and sickly sphere:

Figure 39. Oliver & Rubie Brewster stone (author's collection).

> To the dark and silent tomb
> Soon I hasten'd from the womb;
> Scarce the dawn of life began,
> 'Ere I measur'd out my span.
>
> I no smiling pleasures knew,
> I no gay delights could view;
> Joyless sojourner was I,
> Only born to weep and die.

---

[*] Recall that Dr. Eliot of Boston transcribed a verse from this poem in his common-place book. Dr. Eliot did not identify any source; evidently some version was available (and read) at both ends of the Commonwealth in the late 1700s.

Happy infant! Early blest!
Rest, in peaceful slumbers rest;
Early rescu'd from the cares,
Which increase with growing years;
No delights are worth thy stay,
Smiling as they seem, and gay;
All our gaiety is vain,
All our laughter is but pain.

Are then all your pleasures vain?
Are the none exempt from pain?
Is there no delight or joy,
but your fondest hopes will cloy?

Short and sickly are they all,
Hardly tasted, 'ere they pall?
Lasting only, and divine,
Is an innocence like thine.

Sickly pleasures, all adieu!
Pleasures which I never knew:
I'll enjoy my early rest,
Of my innocence posses'd:
Happy, happy, from the womb,
That I hasten'd to the tomb.

The speaker's perspective prevails, and the baby goes back to its rest, innocent and happy. An earnest and sincere parable of faith, which may or may not have satisfied the mourning parents.

~~~

As mentioned in Part I, American poetry also is found among these epitaphs, though less frequently than English poetry. The earliest example I have found is in Westfield Old Burying Ground:

Sacred to the Memory of
M^{rs}. MARGARET CLAP
Relict of Capt, EZRA
CLAP Who Departed this
Life Sep. 15, 1782, in the 55
Year of her Age

Lamented shade for thee shall Memory mourn
and deathless praise thy hallowed Grave adorn

This stone introduced me to the work of another under-appreciated woman writer of the time: Judith Sargent Murray (1751–1820). Born in Gloucester, she was an autodidact who read history, philosophy, geography, and literature in her parents' library. She became firmly convinced that with proper education, women could be the intellectual and economic equals of men. In her novels, essays, poetry, and plays she was an influential advocate for women's equality, access to education, and the right to control their earnings. Over the years she has been best known for her 1790 essay *On the Equality of the Sexes*. Sargent Murray led a varied life: She married twice, first to a sea captain and merchant whose fortune was destroyed during the American Revolution and died a penniless refugee in Barbados, and then to a Unitarian Minister who had helped guide her family's conversion from Congregationalism years before. She knew Abigail Adams, Ben Franklin, and Martha Washington. She wrote and published continuously, often as the primary breadwinner for her family. Sargent Murray's literary star may have dimmed for a while, but her *Selected Writings* were anthologized by the Oxford University Press (1995); she is due for a revival of interest in her remarkable life and work.

The Clap epitaph quotes Sargent Murray's *Elegiack Lines To the Memory of Mrs. Abigail Jones* which appeared in the March 1790 edition of the *Massachusetts Magazine* under the name "Constantia." Given that Margaret Clap died in 1782, either whoever chose the epitaph had access to an earlier version of the poem, or the stone is back-dated. While I want to learn more about Sargent Murray, this elegy cannot be her finest work. For the most part it is a well-crafted but not particularly original or moving example of its genre. Here is an excerpt with the epitaph verse in context:

> Bright as the Rose, which fades beneath the storm,
> Fair as the gather'd Lily's silver form,
> **Lamented Shade I for thee shall memory mourn,**
> **And deathless praise thy hallow'd grave adorn!**
> With every grace the raptur'd soul to move,
> Caress'd by fortune, happy in thy love;
> Ah! When did fate in equal splendour shine,
> Or what blest Husband knew a joy like thine!

The last stanza, however, moves to another level of art. The poet begins by asking what impious mortal would dare question God's just decision that Mrs. Jones should die—then proceeds to do exactly that, quite effectively:

> Great God of wisdom! On thy just decree,
> What impious mortal dares to question thee!
> Why the blest ANNA yields her valued breath,
> While loathing wretches court the grasp of death.
> While some, whom sad affliction calls her own,
> Beneath this tedious weight of being gross,
> In secret breathe the unavailing sigh,
> And cloud with ceaseless tears the melting eye!
> Or who the hidden springs of fate can find,
> What ruling power instructs the searching mind!
> Why merit droops, and prosp'rous vice beguiles,
> Why pity mourns, and rude oppression smiles,
> And while the living miscreant laughs at woe,
> O'er BEAUTY'S urn the tears of VIRTUE flow.

There is skill and style in Sargent Murray's reverberant ironic contrasts of "merit droops / vice beguiles," "pity mourns / oppression smiles," and the miscreant laughing while Virtue weeps.

A simple, almost stark, little stone in Monson's North Main Street Cemetery introduces us to a prominent writer, educator, and theologian of the time (Figure 40):

> In memory of
> Hiram son of M^r.
> Nathan & M<u>rs</u>. Lucy
> Hoar. who died sept.
> 20th 1794 aged 2 years

Yes we must fade and die.
While virtues strokes shall live,
Transcend this lower [illegible]

The source is Timothy Dwight's *The Conquest of Canäan*. Dwight (1752–1817) was a distinguished American clergyman and educator, a President of Yale and namesake of its Timothy Dwight College. Born in Northampton, he was Jonathan Edwards's grandson—so his pedigree as a devotional writer is impeccable. *The Conquest of Canäan* (1785) is a sweeping, almost Biblical-style allegory of the taking of Connecticut from the British, which some critics regard as the first American epic poem. To be honest, it is a turgid read, but the selection is apt. On the subject of a well-loved child Dwight writes:

Figure 40. Hiram Hoar stone (courtesy of American Antiquarian Society).

> Nature can form the soul, or rough, or fine;
> But all her clouded beauties faintly shine:
> Religion bids a new creation rise,
> Fragrant as spring, and fair as spangled skies…
> **But these must fade: while Virtue's strokes shall live,**
> **Transcend** earth's sky-built tomb, and with the heavens revive.

This is another example of local creativity; note how the composer of little Hiram's epitaph has taken the liberty of adapting the Reverend Dwight's work. I would like to uncover the missing lines, to see how the two texts compare.

Dwight's work brought to my attention a circle of eighteenth-century writers and critics known as the Hartford Wits. Originally a literary society at Yale, the Wits included David Humphreys, Joel Barlow (he of *Meditations on Death*), John Trumbull, Lemuel Hopkins, Richard Alsop, and Dwight. They collaborated on books of political commentary and satire, often lampooning the florid over-wrought literature of the time. They did not merely comment on events; several fought in the Revolution and went on to political careers. As an example of the role literature played in the American town square, this group deserves to be better known today.

Another epitaph whose text originates among the Hartford Wits is in Old Hadley Cemetery (Figure 41):

> This Monument is
> Erected to the Memry
> of
> Doctor Giles Crouch
> Kellogg M.S.S.
> Whose Professional Merit
> has been rarely surpassd
> Whose Philanthropy &

Humanity never.
He was born May 7
1733. died A"gust 28 1793

Oer Halcyon Seas vain Man
His Course pursues,
While hope allures him
While pleasure woos,
Nor sees that veild beneath
the fair disguise
On Death's dark pinions
from the Storm shall rise.

The source is *The Echo, with other Poems, Printed at the Porcupine Press by Pasquin Petronius* (1807). According to the (anonymous) editor's Preface, this anthology of poems and essays includes political satire and deliberate send-ups of the literary conventions of the age. Among the works in the book is *Democracy, an Epic Poem*, by one Aquiline Nimblechops. The introduction to *Democracy* provides a delightful glimpse of the literary and politics of the time:

> The first Canto was printed in New-York, in March, 1794, and at the time excited no inconsiderable share of the public attention. This poem was written in consequence of a tumultuous meeting of the citizens of that place, instigated by a few popular demagogues, for the purpose of prescribing to Congress the adoption of hostile measures against Great Britain. The second Canto, which was of much greater length, was prepared for the press immediately after the appearance of the first, but the timidity of the booksellers, and the peculiar circumstances of the times prevented its publication.

Figure 41. Giles Crouch stone (courtesy of American Antiquarian Society).

And in Canto the Second we read:

> Alas! How fleeting are our schemes of bliss!
> How frail the tenure of our happiness!
> Mid mists of error still involv'd we stray,
> And blindly grope along a slipp'ry way:
> Too oft from specious good our sorrows flow;
> And joy mistaken leads to certain woe.
> Bright smiles the sun, the vernal breezes move,
> And waft a fragrance from the blossom'd grove
> Fair glows each scene around—with pride elate,
> Man spreads the sail and tempts the depths of fate,

> O'er halcyon seas his careless course pursues,
> While hope allures him and while pleasure woos;
> Nor sees that, veild beneath the fair disguise
> On death's dark pinions soon the Storm shall rise.

The text appears on a gravestone dated 1793, but was not published until 1794. Certainly this could be due to a delay between Dr. Kellogg's death and the completion of his gravestone. But how he, or his survivors, became familiar with this obscure anti–Jacobin poem is a matter for purest speculation. It is clear from reading this passage in context that it is tongue-in-cheek, an over-the-top elegy for failed political ambitions. I would not have chosen it to memorialize a respected doctor, but who am I to second-guess? The principle contributor to *The Echo* was Richard Alsop (1761–1815) of Middletown, Connecticut. Perhaps he and Dr. Kellogg moved in the same circles, up and down the Connecticut River. We are unlikely ever to know for certain.[*]

I had an interesting search for the provenance of this bit of American poetry in Sheffield's Barnard Cemetery:

> In MEMORY OF
> Mr. Ephraim Case,
> who departed this
> life May 5th 1801.
> aged 59 years.
>
> *Under this hillock small doth lie*
> *Intered Ephraim Case.s dust.*
> *It will hear the resurrection cry*
> *When death's cold bands asunder burst.*

The *Essex Institute Historical Collections* Volume XXIV (Salem, Massachusetts, 1886) contains an absorbing article: "An 'Epicedium,' composed in 1752 by Reverend John Cleaveland of Chebacco (now Essex), in Ipswich, Mass" by one E.P. Crowell, Professor at Amherst College. The Epicedium was a "Poetical Attempt upon the Life & Death of Mr. Josiah Cleaveland," the Reverend's father, in the form of three hundred and sixty-eight line eulogistic poem. Crowell writes: "To the 'Epicedium' is appended this 'Epitaph'":

> **Under this Hillock small doth lie**
> **Inter'd Josiah Cleaveland's Dust**
> **'Twill hear the Resurrection cry**
> **When Death's cold Bonds asunder burst.**
> No doubt it will triumphing rise,
> Before the Morning of that Day;
> When Christ shall all the World surprize,

---

[*] The Hartford Wits are one of the delightful under-appreciated footnotes of literature that make this project so rewarding for me, and Alsop may be rightly considered a footnote within the footnote. I found this observation from an early-nineteenth-century commentary on the state of American poetry:
> Mr. Alsop made too little effort for literary distinction to acquire much credit or notoriety as a writer beyond the circle of his own acquaintance. His talents have not been displayed to the world at large, nor perhaps sufficiently appreciated by the few who were admitted to his intimacy. His powers were certainly above the ordinary level of our native authors, and had they been prompted to exercise by a strong endeavor to establish a name, rather than an occasional desire for recreation with the pen, would have placed him in a conspicuous rank among his countrymen.

Oh for what might have been, Richard Alsop!

> His Gospel's Voice who wou'dn't obey.
> Then shall this mortal Dust invest,
> A Nature pure, and uncorrupt:
> And enter to the blessed Rest,
> Where's nought their Joy to Interrupt.

It appears the Reverend Cleaveland's pamphlet traveled the length of the Commonwealth between 1752 and 1801.*

Here is a striking bit of American poetry in Agawam Center Cemetery:

> In Memory of
> Cap't Jon'a Worthington
> who died 14th Aug't
> 1809 Aged 65 years
>
> *White cold and lifeless lies the speechless form*
> *which once was with each Godlike virtue warm*
> *Which for the poor and needy wrought relief*
> *And lost its sufferings in another's grief*
> *Applauding seraphs hail thy happier shade*
> *To brighter realms where no rude storms invade*

Whence this somewhat over-the-top panegyric? After collecting so many God-fearing, cautionary epitaphs, I was surprised to find one that portrays the deceased as surrounded by applauding seraphs. I don't know anything about this paragon of virtue, Captain Jonathan Worthington, but I learned that the author of these florid lines was one Paul Allen, who published a collection of "*Original Poems, Serious and Entertaining*" in 1801. One of Allen's works is entitled "*Epitaph for the Grave-Stone of a near and much-respected Relation.*" The Worthington epitaph quotes it, word for word. Allen (1775–1826) was an American author and editor, and a graduate of Brown University. Whether Captain Worthington was the "near and much-respected Relation" for whom this epitaph was penned, or whether an admirer of the Captain's came across Allen's collection and borrowed the verse, I may never know.

This epitaph in Lanesborough's Talcott Cemetery again raises the question of what intermediary text served to make it accessible to whoever found it and selected it:

> Fanny Mason,
> daughter of Reuben and Mary Mason,
> born March 26, 1797, died Jan. 11 1834
>
> *Here let my body sleep and rest,*
> *Within its clay cold bed,*
> *Till with refulgent glory drest*
> *It rises from the dead.*

---

* A series of books and pamphlets in the collection of the Boston Athenaeum make clear that Reverend Cleaveland was an active participant in a long series of back-and-forth disputes with other North Shore ministers. The titles alone are suggestive, including *Chebacco narrative rescu'd from the charge of falsehood and partiality; In reply to the answer printed by order of the Second Church in Ipswich. And falsehood and partiality fix'd on said answer. / By a friend of truth,"* or *Twig of birch for Billy's breech : a letter to the Reverend Mr. William Hobby, a pastor of a church at Reading : being a gentle and necessary correction of him, for his folly and wickedness lately published to the world*, and *A plain narrative of the proceedings which caused the separation of a number of aggrieved brethren from the Second Church in Ipswich, or, A relation of the cause which produced the effects that are exhibited in the Reverend Mr. Pickering's late print, intitled, A bad omen to the churches.* As I mentioned at the outset, this was a time of dire conflict within and between New England churches.

The source is found in the Rev. Timothy Alden's *Collection of American Epitaphs and Inscriptions* (1814). Alden (1771–1839) was a Harvard-educated minister and educator. In 1799 he became pastor of a church at Portsmouth, New Hampshire, and afterwards led schools for young women in Boston, Newark and Cincinnati. In 1817 he founded Allegheny college in Meadville, Pennsylvania. Alden cataloged the New York Historical Society library, compiled two annual registers of New Jersey government and community leaders, and developed a reputation as an antiquarian with the publication of the *Collection*.

Alden quotes at length a memorial essay on the Rev. Abraham Keteltas in Jamaica, New York, "Obiit 30 September 1798." The essay concludes with a short verse:

> Rest from thy labours, now they work is o'er;
> Since death is vanquish'd, now free grace adore.
> A crown of glory sure awaits the just,
> Who serve their God, and in their Saviour trust.

What has this to do with Fanny Mason's epitaph? In his accompanying commentary, Alden goes on to say: "Mr. Keteltas published several occasional discourses…. He frequently wrote poetry for his amusement. As a specimen of his talents in this way, the author of this Collection closes this article with the lines he composed soon after the death of his first born, Jane Keteltas, who died in infancy." And in *that* verse, we find:

> **Then let thy body sleep and rest**
> **Within its clay cold bed**
> **Till with refulgent glory drest**
> **It rises from the dead.**

So we are left to wonder how this elegiac quatrain, written by a minister on Long Island forty or more years earlier, came to Lanesborough. Was it via Alden's anthology (already in print for twenty years—certainly a possibility)? Or a published volume of the Reverend Keteltas's verse, now lost? Or by some other book? And, as ever, in whose library did the intermediary text reside, and who made the choice to have it carved on Fanny Mason's gravestone? By the way, the same lines are also to be found in Dublin, New Hampshire (the Rev. Edward Sprague, died 1817)—just three years after the Reverend Alden's *Collection* was published.

We can end in Lee Center Cemetery, where well into the nineteenth century a text was chosen that harkens back to a much earlier anonymous verse from *The New England Primer*:

> Eliza A.
> dautr of
> Horace T. &
> Releif (sic) B. Moore
> died May 2,
> 1834 AE 2 Ys
> & 2 Ms
>
> *Little Children too,*
> *must Die.*

Recall that *The New England Primer* includes this instructive if dire verse:

> I in the burying place may see,
> Graves shorter there than I,
> From death's arrest no age is free,
> **Young children too must die.**

This is a brutal enough Puritan catechism for a child reader in the 1770s—I am a little surprised that anyone would choose to invoke it as late as the 1830s.

The Graveyard School

You may recall Nathaniel Cotton's verse about "The road through death's dark valley lies / This path the best of men have trod" from the prior chapter. The image of the transition from life to death as a path we all must take appears again in an epitaph that introduces us to the Graveyard School of poetry, a significant category of literature that was widely read and frequently chosen for these stones. As mentioned in Part I, these poems, with their deeply affecting expressions of faith, sorrow and hope, gave colonial New Englanders options for their devotional reading beyond the standard fare of Calvinist sermons and didactic religious tracts.

This point is made dramatically clear in Lee's Center Cemetery, on the gravestone of the daughter of the rock-ribbed Congregationalist minister Alvan Hyde. Harriott Church has for her epitaph not a stern version of The Classic, nor a Bible quotation, but this short verse the poet Thomas Parnell (1679–1718):

> Here lie buried
> the mortal remains of
> Mrs. HARRIOT CHURCH,
> the wife of Mr. Charles Church,
> and the oldest daughter of
> the Rev. Alvan and Mrs. Lucy
> Hyde, who died at her father's
> house, in full hope of a blessed
> immortality, Oct. 14th 1824,
> aged 26.
>
> *The path of death must once be trod by all.*

The source is Parnell's *A Night-Piece on Death* (ca. 1714), which can be considered one of the first, defining works of the Graveyard School of poetry. In his *Night-Piece*, Parnell imagines a pensive solitary tour among a collection of tombs, noting the common fate of all mortal men regardless of their station in life, and finally hearing from Death itself that there is nothing for the virtuous to fear in the short passage from the woes of this life to the pleasures of Paradise.

I will try the reader's patience by presenting the full text, at it introduces all the common tropes of the Graveyard Poets:

> By the blue taper's trembling light,
> No more I waste the wakeful night,
> Intent with endless view to pore
> The schoolmen and the sages o'er:

Their books from wisdom widely stray,
Or point at best the longest way.
I'll seek a readier path, and go
Where wisdom's surely taught below.

How deep yon azure dyes the sky,
Where orbs of gold unnumbered lie,
While through their ranks in silver pride
The nether crescent seems to glide.
The slumb'ring breeze forgets to breathe,
The lake is smooth and clear beneath,
Where once again the spangled show
Descends to meet our eyes below.
The grounds, which on the right aspire,
In dimness from the view retire:
The left presents a place of graves,
Whose wall the silent water laves.
That steeple guides thy doubtful sight
Among the livid gleams of night.
There pass, with melancholy state,
By all the solemn heaps of fate,
And think, as softly-sad you tread
Above the venerable dead,
"Time was, like thee they life possessed,
And time shall be, that thou shalt rest."

Those graves, with bending osier bound,
That nameless heave the crumpled ground,
Quick to the glancing thought disclose
Where Toil and Poverty repose.

The flat smooth stones that bear a name,
The chisel's slender help to fame
(Which ere our set of friends decay
Their frequent steps may wear away),
A middle race of mortals own,
Men, half ambitious, all unknown.

The marble tombs that rise on high,
Whose dead in vaulted arches lie,
Whose pillars swell with sculptured stones,
Arms, angels, epitaphs and bones,
These (all the poor remains of state)
Adorn the rich, or praise the great;
Who, while on earth in fame they live,
Are senseless of the fame they give.

Ha! while I gaze, pale Cynthia fades,
The bursting earth unveils the shades!
All slow and wan, and wrapped with shrouds,
They rise in visionary crowds,
And all with sober accent cry,
"Think, mortal, what it is to die."

Now from yon black and fun'ral yew,
That bathes the charnel-house with dew,
Methinks I hear a voice begin

> (Ye ravens, cease your croaking din,
> Ye tolling clocks, no time resound
> O'er the long lake and midnight ground);
> It sends a peal of hollow groans,
> Thus speaking from among the bones.
>
> "When men my scythe and darts supply,
> How great a King of Fears am I!
> They view me like the last of things:
> They make, and then they dread, my stings.
> Fools! if you less provoked your fears,
> No more my spectre-form appears.
> **Death's but a path that must be trod,**
> **If man would ever pass to God**;
> A port of calms, a state of ease
> From the rough rage of swelling seas.
>
> "Why then thy flowing sable stoles,
> Deep pendant cypress, mourning poles,
> Loose scarfs to fall athwart thy weeds,
> Long palls, drawn hearses, covered steeds,
> And plumes of black, that, as they tread,
> Nod o'er the scutcheons of the dead?
>
> "Nor can the parted body know,
> Nor wants the soul, these forms of woe.
> As men who long in prison dwell,
> With lamps that glimmer round the cell,
> Whene'er their suffering years are run,
> Spring forth to greet the glitt'ring sun:
> Such joy, though far transcending sense,
> Have pious souls at parting hence.
> On earth, and in the body placed,
> A few, and evil, years they waste;
> But when their chains are cast aside,
> See the glad scene unfolding wide,
> Clap the glad wing, and tow'r away,
> And mingle with the blaze of day."

Parnell was an Anglo-Irish poet and clergyman, friends with Pope, Swift, and other contemporary men of letters. Indeed, Pope collected and edited Parnell's *Poems on Several Occasions*. Parnell's works are no longer well-known; even in their time they were considered more pleasing than profound. That said, I very much admire the sequential imagery of the first section of the poem, starting with the unmarked grave of the poor peasant, then the worn stone of the "middle race of mortals," culminating in the lofty marble tombs of the rich and great who can, ironically, no longer appreciate their own monuments.

Parnell also makes Death an engaging character who deprecates his darts and scythe as the mere inventions of men, who then tremble at the product of their own imaginations. This is almost a modern psychological perspective. As an epitaph source, Parnell's work is certainly reasonable: Death makes no distinction between the low and the mighty, and should hold no terror for the pious. With all that said, I find this a fascinating choice for the Reverend Hyde's daughter—one might have expected the old man to have chosen, or encouraged, a more didactic Calvinistic text.

I read another example of a Graveyard School epitaph, not carved in a graveyard but hand-written in a remarkable artifact, the *Account Book* of the John Stevens family of stone carvers in Rhode Island:

> *See here, all pail and ded, she lies;*
> *For ever flow my streaming eyes:*
> *Fly, Hymen, with extinguish'd fires;*
> *Fly, nuptial bliss, and chaste desires*
> *Erminia's fled, the loveli'st mind*
> *Faith, sweetness, wit, together join'd.*
> *Dwelt faith, and wiet, and sweetness thre?*
> *Oh, view the change, and drop a tear.*

The source is a poem by Mrs. Elizabeth Singer Rowe (1674–1737) which appears in *Letters Moral and Entertaining* (II-Letter XIX) entitled "A Letter from Aristus, giving his Friend a Relation of the sudden Death of his new Bride, who was seized in the Chapel while the sacred Rites were performing." The *Letter* concludes with the short poem which Stevens transcribed; it would have been a perfectly apt choice for the grave of a young woman. Overlooked today, in her time Mrs. Rowe was highly regarded for both her literary style and her personal piety. She wrote novels as well as many religious and occasional poems, starting at the precocious age of twelve. She became a prominent defender the rights of women as poets, and an eminent literary figure.[*] Like Barbauld, Carter, and More, Rowe merits renewed attention beyond academic specialists. Her poems reward the reader with their wit, style, and elegance. Her works are not always profound, but they are well-crafted and, on occasion, impassioned. Dr. Johnson admired "the copiousness and luxuriance of Mrs. Rowe."

I do not know if Stevens carved this verse on a customer's gravestone, but I do know the same poem was chosen (and personalized) for a young woman's memorial in Brattleboro, Vermont:

> In Memory of
> M[iss] Susanna Arm[s]
> Dau[r] of M[r] Josiah
> & M[rs] Cynthia Arm[s]
> Who Died April y[e]
> 8th 1790 in y[e] 16th
> Year of her age
>
> *See there all pale & Dead she lies:*
> *For ever flow my streaming Eyes:*
> *Susanna's fled the loveliest Mind*
> *Such Modest worth & sweetness joind*
> *Genius & youth & wit dwelt there*
> *Oh! view ye Change & drop a tear*

Mrs. Rowe's greatest success was another similar, epislatory meditation on death, *Friendship in Death, in Twenty Letters from the Dead to the Living* (1728). It went

---

[*] Incidentally, before she married the poet Thomas Rowe, she was courted by two other writers we have encountered, Matthew Prior and Isaac Watts.

through scores of editions throughout the eighteenth and nineteenth centuries, and I can understand why. The lessons they teach are unimpeachably pious, but they are conveyed via stimulating episodes of adultery, opportunistic rakes, dissipated guardians, cross-dressing seductresses, kidnapping corsairs and ominous Turks, allusions to incest—small wonder they were popular for ladies' private reading. I own a 1760 edition of the *Letters*, printed in London, that binds together *Friendship in Death* and *Letters Moral and Entertaining*. It is dedicated to Edward Young—evidence of the web of relationships amongst these writers.

Mrs. Rowe was also chosen for an epitaph in Dorchester, well east of my usual collecting grounds but worth inclusion here in the interest of building awareness of her work (Figure 42):

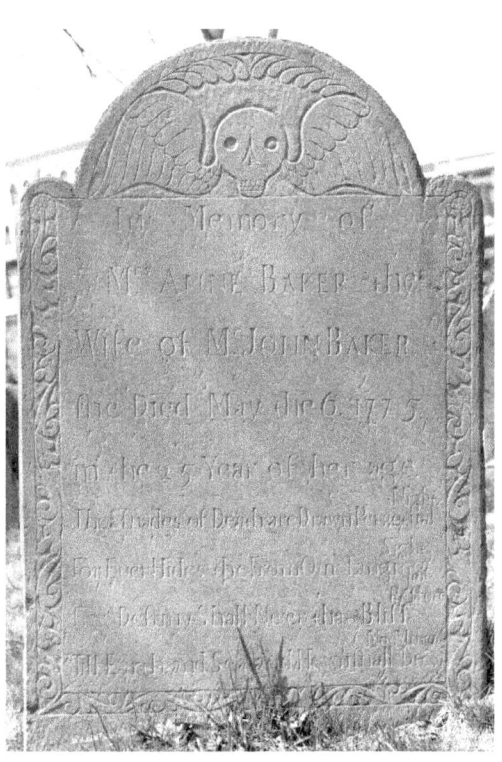

In Memory of
M^{rs}. ANNE BAKER the
Wife of M^r. JOHN BAKER
she Died May the 6. 1775
in the 25 Year of her age.

The shades of Death are Drawn Perpetual Night
For Ever Hides the From Our Langing Sight
Fix'd Destiny Shall Ne'er that Bliss Restore
Till Earth and Sea and Hev'n shall be No More

This is from Mrs. Rowe's *Elegy on the Death of Mrs. Thynne*, a fine example of the smooth meter, elegant rhymes, and calm, controlled emotion that were popular at the time. The *Elegy* begins with a plea for forgiveness for selfishly wishing her virtuous friend back "from celestial joys / to these wild seats of vanity and noise." The lines quoted in the epitaph are spoken by the poet, confirming this can never be; her friend's death is indeed final. Then the poem concludes with these moving and skillfully-composed lines:

Figure 42. Anne Baker stone (courtesy of American Antiquarian Society).

But, sacred friendship, thy superious flame
Shall time outlive, and be unchang'd the same.
When all the fond relations nature knows,
When all the ties that human laws impose,
Are cancell'd, when the mighty league expires,
That holds the universe, when yon gay fires
Have wasted all their glory; thou shalt rise
In triumph o'er the ruins of the skies...

Another of the leading figures of the Graveyard School was chosen for a splendid marble monument in Sheffield's Barnard Cemetery (Figure 43):

Here lies deposited
the body of
Major General
JOHN ASHLEY
who died Nov. 5 1799
in the Sixty fourth
year of his Life.

Make the extended skies your tomb,
Let Stars record your worth,
Yet know vain mortals all must die,
As nature's sickliest birth.

This rich, resonant verse can also be found in Lanesborough (Solomon Williams, also 1799) and earlier in Lancaster (1789). It is from James Hervey's *Meditations Among the Tombs*, a work we discussed in passing earlier. Hervey (1714–1758) was born near Northampton and educated at Lincoln College, Oxford—the Cradle of Methodism. He did indeed come under the influence of the Oxford Methodists, but in the end became a conventional Anglican. Hervey took orders in 1727, and became

Figure 43. John Ashley stone (author's collection).

a well-regarded parish priest and a prolific writer of devotional texts. *Meditations* is the work that established Hervey's place among the Graveyard Poets; it is often excerpted or referred to by other writers of the school. William Blake was also an admirer, and painted an elaborate *Epitome of James Hervey's Meditations among the Tombs* between 1820 and 1825.

Hervey incorporates all the essential motifs of the Graveyard School. He begins by describing, to an unnamed Lady, his visit to an empty church (reportedly St. James, Kilkhampton in Cornwall). Then in simple language and with commonplace imagery he shares "a train of meditations, serious, and mournfully pleasing" on the need to prepare for death amid the uncertainty of life:

> How thin is the partition, between this world and another! How short the transition, from time to eternity! The partition, nothing more than the breath in our nostrils; and the transition may be made in the twinkling of an eye. Poor Chremylus, I remember, arose from the diversion of a card-table, and dropt into the dwellings of darkness. One night, Corinna was all gaiety in her spirits, all finery in her apparel, at a magnificent ball. The next night she lay pale and stiff, an extended corpse, and ready to be mingled with the mouldering dead....

After a lengthy discourse on death, mourning, and above all how to be a good Christian, Hervey makes a point of ending on a positive note:

> Now, madam, lest my meditations set in a cloud, and leave any unpleasing gloom upon your mind; let me once more turn to the brightening prospects of the righteous.... The righteous seem to lie by in the bosom of the earth, as a wary pilot in some well-sheltered creek, till all the storms which infest this lower world are blown over. Here they enjoy safe

anchorage; are in no danger of foundering amidst the waves of prevailing iniquity; or of being shipwrecked, on the rocks of any powerful temptation. But ere long, we shall behold them hoisting their flag of hope; riding before a sweet gale of atoning merit, and redeeming love; till they make, with all the sails of an assured faith, the blessed port of eternal life.

Hervey was extremely popular—his works might have been composed expressly for private devotional reading, and can be found in many colonial libraries.

The full poem reads:

> **Make the extended Skies your Tomb,**
> **Let Stars record your Worth:**
> **Yet know, vain Mortals, all must die,**
> **As Nature's sickliest Birth**.
>
> Wou'd bounteous Heav'n indulge my Pray'r,
> I frame a nobler Choice;
> Nor, living, wish the pompous Pile,
> Nor dead regret the Loss.
>
> In thy fair Book of Life divine,
> My God, inscribe my Name:
> There let it fill some humble Place,
> Beneath the slaughter'd Lamb.
>
> The Saints, while Ages roll away,
> In endless Fame survive;
> Their Glories, o'er the Wrongs of Time,
> Greatly triumphant, live.

I have also found the third verse chosen for a grave in Lanesborough (Abiah Hawley, died 1797). This poem was put to music and served as a hymn. It has some of Watts's triumphal spirit, though the meter and imagery are more complex.

A passage from another work by Hervey was chosen for a child's grave in Amherst's West Cemetery (Nancy Nichols, 1796, aged 3 years)

> *Sweet are ye charms adorn'd cheek*
> *And sparkling in the Eye*
> *Swift from ye lovely finished form*
> *The transient graces fly*

This is from *Reflections on a Flower Garden*, in which Hervey contemplates how everything in the garden gives way from one season to the next, reminding the reader gently that the same changes must come to human beings in their season:

> **Such are the Charms, that flush the Cheek,**
> **And sparkle in the Eye:**
> **So, from the lovely finished form**
> **The transient Graces fly**.
> To this the Seasons, as they roll,
> Their Attention bring:
> They warn the Fair; their ev'ry Round
> Confirms the Truth I sing.

Reading Hervey's works, I can see how Colonial readers embraced his kind yet firmly orthodox instruction in the path to salvation. One scholar of colonial reading habits is eloquent on the subject:

The one author who excited the religious feelings of colonial American women (and men) more than any other during the second half of the eighteenth century was James Hervey. After Hervey's *Meditations and Contemplations* appeared at mid-century, it could be found from New England to Georgia. Hervey had designed the work specifically for female readers....

While modern readers may find it difficult to understand Hervey's immense popularity, it becomes more comprehensible when seen within the context of early American devotional practice. Hervey helped revitalize the colonial woman's closet devotions. Imagining one's inherent sinfulness had become increasingly difficult by the mid-eighteenth century. Readers needed tangible, concrete subject matter upon which they could focus their religious meditations. Hervey provided many examples of everyday subjects which could be used as a basis for spiritual meditation. One spring evening in 1755, Esther Edwards Burr, for example, wrote in her journal, "How extreamly the silence of the Night resembles the silence of the grave. Mr Hervy has most butifully painted in his Contemplations on the nig[ht]." ... Reading Hervey, she could take time on ... quiet, lonely nights to listen to the night and imagine the silence of the grave.[*]

This image of a woman reading Hervey in her few and treasured moments of privacy came vividly to mind when I encountered this prose passage from *Meditations among the Tombs* chosen for an epitaph in Longmeadow Cemetery:

> In Memory of
> MRS. SARAH ELY
> Who died Dec, 12, 1777.
> in her 23, Year.
>
> *Oh! trust not in Youth,*
> *or strength, or in any thing*
> *Mortal;*
> *For their is nothing certain*
> *Nothing to be depended on*
> *beneath the unchangeable*
> *GOD*

I will quote the context at some length as it gives you a good idea of the spiritual and sentimental style that Hervey favored, and that his readers so treasured. As he wanders through the church, the narrator comes upon a "sepulchral stone [that] tells a most pitiable tale indeed! ... His age twenty-eight; his death sudden, himself cut down in the prime of life, amidst all the vivacity and vigour of manhood." Hervey goes on with a remarkable combination of religious devotion, macabre effect, and barely-suppressed eroticism that must have moved his readers in several ways:

> Perhaps the nuptial joys were all he thought on.—Were not such the breathings of his enamoured soul? ... In the midst of such enchanting views, had some faithful friend but softly reminded him of an opening grave ... how unseasonable would he have reckoned the admonition? yet, though all warm with life, and rich in visionary bliss, he was even then tottering upon the brink of both. — Dreadful vicissitude! to have the bridal festivity turned into the funeral solemnity! ... Who can tell, but the bride-maids, girded with gladness, had prepared the marriage-bed? Had decked it with the richest covers, and dressed it in the pillows of down? When — **Oh! trust not in youth, or strength, or in anything mortal; for there is nothing certain, nothing to be depended on, beneath**

---

[*] Hayes, *A Colonial Woman's Bookshelf.*

the unchangeable God—Death, relentless Death, is making him another kind of bed in the dust of the earth. ... In vain does the consenting fair one put on her ornaments, and expect her spouse. ... Go, disappointed virgin! Go, mourn the uncertainty of all created bliss! Teach thy soul to aspire after a sure and immutable felicity!

I wonder if perhaps a young Sarah Ely dog-eared this passage and copied it out in a commonplace book. I have an 1807 edition of Hervey's works that binds *Meditations Among the Tombs* and *Reflections on a Flower-Garden* with *A Descant Upon Creation, Contemplations of the Night, Contemplations on the Starry Heavens*, and *A Winter-Piece*. The settings vary but the kind-hearted encouragement of religion and spiritual reflection is consistent.

In Ludlow Center Cemetery, I read this interesting verse for a young brother and sister. Researching its origin took me into a wondrous thicket of half-forgotten writers:

> This stone is erected
> to the memory of a son
> and a Daughter of Capt.
> Joseph and Mrs. Mary
> Miller (viz) Wilder, who
> died Oct. 13 1786 in the 5
> year of his age.
> And Joanna who died Dec
> 10, 1787, in the 3 year of her age
>
> *When death receives the dire command*
> *None can elude or stay his hand*
> *Nor can a hope or beauty save*
> *From the dire conquest of the grave.*

Tracing this one quatrain led me to some unexpected revelations concerning not just authorship, but the way these works were borrowed and re-used by editors and publishers. The first two lines appear in a mere footnote to the 1812 "New Correct Edition" of the Rev. William Dodd's *Reflections on Death* (originally published 1763):

> **When death receives the dire command**
> **None can elude or stay his hand**;
> For when his dread commission's seal'd,
> The youngest, healthiest, all must yield.
> --- Rur. Christian

Earlier editions of Dodd's *Reflections* contain several passages from other Graveyard poets as chapter headings or footnotes, but this is the only edition I have found that quotes this particular verse. The "New Correct Edition" has a short introductory paragraph that states:

> The Notes and Illustrations added to this edition, it is hoped, will not be thought altogether superfluous, or wholly unnecessary, as the editor has aimed, in and by them, to make the treatise in general more agreeable to the tenets of the truly pious and evangelical reader.

So apparently the "Rur. Christian" verse is an "editor's choice" addition to the original text, to make it more appealing to the pious reader. Let us try to untangle these several intertwined strands.

First, who is the Rev. William Dodd, the author of the original *Reflections on Death*? Dodd (1729–1777) was a fashionable preacher known as the "Macaroni Parson" for his extravagant lifestyle. His profligacy drove him into debt, and he resorted to forgery in an attempt to restore his finances. He was discovered, convicted, and hanged at Tyburn. Samuel Johnson was referring to Dodd when he famously remarked to Boswell: "Depend upon it, Sir, when a man knows he is to be hanged in a fortnight, it concentrates his mind wonderfully."

Dodd's *Reflections* was a popular work for many decades in the eighteenth century. It consists of a series of didactic vignettes that tell the edifying stories of fictional archetypes (the doomed Avaro who indulged his children but neglected their religious training, the blessed Pulcheria whose parents "omitted no opportunity to cultivate her mind, and early to lead her into the pure and peaceful paths of sacred wisdom") as they face death. Each character's story reinforces the lesson that death is a welcome transition to paradise for those who have lived a Christian life, but a wretched and remorse-filled calamity for those who esteemed insubstantial pleasures and pursuits.

The editor who in 1812 inserted that extraneous verse into Dodd's book borrowed (not to say "lifted") it from George Wright's *The Rural Christian* (1772), a poem in four books that celebrates the wonders and force of Nature, and invites the reader to reflect on how sunshine, floods, fields, even the dew demonstrate both the power of God and the transience of human life. Here is the verse as it appears in Book I of *The Rural Christian*—similar to the first two lines of the Dodd editor's version, though slightly altered:

> See how precarious is the life of man,
> Short and uncertain is our earthly span;
> A few more years, or weeks, or moments past,
> And you (tho' now in health) may breathe your last;
> For know, O man, when 'tis thy Maker's will,
> "A fly, a grape-stone, or a hair may kill [Prior's *Variety of Deaths*]."
> **When Nature's foe receives the dire command,**
> **None can elude or stay the tyrant's hand.**
> Thou must not youth, on numerous years depend,
> For unknown accidents thy steps attend;
> Disorders numberless await thee here,
> Thy greatest pleasures may thy bane appear.

Note the quotation marks and parenthetical comment in the sixth line in this passage (the parenthetical appears as a footnote in my copy of *Rural Christian*). Here Wright directly quotes a line from Matthew Prior's *Ode to the Memory of George Villiers; Drowned in the River Piava 1703*. In that elegantly-turned elegy, Prior describes the impossibility of avoiding Death the great tyrant once "obedient Nature knows his Will":

> Some from the stranded Vessel force their Way;
> Fearful of Fate, they meet it in the Sea:
> Some who escape the fury of the Wave,
> Sicken on Earth, and sink into a Grave:
> ...Each charging Season does it's Poison bring,
> Rheums chill the Winter, Agues blast the Spring:

> Wet, Dry, Cold, Hot, at the appointed Hour,
> All act subservient to the Tyrant's Pow'r:
> And when obedient Nature knows his Will,
> **A Fly, a Grape-stone, or a Hair can kill**.

The second couplet of the Dodd editor's verse appears in a *different* Wright work, *Solitary Walks* (1774). This somewhat rambling account, in prose and poetry, of a contemplative walk through a graveyard includes this passage:

> Come, ye in health, who neither know
> Affliction, trouble, pain or woe,
> And see from every tomb around,
> (With which these dreary realms abound)
> No age or station is secure,
> No art a moment can insure,
> **When death has got his warrant seal'd.**
> **The youngest, healthiest, all must yield.**

Wright acknowledges a debt to Hervey's *Meditations*, and rightly so. Indeed, Wright's third book, *Pleasing Melancholy or a Walk Among the Tombs in a Country Churchyard* (1793) is explicitly sub-titled "In the stile and manner of Hervey's *Meditations*." This is a lovely book in its own right, combining a thoroughly Hervey-esque stroll through a graveyard with a choice selection of instructive epitaphs.

George Wright fascinates me. I can discover nothing about his biography. He wrote about a dozen books in the 1770s, '80s, and '90s on subjects like *Retired Pleasures, or the charms of rural life*; moral and entertaining miscellanies for ladies (1793) and gentlemen (1797), the seasons, and *Walking amusements for chearful Christians*. As far as I can tell he was a reasonably if not exceptionally skilled versifier and essayist who found a ready market for spiritually edifying books in the style of James Hervey and set about earning a living writing them. Indeed, his Preface and conclusion to *Solitary Walks* provides an excellent summation of the religious doctrine that he, Hervey, Young, Dodd, and a host of contemporaries sought to impart to their many readers:

> Man, as a rational being, endow'd with an immortal soul, and form'd for an eternal duration, should make serious reflection his daily employ; ... while the sacred writings assure him of a world to come; how reasonable then is a life of piety and meditation?

> ...That there is a *future* state, few, if any, will be so bold as to deny, tho' they may seem, or wish, to disbelieve it; the present unequal distribution of rewards and punishments in *this* world, together with the constant thirst and desire in man after some *future* good, prove the necessity, as well as the certainty of it.

> If there is, then, an hereafter, an eternity of happiness and misery *beyond* the grave; and if religion only will bring us to the *former*, and impiety subject us to the *latter*, how solicitous should we be *to know the things which belong to our eternal peace* ... how careful of not encouraging evil thoughts....

> Let us seriously reflect on that solemn transaction, which we must soon realize, of exchanging corruption for incorruption, and ... enter the boundless ages of eternity.... Reader, whoever thou art, whether young or old, high or low, rich or poor, prepare to *die*, for it will soon by *thy* lot. Let Religion be thy guide, the real Christian thy character, and Piety thy truest wisdom; live holy, die daily to sin, watch they heart, guard thy senses, redeem time, Love CHRIST, and long for heaven; for thus acting thou wilt approve thyself to GOD, and be placed after death, and the right-hand of Omnipotence in glory.

I would like to know more about him; if any reader knows of a George Wright Society, I should like to join.

Close reading of Hervey, Dodd, and Wright together is a solitary pursuit, I admit, but instructive. Each writer uses the same narrative devices—a solitary tour of graves which inspired vignettes on the lives and deathbeds of sinners and saved—to drive home the same religious messages. Their works are, to one degree or another, pastiches of quotations from Scripture, other Graveyard poets, and one another. At times the rhymes and lessons become almost interchangeable, but I suppose the same is true of certain genres of television or film or fiction today. The sheer volume of similar books suggests how in-demand this style of literature was with contemporary readers.

All this being said, the origin of the *second* couplet of the Wilder epitaph is unknown to me.

Here is a verse that appears twice in Longmeadow Cemetery, showing the influence of the Graveyard School on an individual who apparently composed his own epitaph. Abigail Colton's carver included a little manicule pointing to the first line (Figure 44):

In Memory of
M[rs]. ABIGAIL
Wife of
Ca[pt]. SIMON COLTON
Who died
May 3rd. 1760
Aged 46 Years.

Here, Reader, mark
(Perhaps now in thy Prime)
the stealing Steps
of never-standing Time:
Thoul't be what I am;
catch the present Hour:
Employ that well
for that's within thy Power

Figure 44. Abigail Colton stone (author's collection).

The author is one Edward Bond, who apparently composed it for his own tomb. An editor named William Toldervy included it in his anthology of *Select Epitaphs* (1755), and it can be found in several nineteenth-century anthologies. The full text reads: "In Armagh church-yard, the following Inscription is placed under a dial erected over the grave of Edward Bond, esq., Who ordered one hundred pounds to be given to the Poor, instead of a pompous funeral, 1744":

No marble pomp, no monumental praise;
My tomb this dial, my epitaph these lays.
Pride and low mould'ring clay but ill agree;
Death levels me to beggars; kings to me.
Alive, instruction was my work each day;
Dead, I persist instruction to convey.

> *Here, Reader! mark (perhaps now in thy Prime)*
> *The stealing Steps of never-standing time:*
> *Thoul't be what I am; catch the present hour:*
> *Employ that well, for that's within thy Power.*

We hear the familiar admonition from The Classic, to make good use of our time while it is in our power. The familiar Graveyard School trope of death leveling all is finely rendered here—you can almost see the speaker tumbling down to the level of the beggar, even as kings fall down on him from above.

Note that the verse went from its creation in Ireland, into print, and over to Longmeadow in the space of just sixteen years. William Toldervy (1721–62) was a Shropshire-born Londoner who combined a faltering career in the linen trade with writing for the bookseller William Owen. He wrote three books—*Select Epitaphs* (1755), *The History of Two Orphans* (1756), and the unfinished *England and Wales Described* (1762).

The line about the stealing steps of never-standing time enjoyed a long life. The anonymous contributor of an item on watch papers (tiny notes contained in a watch case) to *Notes and Queries, a Medium of Intercommunication for Literary Men, General Readers, etc.* (London, December 23, 1871) includes "the following verses printed on satin":

> Here, reader, see in youth, in age, or prime,
> The stealing steps of never-standing Time:
> With wisdom mark the moment as it flies,
> Think what a moment is to him that dies.
> 1823

But enough about watch papers. This passage from one of the foremost works of the Graveyard School appears in Lee Center Cemetery:

> In memory of Miss Ze-
> rujay Crocker who died
> Sep 2nd 1798 in the 21st
> year of her age
>
> *Tis long since death had*
> *the majority. Yet strange*
> *the living lay it not to heart.*

The source is *The Grave* by Robert Blair (1699–1746), which I would place next to Parnell's *A Night-Piece on Death* as a quintessential Graveyard School poem. Compared to Collins and Logan, Blair has a somewhat bland biography.[*] The son of a Scottish minister, he had enough family wealth to spend his days gardening, studying English poets, and writing a grand total of three poems of his own. *The Grave* was his one enduring success, highly popular in his time and later printed in an edition with splendid illustrations by William Blake. *The Grave* appears in full in *Elegant Extracts* and Murray's *English Reader*; passages from it are quoted in many devotional books including Wright's.

The Grave is too long to reproduce in its entirety here, but compared to many other Graveyard poems it displays original imagery and superior literary merit. I commend it to your attention. Here is the Crocker epitaph in context:

---

[*] Then again, who hasn't?

> Death's shafts fly thick! Here fall the village swain,
> And there his pamper'd lord! The cup goes round,
> And who so artful as to put it by?
> **'Tis long since death had the majority,**
> **Yet, strange, the living lay it not to heart**!
> See yonder maker of the dead man's bed,
> The sexton, hoary-headed chronicle!
> Of hard unmeaning face, down which ne'er stole
> A gentle tear...
> ...Thus hand in hand
> The sot has walk'd with Death twice twenty years;
> And yet ne'er younker [youngster] on the green laughs louder,
> Or clubs a smuttier tale: when drunkards meet,
> None sings a merrier catch, or lends a hand
> More willing to his cup. Poor wretch! he minds not
> That soon some trusty brother of the trade
> Shall do for him what he has done for thousands.

I very much like the description of the lord as "pamper'd"—not haughty or lofty, but spoiled. The old sexton (a clear nod to the memorable gravediggers in *Hamlet*) may receive more characterization than is required to drive home the moral of the poem, but identifying him as a sot is a nice touch. The image of Death's cup being passed around, and none of us clever enough to avoid our turn, is very effective. I also admire the following passage, which deplores our lack of concern for the inevitable change we will soon be facing:

> Never to think of Death and of ourselves
> At the same time!—as if to learn to die
> Were no concern of ours. O more than sottish!
> For creatures of a day in gamesome mood
> To frolic on eternity's dread brink,
> Unapprehensive; when, for aught we know,
> The very first swol'n surge shall sweep us in!
> Think we, or think we not, time hurries on
> With a resistless unremitting stream,
> Yet treads more soft than e'er did midnight thief,
> That slides his hand under the miser's pillow,
> And carries off his prize.

Remember that midnight thief with his hand under your pillow, the next time you feel gamesome and inclined to frolic on eternity's dread brink.

Another epitaph from another Graveyard poem is found in Lee Center Cemetery as late as 1822:

> In memory of
> Mrs. LYDIA BARLOW.
> who died March 1ˢᵗ 1822
> aged 25
>
> *There is a calm for those that weep,*
> *A rest for weary pilgrims found,*
> *And while the mouldering ashes sleep,*
> *Low in the ground;*
> *The soul of origin divine,*

Gods glorious image freed from clay,
In Heavens eternal sphere shall shine,
A star of day.

The source is a poem also entitled *The Grave* (1804), this one by James Montgomery (1771–1854). Montgomery was a poet, hymn writer, and politically active humanitarian, once jailed for insurrection after publishing a poem that celebrated the fall of the Bastille. His wrote poems in opposition to the slave trade and the exploitation of chimney sweeps. His best-known contribution to hymnody today is the Christmas carol *Angels from the Realms of Glory*. *The Grave* was set to music and also became a popular hymn. Here is an abridged version:

THERE is a calm for those who weep,
A rest for weary pilgrims found,
They softly lie and sweetly sleep
Low in the ground.

The storm that wrecks the winter sky
No more disturbs their deep repose,
Than summer evening's latest sigh
That shuts the rose.

I long to lay this painful head
And aching heart beneath the soil;
To slumber in that dreamless bed
From all my toil.

…

Hark!—a strange sound affrights mine ear;
My pulse,—my brain runs wild,—I rave;
—Ah! who art thou whose voice I hear?
"I am THE GRAVE!"

"The GRAVE, that never spake before,
Hath found at length a tongue to chide;
O listen!—I will speak no more:—
Be silent, Pride!

"Art thou a wretch of hope forlorn,
The victim of consuming care?
Is thy distracted conscience torn
By fell despair?

…

"Lash'd by the furies of the mind,
From Wrath and Vengeance wouldst thou flee?
Ah! think not, hope not, fool, to find
A friend in me.

…

"I charge thee, LIVE!—repent and pray;
In dust thine infamy deplore;
There yet is mercy;—go thy way,
And sin no more.

"Art thou a Mourner?—Hast thou known
The joy of innocent delights,
Endearing days for ever flown,
And tranquil nights?

"O LIVE!—and deeply cherish still
The sweet remembrance of the past:
Rely on Heaven's unchanging will
For peace at last.

"Art thou a Wanderer?—Hast thou seen
O'erwhelming tempests drown thy bark?
A ship-wreck'd sufferer, hast thou been,
Misfortune's mark?

"Though long of winds and waves the sport,
Condemn'd in wretchedness to roam,
LIVE!—thou shalt reach a sheltering port,
A quiet home.

"To Friendship didst thou trust thy fame
And was thy friend a deadly foe,
Who stole into thy breast to aim
A surer blow?

"LIVE!—and repine not o'er his loss,
A loss unworthy to be told:
Thou hast mistaken sordid dross
For friendship's gold.

...

"Did Woman's charms thy youth beguile,
And did the fair one faithless prove?
Hath she betray'd thee with a smile,
And sold thy love?

"LIVE!— 'twas a false bewildering fire:
Too often Love's insidious dart
Thrills the fond soul with wild desire,
But kills the heart.

...

"——Whate'er thy lot—whoe'er thou be,—
Confess thy folly,—kiss the rod,
And in thy chastening sorrows see
The hand of God.

"A bruisèd reed He will not break;
Afflictions all His children feel:
He wounds them for His mercy's sake,
He wounds to heal.

"Humbled beneath His mighty hand,
Prostrate His Providence adore:
'Tis done!—Arise! He bids thee stand,
To fall no more.

"Now, Traveller in the vale of tears,
To realms of everlasting light,
Through Time's dark wilderness of years,
Pursue thy flight.

"**There is a calm for those who weep,**
A rest for weary pilgrims found;
And while the mouldering ashes sleep
Low in the ground,

> "The Soul, of origin divine,
> God's glorious image, freed from clay,
> In Heaven's eternal sphere shall shine
> A star of day!
>
> "The Sun is but a spark of fire,
> A transient meteor in the sky:
> The Soul, immortal as its sire,
> Shall never die."

The same verse was chosen several times in Lancaster, so either the hymn or the poem was known far across Massachusetts. Montgomery creates a stirring, vibrant tone—quite different to the more somber and introverted Graveyard poems. He animates the Grave, giving it a voice that calls upon the reader to LIVE, not to fear impending danger. The message, as always, is to make good use of our time in life to prepare for death, but the tone is unique. I like to think that sad, bereft, doubting, perhaps sinning readers found not just spiritual comfort in Montgomery's words, but a vivifying call to action and salvation.

A verse from the same poem was chosen for a partially customized epitaph in the South Cemetery in West Stockbridge:

> This humble stone
> is inscribed
> to the memory of
> Mr. SAMUEL BOYNTON
> who died Nov. the 12th 1793
> in the 43rd year of his age
>
> *The once lov'd form that lies in ruins here*
> *Speaks from the tomb his warnings* [illegible] *hear*
> *Be still be humble kiss the chastening rod*
> *And in your deep afflictions see the hand of GOD*

The opening lines (which I cannot identify), though partially obscured by time and weather, still convey a powerful image of the ruined dead speaking words of warning. The second couplet appears in the middle of *The Grave*:

> Whate'er thy lot, where'er thou be,
> Confess thy folly—**kiss the rod;**
> **And in thy chastening sorrows see**
> **The hand of God.**

Note the distinctive meter of the whole poem, where every fourth line has just two solemn beats (low/ground, silent/pride, Death/Hell, etc.). This stanza makes highly effective use of this device, landing us squarely under the hand of God.

I must mention here another poem by Montgomery that was used in an epitaph in Longmeadow Cemetery. The grave itself is a remarkable monument, a rectangular column with text on all four sides, surmounted by a tall four-sided pyramid. Note the lengthy eulogy that lists the virtues of the late Reverend Stokes in meticulous detail. This is one of several examples of the townspeople of early Longmeadow paying for substantial memorials to their leaders, lay and clerical (Figure 45):

Figure 45. Richard Stokes stone (author's collection).

Sacred
to the memory of
the Rev. RICHARD
SALTER STOKES
Pastor of the Church
in Longmeadow.
He was born
at Mansfield Conn
Aug. 30th 1763.
Graduated at Yale
College in 1783.
Ordained Dec 7, 1785.
died Oct. 3, 1819.

In the private rela
tions of life He emi
nently illustrated
the graces of the
Christian character.
As a minister of Christ
He was distinguish
ed for his appropri
ate perspicuous and af
fectionate Exhibition
of Evangelical Truth,
for propriety rich
ness and fervor in social
prayer, and for his in
structive conversation
and Christian sympathy;
in pastoral duties.

In testimony of
their affectionate
remembrance of
his personal worth
& high regard for
his Ability, Zeal,
and Usefulness as their
Christian Pastor,
his mourning
Congregation
Erect this
Monument.

RELIGION,
Her Almighty breath Amidst that calm
of sweet repose
Rebuked the winds
and waves of death; to Heaven his
gentle spirit rose.
Blessed are the
dead who die in the
Lord, for they rest
from their labour
& their works do
follow them.

The first half of epitaph is from Montgomery's *The Pillow*. This is a strange poem, a cautionary tale about a deceased young man who has suffered many disappointments in life and confides his woes to his pillow, not his friend the anonymous narrator. The poem ends as the poor fellow is consumed by despair and illness:

> And as his evening sun declined,
> The shadows deepen'd o'er his mind.
> What doubts and terrors then possess'd
> The dark dominion of his breast!
> How did delirious fancy dwell
> On madness, suicide, and hell!
> There was on earth no power to save
> --- But, as he shuddered o'er the grave,
> He saw from realms of light descend
> The friend of him who has no friend,
> Religion!—Her almighty breath
> Rebuked the winds and waves of death;
> She bad the storm of phrensy cease,
> And smiled a calm, and whisper'd peace:
> Amidst that calm of sweet repose,
> To heaven his gentle spirit rose.

The protagonist does not live, but at least he is saved by the last-minute appearance of Religion. The second part of the epitaph, which comes as something of an anti-climax, is the familiar verse from Revelation we saw in Scripture section. It is a testament to Montgomery's long-extinguished fame that one of his verses was chosen for this most impressive monument, above a host of other possible texts.

This beautiful and moving verse from perhaps the most enduringly popular Graveyard poem was chosen for a young man's grave in the Norton or Old East graveyard in Otis (Figure 46):

JAMES. W. MERRILL:
son of
Doct. Michael & Artemesia
Merrill. who died August
19. 1822 aged 19 years.

Here rests his head upon the lap of earth,
A youth to fortune and to fame unknone
Fair science frown'd not on his humble birth
And melancholy marked him for her own.
Large was his bounty, and his soul sincere.
Heaven did a recompence as largely send:
He gave to misery all he had—a tear:
He gain'd from Heav'n (t'was all he wishd)
a friend.

This is stone is late for my collecting, decorated with the stylized willow drooping over an urn that became commonplace on stones in the nineteenth century.

Figure 46. James Merrill stone (author's collection).

But the choice of epitaph is so superb I must include it. The source is Thomas Gray's masterpiece, *Elegy Written in a Country Church-Yard.* To introduce Thomas Gray (1716–1771), I cannot improve upon this description from my old college *Norton Anthology of English Literature*[*]: "The man who wrote the English poem best known and most loved by unsophisticated readers was oddly enough a scholarly recluse who lived the quiet life of a university professor in the stagnant atmosphere of mid–18th-century Cambridge, where toward the end of his life he held the Professorship of Modern History without feeling called upon to give a single lecture." Educated at Eton and (barely) Cambridge, Gray wrote few but exquisite odes and elegies in a carefully-crafted voice of solitary, brooding melancholy. The *Elegy Written in a Country Church-Yard* is his great masterpiece, a disquisition on death as the shared fate of the mighty and the lowly that has never lost its appeal among general readers.

As a matter of fact, the source for James Merrill's memorial text is not found in the body of that pensive, philosophical poem but an epitaph that appears at its end. The narrator of the *Elegy*, contemplating the rural graveyard, reflects that while the rustics buried there might have become great and famous men under other circumstances, as it is "their lot forbade," and

> Far from the madding crowd's ignoble strife,
> Their sober wishes never learn'd to stray;
> Along the cool sequester'd vale of life
> They kept the noiseless tenor of their way.

Soon the first speaker gives way to a second, who addresses the first and speculates that perhaps someday "by lonely contemplation led / Some kindred spirit shall inquire thy fate." Gray then conjures a vision of some local graybeard describing the restless spirit of the original poet, pointing to his gravesite, and inviting us to "Approach and read (for thou can'st read) the lay / Grav'd on the stone beneath yon aged thorn." James Merrill's stone bears an exact quotation of the first two stanzas of this imagined epitaph; the final one reads:

> No farther seek his merits to disclose,
> Or draw his frailties from their dread abode,
> (There they alike in trembling hope repose)
> The bosom of his Father and his God.

As a choice of epitaph for such a remote rural graveyard, this cannot be surpassed. I do not know anything about Doctor Michael Merrill, but I am convinced he knew and admired Gray's *Elegy*, and that he is the one who chose it for the grave of his young son. I must have re-read that poem dozens of times over the years, but it took James Merrill's gravestone to make me appreciate the power of those last lines, with their poignant demand that we leave the soul of the deceased young man with all its frailties alone, in the deep hope that it rests peacefully in paradise with his God.

I have also found an American example of (or, possibly, lampoon of) Graveyard poetry, in Lee Center Cemetery (Figure 47):

> In memory of Miss Re
> member Tobey: Daut^r to

---

[*] M. H. Abrams, General Editor: *The Norton Anthology of English Literature, Third Edition.* (New York: W. W. Norton & Company, 1974).

Mr Stephen & Mrs Lydia
Tobey; who died Feb 6th
1799. in the 22 year of
her age.

The blooming cheeks the lovely charms
Lie clasp'd in death's cold icy arms

This stone was Erected
by Seth Backus Junr

Figure 47. Remember Tobey stone (author's collection).

What do you suppose is the backstory here? Who is Seth Backus, Jr.? Perhaps her fiancé, heartbroken and left behind, or maybe the stone carver, leaving behind an intrusive advertisement?

The identical verse appeared in Lee a few years earlier, on a common stone for Mercy (d. 1795, aged 4) and Joseph Crocker (d. 1796, aged 7 months), and again for Bulah Peet (d. 1799). It is not used only in Lee; it was chosen in at least twice in Connecticut. The source is a vivid, lengthy, and completely forgotten poem by Joel Barlow (1754–1812) called *Meditations on Death and the Grave* (1790). Barlow was born in Redding, Connecticut, where the local high school is named after him. He graduated from Yale and became a Jeffersonian diplomat and politician. Barlow was one of the Hartford Wits mentioned earlier; some of the works for which he was popular in his time included *The Anarchiad*, a work of political satire, and *The Vision of Columbus*. He also edited a book of Isaac Watts's psalms and hymns, expressly to adapt them for use in the United States. Today Barlow enjoys a modest literary fame for his mock-epic *The Hasty-Pudding*.

Meditations on Death and the Grave is an odd work. It goes on for more than two hundred lines, erratic in scansion, rhyming, and tone. When all is said and done, it is not really worth reading. For its curiosity value I have tried to find a contemporary edition of this poem, but without success. It appears in a 15-volume *Collected Writings* edition, but that seems like a lot of Barlow to take on board, for one mediocre poem. Here are a few representative stanzas, from which you may form your own opinion:

> I crave your calm attention now
> Till I reveal my Mind to you,
> And tell you where my Thoughts were led
> Out in the Tombs among the dead.
>
> 'Twas when the Care of Life had fled
> And Night's dark curtain spread his shade,
> And sweet Repose had clos'd mine Eyes
> I heard a voice that bid me rise—

Arise, go view your other Bed
That death is making with the dead:
Another dwelling you must have,
Though little thought on, 'tis the Grave.

...

How strangely did this sight appear
To see the great and small lie here?
The rich, the poor, the bond and free
In band of Harmony agree.

There lay the gallant and the brave
Both mouldering in the silent Grave.
The Fool, the Beggar fill'd a seat
As high as any in this Court.

There mighty Kings and Princes lay
Chain'd down in silence in the Clay.
There Counsellors and Judges cease
To grant Advice or give release.

There I beheld the highest trust,
Pull'd down, lay level'd with the Dust,
The great, the mighty and the proud,
They all lay equal'd in the croud.

...

The slandrous and backsliding Tongue
Lay bound in silence in the Tomb:
the furious Temper's cease to rage
And lay in Death's cold gloomy shades.

...

There I beheld and lo I found
A lovely youth lye in the Ground:
'Twas but a little while before
I saw him flourish like a Flower.

But O the shaft of Death was flung
And cut the tender Flower down.
Death's sharpen'd Arrows gave the wound,
And now he moulders in the Ground.

The lovely Flesh, the sparkling Eyes
Lay mouldering in Eternity;
The blooming Cheek that once was worn
Is now a Feast for odious Worms.

The lovely Frame the active Hands
Lay bound in Death's cold Prison Bands,
The burning Flesh, the charmless Tongue
Lay mouldering in the silent Tomb.

The tender Skin, the curious Frame,
The blooming Countenance was gone,
The softest Flesh, the lovely Charms
Lay clasp'd in Death's cold icy arms.

...

What Millions! Millions! had been slain
By Death, that conquering, mighty King?

> What crowds of num'rous corps I found
> Lay cold and mouldering in the Ground.
>
> ...
>
> But O I saw ten thousand run,
> Stupid as stocks they do go on
> In the broad Road that leads to Hell,
> Where tortured Souls in Torment dwell.
>
> What precious Moments do they waste
> To please their sinful carnal Taste?
> Forgetful that their Souls must live
> Eternally beyond the Grave.
>
> ...
>
> Trembling and sorrow seiz'd me round,
> In Prayer I fell upon the Ground.
> My Soul addrest God's holy Throne,
> To shower his blessed Spirit down.
>
> ...
>
> Shew Sinners their undone Estate;
> Their precious Souls now lie at stake;
> A few more sinful steps remains
> And they'r in everlasting Flames.
>
> Arise dead Souls, and beg of God,
> To teach you how to read his Word,
> And change your Heart by power Divine
> That in your Heart may honor him.

It is hard what to know to make of this work, and its choice as an epitaph. Barlow obviously knew the messages of The Classic—the sudden flight of the arrow of Death, and the importance of not letting the distractions of Life draw your attention away from the certainty of Death. He also makes use of all the common tropes of the Graveyard poets, reviewing the standard cast of characters that illustrate how all are equal in the Grave. I supposed he must have known Dante and Milton and medieval Danse Macabre paintings, as their images shape his dream. But keep in mind that one of the goals of the Hartford Wits was to ridicule highfalutin style wherever they found it. It may be this whole fifty-seven-stanza epic is not simply bad, but a deliberately sarcastic parody of the Graveyard School. If so, that subtlety was lost on Seth Backus, Jr.

~~~

Of all the poets I have encountered in these graveyards, Graveyard School or otherwise, familiar or new to me, the single most often-quoted is Edward Young (1683–1765). I had not heard of, let alone read, Young before beginning this project. As far as I can tell he is known today primarily among academic specialists, but he was astonishingly popular and widely read in his day. Born near Winchester and educated at New College, Oxford, Young for many years struggled to earn a living, first as a writer, then as a clergyman, succeeding in neither vocation. Despite his lack of success, he kept introducing his works with fawning dedications to the great and good, unflaggingly convinced that for some reason he deserved their lucrative patronage. By the 1730s he had attained a modest living and a well-connected wife. She died in

1740, and in 1742 he was inspired to write his one tremendously successful work, *The Complaint, or Night Thoughts on Life, Death and Immortality.*

Its success was immediate and its influence enormous. It was translated into all major European languages and appeared in countless editions and anthologies. Young is extensively excerpted in *Elegant Extracts* and Murray's *English Reader,* and his lines are "sampled" by countless other devotional writers and editors. *Night Thoughts* became a classic of French Romantic literature, and Goethe and Burke were among the writers moved by its treatment of the Sublime. It is long and uneven, but at its best it contains brilliant writing. William Blake was a great admirer, and produced superb watercolor illustrations for a special edition of *Night Thoughts.*

I own a copy of the third edition (London, 1773); a prior owner inscribed a few marginal notes and corrections to the text, and hand-drew several delightful little manicules to indicate favorite passages. This telltale evidence of a deeply engaged reader (and book owner) from two hundred and fifty years ago adds another little bit of life to the otherwise lost world of writing, publishing, reading, and re-use of literature that produced these epitaphs.

While *Night Thoughts* was not the earliest work of the Graveyard School, it firmly established the genre as appropriate for pious readers and devotional study. This influence is clearly demonstrated by the extensive use of Young's work for epitaphs, across many miles and decades. Indeed, as noted above Mrs. Rowe dedicated her *Letters* to Young.

Let us begin with a stone in the Old Hadley Cemetery (Figure 48):

> Here lies Interrd
> the Remains of
> *MRS SUBMIT* GAYLORD
> Wife of
> Mr. SAMUEL GAYLORD
> who died Oct, 21, 1766
> In Her 24, Year.
>
> ---
>
> *Death,s terror is*
> *the Mountain Faith removes*
> *tis Faith disarms*
> *Destruction,*
> *Believe & look*
> *With triumph on the tomb*

The source is a paean to Faith in *Night the Fourth*:

Faith builds a bridge across the gulf of death,
To break the shock blind nature cannot shun,
And lands thought smoothly on the farther
   shore.
Death's terror is the mountain faith removes;
That mountain barrier between man and peace;
'Tis faith disarms destruction; and absolves
From ev'ry clam'rous charge the guiltless tomb.

Figure 48. Submit Gaylord stone (author's collection).

I do not know the source of the fragmentary command to believe and look. This is one of the instances that makes me reflect on just whose voice we are hearing when we read the verse—should we attribute this stirring testimonial of Christian faith to Submit herself, or is it a first-person testimony by her surviving husband of the strength of *his* faith, to overcome his sorrow at the loss of his wife? Or is it a timely little sermon recommended by the local minister? As ever, we cannot know, we can only read and speculate.

Here is a memorial of the same vintage, from Montague's Old South Cemetery. It is a lovely double-headed stone; the text runs below two carved heads (Figure 49):

> In Memory of 2 Sons
> of y^e Revd Judah & Mrs.
> Mary Nash who died at
> y^e Birth the one on y^e
> Right hand Septr 8th, 1764,
> on y^e left Decr. 17th, 1766
>
> *Our birth is nothing
> but our Death begun.*

Note that neither stillborn brother is named. The source is *Night the Fifth*:

> While man is growing life is in decrease:
> And cradles rock us nearer to the tomb.
> **Our birth is nothing but our death begun**.

Young's image of infancy's cradle rocking us straight to the tomb is frighteningly effective. This was an essential lesson for Calvinist readers: the death of an infant reminds us how fleeting life is. I give the Reverend Nash credit for not shirking this sentiment in the case of his own two stillborn sons. The choice of a passage from Young, instead of a Bible verse, for the gravestone of a minister's children indicates of how acceptable Young's works were as a form of religious instruction, as appropriate as a verse from Job or a passage *The New England Primer*, even as he provides a more lyrical, emotional language for the reader to experience.*

Figure 49. Nash sons stone (courtesy of American Antiquarian Society).

Young was frequently chosen for epitaphs in Northampton's Bridge Street Cemetery. Here is passage from *Night the Second*:

> In Memory of
> Cap NOAH WRIGHT
> who died July 27
> AD 1775 in the
> 76 year of his age.
>
> *Life like the Solar Shadow
> Speeds away from Point
> To Point.*

---

* My respect for Reverend Nash, and my sympathy for him and his wife, only increases when I recall that they had a son born in 1767 who survived childbirth only to die at age 10.

The Graveyard School

Tho seeming to stand still
Thus soon Man's hours are
Up, and we are gone.

This is an intriguing and complicated verse. What exactly is a Solar Shadow? An eclipse, perhaps? Or one's own shadow, lengthening faster and faster as the sun goes down? Either way Young skillfully evokes the cosmic power of the solar system: our shadow before us appears to static, but in fact it and we are spinning through space all the time. And then, quite suddenly, our time is up and we are gone.

Here is another epitaph from *Night the Second*, also in Northampton:

> In Memory of
> Mr. CALEB STRONG
> who Died Feb^r 13
> A.D. 1776 In
> the 66th year of
> his Age.
>
> *Man's Home is in the*
> *Grave,*
> *Here dwells ye Multitude,*
> *we gaze around,*
> *We read their Monuments,*
> *we sigh, & while*
> *We sigh, we sink*

I have found two versions of the same text, from the same year and the same town. And yet, based on the carving of the gravestones and two different renderings of the text, I assume they are the work of two different stone cutters. Young's original text reads:

> Life's little stage is a small eminence,
> Inch-high **the grave above; that home of man,**
> **Where dwells the multitude: We gaze around;**
> **We read their monuments; we sigh; and while**
> **We sigh, we sink;** and are what we deplor'd...

Upon close reading, Caleb Strong's epitaph shifts Young's meaning in a material way. Young is referring to the mortal world, a little stage inch-high *above* the grave, where we multitudinous mortals scurry about on our business—until we come into a graveyard, see the monuments all around, and are reminded of our inevitable fate. Re-used as an epitaph, the lines omit the key word "above" and now describe the grave as the home into which all men come to dwell. Who do you suppose took it upon him or herself to modify the source text in this way?

A selection from *Night the Third* was chosen in Northampton (where Young was clearly popular), as well as Monson and Deerfield, twenty-five years apart. In these instances, the quotation is exact:

> In memory of
> Mr. EBENEZER PRESCOTT
> who died in Dorchester
> Oct. 15th 1776
> in the 60th year of his age.
> and of

> Mrs. JERUSHA PRESCOTT
> wife of Mr. Ebenezer Prescott
> who died in this Town
> Oct. 15th 1779
> in the 56th year of her age.
> *"Life makes the soul dependant on the dust*
> *Death gives her wings to mount above the spheres."*

The passage in context reads:

> **Life makes the soul dependent on the dust;**
> **Death gives her wings to mount above the spheres.**
> Through chinks, styled organs, dim Life peeps at light;
> Death bursts the involving cloud, and all is day;
> All eye, all ear, the disembodied power.
> Death has feign'd evils Nature shall not feel
> Life, ills substantial, Wisdom cannot shun.
> Is not the mighty mind, that son of heaven,
> By tyrant Life dethroned, imprison'd, pain'd?
> By Death enlarged, ennobled, deified?
> Death but entombs the body; Life, the soul.

Notice how Young develops a theme we have heard in Scripture, hymns and other poems, that the death is a liberation from the sufferings of life for the righteous. Here Death is a release from mortal woes, a glorious chance to soar, a freeing of the soul from the *entombment* of life.

Another text of Young's appears over the hills in Lanesborough's Center Cemetery:

> SACRED to the Me
> mory of Mrs. SARAH
> the Amiable Consort
> of Lieu^t. CALEB SMITH
> Who died June ye 5th, 1779
> in ye 24 year.
> *O! What a sweet temper and mild*
> *When grim death approach she smiled,*
> *What tho' short thy date*
> *Virtue, not rolling suns*
> *The mind matures.*

I have not been able to identify the first two lines, but the last three are from *Night the Fifth*:

> **What tho' short thy date?**
> **Virtue, not rolling suns, the mind matures.**
> **That life is long, which answer's life's great end**.
> The time that bears no fruit, deserves no name;
> **The man of wisdom is the man of years**.
> In hoary youth Methuselahs may die,
> O how misdated on their flattering tombs!

Slight variations of this same text appear in Northfield, Stockbridge, and Sheffield over the ensuing twenty-five years. This diffusion of a single Young text, across decades and scores of miles, demonstrates the extensive and appreciative readership his work enjoyed. Indeed, it is a testament to both the reach and the duration of Young's popularity that Abigail Adams quotes these same lines in a letter to a bereaved friend dated May 8, 1798:

> It becomes us then to be silent, and adore the hand which strikes our comforts dead. To be insensible to our loss is not requir'd of us by Him who made and knows our Frame, and whom we are told in holy writ wept at the loss of a Friend, to mourn is the State of humanity. But we have comfort in this that we mourn not as those who have no hope. Tho our dear young Friend [and others] ... have gone before us we have a rational hope from their lives and conversation, that the period of their duties were compleat, what tho short their date:
>
> > "Virtue, not rolling Suns, the mind matures,
> > That life is long which answers Life's great End."

Elsewhere, Adams quotes a passage from *Night the Second*. On this occasion, the subject is the death of her own father, as she writes to John Thaxter:

> Braintree October 20. 1783
>
> To you my young Friend upon whom the parental ties are strong and unbroken; who never yet knew the agonies which attend the loss of a fond Mother; or the pangs which rend the filial Heart Bereaved of a dear and venerable Father, to You I say, may Heaven long continue those blessings, nor teach you, experimentally to Sympathize with your afflicted Friend.
>
> My dear parent is no more! His illness was Short and accute, his patience resignation and Submission, exemplary.... Even in his last hours, he retaind that Cheerfullness which had distinguishd him through his Life. I never before past through so painfull and yet so instructive a Scene, I reflect upon the last fortnight of his Life with a melancholy satisfaction and pleasure.
>
> > "Sweet peace and Heavenly hope, and humble joy
> > Divinely beamd on his exalted Soul."

The source for this second Adams quotation in *Night Thoughts* is:

> **Sweet Peace, and heavenly Hope, and humble Joy,**
> **Divinely beam on his exalted soul**,
> Destruction gild, and crown him for the skies,
> With incommunicable lustre bright.

The same text was chosen for a grave in Northampton's Bridge Street Cemetery, twice, more than twenty years later (Young keeps bringing us back to Northampton, and vice-versa):

> In Memory of
> JULIA A. STRONG
> daugher of Caleb Strong, and Sarah, his wife,
> whose life was employed in active benevolence, and who
> died in full hope of a happy immortality,
> October 1st, 1818, aged 25 years.
>
> *Sweet peace, and heavenly hope, and humble joy,*
> *Divinely beamed on her enraptured soul,*
> *And crowned her for the skies.*

The eulogistic prose of this memorial strikes me as a good summary of the ideal Christian's experience and expectations: a life of active benevolence, and a death full of hope of paradise to come.

Also in Northampton is this short passage which, out of all proportion to its brevity, moves us to contemplate the vastness of eternity:

> Here lies the Body
> of Deacon
> Ebenezer Hunt
> who died FEbRy 21
> 1788 in the 85th Year
> of his age
>
> *The Moments seize; a*
> *Moment you may wish when*
> *Worlds want wealth to buy*

The text is from another part of *Night the Second*:

> Throw Time away?
> Throw Empires and be blameless. **Moments seize;**
> Heaven's on their wing. **A moment you may wish,**
> **When Worlds want Wealth to buy**.

Here again Young uses, and expands upon, a key message from hymnody and The Classic: Far better to throw away the greatest wealth and power you can have in this vain and insubstantial world, than to waste one moment that might very well be your last, and as such should be spent preparing your soul for eternity. Every moment carries eternity on its wings, and there is no repentance in the grave. There may even be a faint echo of Marvell's "Time's winged chariot drawing near." While it may be a stretch, I wonder if Thoreau read Edward Young and had this passage in mind, consciously or otherwise, when he wrote: "As if you could kill time without injuring eternity."

The Elijah Bordwell stone in Montague's Old South Cemetery is astonishing in several respects. First, the long memorial text describes in riveting detail the circumstances of poor Elijah's harrowing death. There is then a short two-line verse, the first by Young and the second I believe original. Finally, the whole is surmounted by a wonderful carved clock face, a decoration I have not seen anywhere else. A friend of mine, a skilled horologist, points out that this an old-fashioned one-handed clock pointing to 12:00, indicating Bordwell's day has ended (Figure 50):

> In Memory of Mr. Elijah Bordwell
> who died Janry 26th 1786 in ye 27th
> Year of his Age, having but a few days
> survivd ye fatal Night when he was
> flung from his horse & drawn by ye stirrup
> 26 rods along ye path as appear'd by ye place
> where his hat was found & where he had
> Spent ye whole following severe cold night
> treading ye Snow in a Small Circle. the
> family he left was an aged father a Wife
> & 3 Small Children.

On this Side Death Man's Dangers never cease
Beyond ye Virtuous Share eternal Peace.

The first line is the one Young quotation I have seen that is not from *Night Thoughts*. Rather it is from one of his early works, a lengthy patriotic panegyric in rhyme entitled *Poem on the Last Day* (1713), dedicated (quite fulsomely) to Queen Anne. Referring to this mortal, fallen world, Young writes:

This is the scene of combat, not of rest,
Man's is laborious happiness at best;
On this side death his dangers never cease,
His joys are joys of conquest not of peace.*

Figure 50. Elijah Bordwell stone (courtesy of American Antiquarian Society).

The second line of the epitaph retains the rhyme of "cease/peace" but otherwise presents a completely different image, tightly contrasting the dangers of this existence with eternal peace for the virtuous in the life to come. There may be an echo here of St. Augustine's *City of God* (Book XIX, Chapter X: The Reward Prepared for the Saints After They Have Endured the Trial of Life): "There [in Heaven] the virtues shall no longer be struggling against any vice or evil, but shall enjoy the reward of victory, the eternal peace which no adversary shall disturb." Mere speculation, certainly, and no doubt a long shot, but it is surely not out of the question that a devout citizen or minister in early Montague had read this passage from Augustine, and dog-eared it as appropriate when mourning one who has suffered greatly. At any rate, between the artful carving and the quantity of text, this is an impressive and probably quite expensive monument. I wonder if the carver was a friend of Bordwell's.

In Provincetown there is a double-stone for a young sister and brother who died within a month of each other, presumably from an unnamed contagion:

MARCIA GIBBS and HENRY GIBBS
Nov. 17th and Dec. 14th 1791
Aged 4 Years and 8 Years

Insatiate Archer could not one suffice?
Thy shaft flew twice, & twice my peace was slain;
And twice, ere twice yon moon had fill'd her horn.
Young

This is one of the infrequent instances where the author of the epitaph text is explicitly named. The original passage, in *Night the First*, refers to three deaths;

---

* Reading these early, awkward attempts at heroic couplets, we can understand why Young took up blank verse for his greater work.

someone in Provincetown had access to this text and made the necessary, simple revisions:

> **Insatiate archer! could not one suffice?**
> **Thy shaft flew thrice, and thrice my peace was slain;**
> **And thrice, ere thrice yon moon had filled her horn**.

The same lines were chosen in Greenfield on the graves of three young brothers (Daniel, Guy, and Stephen Clay) who died within a week of each other, of smallpox, in August 1802 (Figure 51). Pause for a moment, reader, and try to imagine the feelings of Lucinda and Daniel, the boys' bereaved parents, as they commissioned the three little gravestones that stand today side by side.

The insatiate archer is also found in Westfield Old Burying Ground, where a widower buried two wives and a child, this time "thrice" as in the original:

> Sacred to the Memory of Mrs.
> Dolly Wife of Mr. JOHN ATWATER
> who Died June 26 1787 in ye 33d
> Year of her Age. Also Dolly dautr
> of Mr. JOHN and Mrs. Dolly ATWATER
> Died Sept. 4 1787 Aged 6
> Years & 6 Months. Also Mrs.
> Anna 2nd Wife of Mr. JOHN ATWATER
> Who Died Feb. 17 1790 in ye 25
> Year of Her Age
>
> *Each moment has its sickle, emulous*
> *Of Time's enormous scythe, whose ample sweep*
> *Strikes empires from the root each moment plies*
> *His little weapon in the narrow sphere*
> *Of Sweet domestick comfort and cuts down*

Figure 51. Clay children stone (courtesy of Bob Drinkwater).

> *The fair blooms of sublunary Bliss*
> *Death great Proprietor of all tis thine*
> *To tread our empire, and to quench the stars.*
> *Insatiate archer! could not one suffice*
> *Thy shaft flew thrice & thrice my peace was slain*
> *I tremble at the blessing once so dear*
> *& every pleasure pains me to the heart*

This text contains three distinct sections, all from *Night the First*, spliced together. Note how much text this amounts to. Someone spent a lot of time to compose this, and money to have it carved. The imagery of the first section is terrifying, contrasting the sickle with the enormous scythe, and showing the little weapon flying its lethal way through the narrow sphere of domestic comfort.

These verses could have been written expressly for the bereaved John Atwater's use. Indeed, we have to wonder, who did the splicing? Reading the original texts, I can understand how Young's language and imagery resonated, and it does leave one wondering a bit why he is so forgotten today. Hervey and Wright and the elegant elegists with their well-turned couplets urged their readers to consider the sublime; Young's work aspires to *be* sublime.

The archer also appears in the Berkshires, first in Richmond's Center Cemetery, on a stone with an unusual wavy border (Figure 52):

```
       To the Memory
             of
     Mrs. ZERUJAH CHIDSEY
          Consort of
      Mr. JOSEPH CHIDSEY
      who died November
          21st AD 1771
     in the 31st Year of her
             age.
```
The insatiate Archer did not spare
A tender Mother and a Consort dear.

The identical lines appear in Sheffield's Plain Cemetery, twenty miles away and twenty years later, on the grave of Juliann Dibble (d. 1793, of smallpox, at age 29). This is perfect example of a local hand taking a phrase from a source text and transforming it into an original composition. The insatiate archer was so widely recognized that no further reference was needed to ground this short memorial in Young's work— any contemporary reader would have caught the reference.*

Figure 52. Zerujah Chidsey stone (author's collection).

---

* Young's cry "insatiate Archer, could not one suffice?" became a common phrase throughout the nineteenth century, used to poke fun at someone prone to repetition ('Stop saying the same thing over and over! I heard you the first time!').

Here is a stone in Shelburne's Hill Cemetery with a passage from *Night the Third*:

> In Memory of Mrs.
> Naomy Consort of
> Mr. Elisha Barnard
> who died July
> 1796, in the 28
> Year of her Age.
>
> *Smitten Friends*
> *Are Angels Sent on*
> *Errands full of Love,*
> *For us they languish &*
> *For us they die.*

This choice of epitaph provides another glimpse into the different ways a text might make it from book to gravestone. This exact passage can be found in Knox's *Elegant Extracts*. The same quotation from Young also appears in a sermon preached by the Rev. Jonathan Homer of Newton Massachusetts in December 1792 "upon the death of a very dear and promising child." Homer's sermon was subsequently published as *The Mourner's Friend*, in order to provide consolation and advice to parents of deceased children. It is entirely possible that a copy of this pamphlet made its way into the library of the minister in Shelburne. Thus by 1796 Naomy Barnard's epitaph might have been sourced from either *Night Thoughts*, *Elegant Extracts*, or *The Mourner's Friend*.

Here is an extraordinary epitaph from Longmeadow Cemetery. It is carved on a big flat table-tomb (one of several in Longmeadow) whose carving is still wondrously well-preserved, despite two-and-a-quarter centuries' worth of snow, rain, and lichen. Consider the effort and expense that went into composing and carving this generous eulogy. It was not her husband's work; Lucy was Samuel's relict (i.e., widow) so it must have been commissioned by her surviving friends and admirers. The litany of Christian virtues is comprehensive and apparently sincere:

> Sacred to the Memory of
> Mrs. Lucy Colton
> Relict of Mr. Samuel Colton, Merchant
> She died Dec. 7 A.D. 1799. AEt. 57.
> She possessed a mind much above
> the command standard and
> practiced the social virtues
> in an eminent degree. She was an
> affectionate and faithful Partner
> Parent and Friend. Being
> liberally endowed, she judiciously
> and liberally contributed to public
> purposes and caused the heart of the
> Widow and the Fatherless to rejoice
> Thus she honored the Lord with her
> Substance and her Memory is blessed.
> She was an understanding Believer
> in the doctrines of Christianity

> Serious attendant on Divine
> Instruction, & died in the hope of an
> immortal and glorious life.
>
> *Death great Proprietor of all tis thine*
> *To tread out Empires, and to quench the stars.*
> *The Sun himself by thy permission shines*
> *And, one day, thou shalt pluck him from his sphere.*

Whoever created this monument piously expresses the hope of resurrection and salvation for Lucy Colton; piously, but also quite confidently don't you think? There follows a shift to the marvelous, sonorous language of Young's *Night the First*. Permit yourself the pleasure of reading it aloud; you can't mistake the drama, and the breadth of Young's imagination is truly cosmic. Death, the great Proprietor, will someday extinguish the Sun itself.

This may seem like a bleak sentiment for an exemplary Christian woman who died in the hope of immortality. However I believe the message this epitaph choice intends to send is that while Death is awesomely powerful, so powerful he can even pluck the Sun from the Spheres, for the true Christian there will then come an end of times followed by an eternity in Heaven.

Interestingly, in the source text the language of Lucy Colton's epitaph immediately precedes the "insatiate archer" passage on the gravestones just mentioned. The poet is bemoaning the sublunary bliss that he enjoyed before being bereft by the loss of three loved ones. Young asks of Death, given his awesome power:

> Amid such mighty plunder, why exhaust
> Thy partial quiver on a mark so mean?
> Why this peculiar rancor wreak'd on me?
> Insatiate archer! could not one suffice....

In Stockbridge Cemetery, a passage from *Night the First* was used on the double head-stone of two children:

> Charles Brown and Frederic Brown
> Died 1800
>
> Children of Mr. HENRY and Mrs. MARY BROWN
>
> *Sweet smiling buds that open'd bloom'd and died*
>
> *Bliss there is none but unprecarious bliss*
> *That is the Gem. Sell all and purchase that.*

How strange, condensed, and inscrutable are these two lines from Young, and what a contrast to the open sentimentality of the sweet smiling buds. Here is the passage in context:

> Vain are all sudden sallies of delight;
> Convulsions of a weak distemper'd joy.
> Joy's a fix'd state; a tenure, not a start.
> **Bliss there is none, but unprecarious bliss:**
> **That is the gem: sell all, and purchase that.**

Young's message is that most of what seems to make us happy is actually sudden, fleeting, precarious—like the lives of the Brown children. The only true bliss is the happiness of the virtuous Christian in Heaven; rid yourself of everything else in order to attain it. I hope Mary and Henry Brown found comfort in the thought, and were able to embrace it.

An exact quotation from *Night the Fifth* is used twice, eleven years apart, once again in Northampton's Bridge Street Cemetery:

> In Memory of
> Mr. JOSEPH HUNT BRECK,
> who departed this life November 10th, A.D. 1801,
> in the 36th year of his age.
>
> *That life is long which answer's life's great end,*
> *One eye on Death, and one full fixed on heaven,*
> *Becomes a mortal and immortal man*

This is a softer, more lyrical, but still admonitory version of The Classic—mortal men should not waste glances on the paltry pleasures and glittering toys of this earth, but keep their attention on Death and Eternity. The first line of Breck's epitaph, "That life is long…" is also from *Night the Fifth*, but it is not adjacent to the next two lines. It seems especially appropriate for a young person's grave; Breck was only thirty-six.

In Sheffield's Barnard Cemetery, this respectful epitaph for a venerable old soldier splices together two different passages from Young:

> This
> Monument is erected
> to perpetuate the memory of
> Col. JOHN ASHLEY
> who departed this life
> September 1st, 1802, in
> the 93d year of his age.
>
> *Virtue alone has majesty in death,*
> *And triumphs most when most the tyrant frowns;*
> *Earth highest station ends in Here he lies*
> *And dust to dust concludes her noblest song.*

We have already seen the last two lines from *Night the Fourth*; the first are from *Night the Second*:

> Whatever farce the boastful hero plays,
> **Virtue alone has majesty in death,**
> And greater still, **the more the tyrant frowns**.

In context, this passage refers to a young man taken in "a sudden rush from life's meridian joys," not an old man of ninety-three years. But the choice is still apt; Colonel Ashley clearly had the respect of his memorialist, and we understand that his majestic virtue stands apart from, and above, the boastful player. Interestingly, the identical "edited" quatrain was chosen for a gravestone just up in the road in Great Barrington's Mahaiwe Cemetery only a few years later (John Gibson, died 1806).

In Old Hadley Cemetery, a passage from Young was chosen for a daughter of Jonathan Edwards:

> This monument is
> erected in memory of
> Madam Susanna Porter
> widow of the Late honorable Eleazer Porter Esqr &

daughter of the Rev. Jonathan
Edwards, late President of
New Jersey College, who died
May 2d 1803 in the 63d year
of her age.

Were Death denyed, poor man would live in vain
Death gives us more than was in Eden lost
This King of Terrors is the Prince of Peace.

The lines are from the end of *Night the Third*, the culmination of a long exaltation of Death as a welcome release from the burdens of Life, which keep us in darkness, fear, and worldly worries:

Death is the Crown of Life;
Was Death deny'd, poor Man would live in vain;
Was Death deny'd, to live would not be life;
Was Death deny'd, even Fools would wish to die.
Death wounds, to cure: We fall; we rise; we reign!
Spring from our Fetters; fasten in the Skies;
Where blooming *Eden* withers in our sight:
Death gives us more than was in *Eden* lost.
This King of Terrors is the Prince of Peace.
When shall I die to Vanity, Pain, Death?
When shall I *die*?—When shall I live for ever?

I do not know what Jonathan Edwards would have thought of this choice of epitaph by (or for) his daughter. He had died forty-five years earlier, so he had no say. But the sentiment of being impatient to die, eager to die in order to enjoy the benefit of death (i.e., eternal life) does not sound like one he would endorse. Ideas change in a half-century.

Young is still being chosen well into the nineteenth century, as in this verse for a young man in Longmeadow:

In
Memory of
SIMEON C. BLISS
who died
MAY 5, 1838.
AEt. 26

No warning giv'n!
Unceremonious fate!
A sudden rush from life's meridian joys!
A wrench from all we love from all we are!

The forceful drama of the blank verse lines are unmistakably Edward Young's. Who cannot grasp and envision the sudden rush away from our everyday pleasures? It is as if an alarm has sounded, and everyone has to leap up from whatever we are doing and run out into the street ... or in this case, the grave.

All in all, I have found Young chosen for epitaphs more or less continuously from 1770 to almost 1840. While there is some repetition in the choices, I am struck by how many different passages from his work served rural New Englanders to express their grief and their devotion, over the course of seventy years. We know they had access to his work: *Night Thoughts* appears in the Reverend Storrs estate and also in private book inventories of the time. As noted, readers could find plenty of Young poetry in *Elegant Extracts* and Murray's *English Reader*—but I have found far more passages from Young in these graveyards than appear in those two books.

I have commented on the duration of Edward Young's popularity with these readers, and his relevance to their spiritual needs. Let me end my comments on him by observing that a full century later, the British poet and novelist Edmund Blunden (1896–1974) recalls in *Undertones of War* (1928) that he found great consolation in reading Young in the trenches of World War I:

> During this period [of intensive shelling in September 1917] my indebtedness to an eighteenth-century poet became enormous. At every spare moment I read in Young's *Night Thoughts on Life, Death and Immortality*, and I felt the benefit of the grave and intellectual voice, speaking out of a profound eighteenth-century calm, often in metaphor which came home to one even in a pillbox. The mere amusement of discovering lines applicable to our crisis kept me from despair.

I encourage you to try Young yourself. His numinous language still has great power to inspire and move, however far removed most of us are from the particular religiosity of his contemporary readers.

Recurring but Unidentified

As mentioned in Part I, another common category of epitaph consists of verses that occur more or less identically across time and distance, but for which there is no single identifiable source or author.* Some appear so often that I have developed a policy of "catch and release"—I cannot even be bothered to record them anymore. Others are just infrequent enough to bring a smile of recognition when I find one: "Well look here, it's my old friend 'Go home, dry tears'!" Still others recur only a few times, in a few adjoining towns; reading these brings me quite close to an elusive and ultimately inaccessible anonymous author.

We can start early, in 1740, with "A Law Eternal doth decree." I have found this little couplet four times over more than fifty years in the 1700s, in four separate towns, none far away from the other. It has an almost psalm-like ring to it, but I have found no source text. The first example is in the Westfield Old Burying Ground:

In Memory of
Mrs RHODA, wife
Of Deacon ELDAD
Taylor, died June ye 22nd, 1740,
In ye 29th year of her age

A law eternal doth decree,
That all things made shall mortal be.

The last instance I have found is in Blandford Cemetery in 1802. This is not the most profound message you will ever read in these cemeteries, but it provides a glimpse into a world of writing and reading in early rural New England. Whatever its merits as poetry, the fact is someone took the time to compose it, someone else deemed it worth the expense of publication and distribution, and others read it and were moved by it and paid to have it carved on a loved one's gravestone.

A similar example of a popular, widely-seen, but ultimately un-sourced verse was chosen several times up and down the Connecticut River; here is an early version from Enfield:

In Memory of
Mr. DAVID SABIN
who died

---

* I will largely refrain from showing multiple examples of these epitaphs –the reader will have to trust me that that they recur over and over, and that I could provide many instances to prove the point. Nor have I included every example of recurring epitaph I have collected; I have tried to limit myself to the particularly common or distinctly interesting.

Oct 28, 1749
Aged 52 Years

This stone stands but to tell
Where his dust lies, not what he was.
When saints do rise that day will show
The part he acted here below

This stone been attributed to the Stebbins carving shop, and it appears on Stebbins stones in South Hadley (the Rev. John Woodbridge and his two wives, 1786) and again in Enfield (Benjamin Eastman, died 1792). It also can be found in Longmeadow, Agawam, and Westfield; I'm not sure if those can also be attributed to Stebbins. As mentioned in Part I, this may be an example of a carver's "house stock" of verse, or alternatively it could have been familiar to, and used by, a range of area carvers.

One of the more interesting examples of this category, for its subtle but noticeable variations, is "Go home, dry tears." The earliest example I have read is in Northfield Center Cemetery:

In Memory of Mrs. Sarah Belding
The wife of Mr Jonathan Belding
Who died June 17 1762 in ye 31 year of her age

Depart my friends
Dry up your tears,
I must lie here
Till Christ appears

It appears again, over the hills in Lee Center Cemetery, in 1788:

Mrs
Rebecca, wife
of Mr Oliver Hatch
died May 1st 1788
In the 33d year
of her age.

Farewell my friends
dry up your tears
My dust lies here
Till Christ appears

You can read this slight variant up in Williamstown's South Lawn Cemetery:

Mr. Stephen Bennett.
died July 27, 1796:
in the 24 year of
his age.

Go home my friends
Wipe off your tears
Here I must lie
Till Christ appears

And so on, through the 1830s, in Massachusetts, New York, New Jersey, and Connecticut.

Clearly this verse was widely available in print over many decades. We can understand the its popularity as an epitaph. It provides a simple, hopeful message to surviving friends: "Do not worry, do not be sad. There is nothing more you can do now. I must lie in this grave awhile, but then the resurrection will follow." Note that this encouraging message is put into the mouth of the deceased who of course cannot speak—the obvious but recurring irony of so many of these epitaphs.

Note also the many slight variations employed, across time and distance. I quite like the shifts in movement or agency between the "Farewell" message—the deceased is the one in motion, leaving us behind, bidding us adieu—and the "Depart" message—the deceased knows we are standing there reading his stone, mourning, and bids *us* to go hence, back to the world. Then "Go home"—now the message is even more specific: "I know you, and I know where you live. Go there and comfort yourself amongst your family, you needn't linger here." It also becomes more intimate, in a way; to "dry off" your tears is perhaps a bit poetic, a bit fancy; to "wipe off" your tears is more immediate, more literal.

Here is a gently comforting version from the tiny disused Townsend Cemetery in Hancock:

> In memory of
> Reuben Ely
> Who departed this life
> Feb the 22nd, 1799
> In the 90th year
> of his age
>
> *Go home dear friends*
> *Lament no more*
> *I am not lost*
> *But gone before*

The "gone before" sentiment seems ahead of its time here; the notion that the deceased are not lost to us forever, just gone ahead to a place where we will meet again, became widely popular in the mid-nineteenth century and in the aftermath of the Civil War.

Lastly, here is a version from Lanesborough. I cannot find it in Josephine C. Frost's collection, but I still have my youthful hand-transcription of it, in mediocre Palmer Method cursive script, on a fading sheet from a yellow legal pad:

> N. P. Talcott
> 1841
> Age 39
>
> *Suppress your grief, dry up your tears*
> *His dust must rest till Christ appears*
> *My friends be still and eye the rod*
> *And know the hand that struck was God.*

The message is still to reconcile yourself, but the tone is not quite as comforting. The command to suppress our grief is stern, the voice of a minister enjoining us to force our minds away from the noise and frivolous distractions of the mortal sphere. That pulpit tone is also heard instructing us to eye the rod and never question God's handiwork. Tellingly, the voice in the text shifts from the first-person representing the deceased, to a third-party speaker ("*his* dust must rest"). The one speaking to "my friends" in this epitaph is a voice of authority, not poor N.P. Talcott.

To conclude this perhaps overly-thorough discussion of one simple verse, recall for a moment The Classic, and compare it to "Go home, dry tears." The former typically addresses itself to an unspecified and unknown Reader or passer-by, the latter to known friends. As such, The Classic serves as a literally timeless warning. "Go home" is carved to endure but also to convey a message from the deceased to her/his surviving loved ones at a point in time. The Classic calls upon us to reflect on our imminent death and the risk of eternal suffering; "Go home" bids us to cheer up and live amongst the living. Two dramatically different choices, vividly illustrating the range of contemporaneous attitudes towards death.

Another widely distributed but un-sourceable text is "Death is a debt to Nature due." The earliest version I have found is in Westfield's Old Burying Ground:

> In Memory of
> Mrs. JOANNA
> Wife of Ens.
> MATHEW NOBLE
> who died Nov
> 1st, 1763, in her
> 67th Year
>
> *Death is a Debt*
> *to Nature Due,*
> *Which I have paid*
> *& so must you.*

At about the same time a variation of this trope was incorporated to an apparently bespoke memorial in Great Barrington's Mahaiwe Cemetery—a stately old burying ground with a colonial-era section close to Route 7 but somehow a little sheltered from the traffic, its later stones and Victorian mausolea spread across a little lea, its far edge abutting by a café and gas station, with a shopping mall just beyond. Here the debt is held specifically by death, not generally by nature:

> Sacred
> to the memory of
> Brig'dr Gen'l Joseph Dwight
> Died June 9 1765
> AE 62
>
> *Tho great in council and in arms,*
> *Tho pious, good and just,*
> *Yet death its cruel debt demands,*
> *Dwight slumbers in the dust.*

The last instance I have found is in Lanesborough Center Cemetery, at the beginning of the 1800s:

> Mrs. Polly perkins,
> wife of Mr. Joseph B. perkins,
> died June 21, 1802,
> in her 41st year.
>
> *Death is a debt to nature due,*
> *Which I have paid and so must you.*

I have found it many other times in the intervening years. Death as a debt to nature was a commonplace expression in America at the time these epitaphs were carved. In 1702, Cotton Mather wrote in one of his histories: "He did, at length, pay one debt, namely, that unto nature, by death" and in 1731 a journal-writer noted: "Death was a Debt due to Nature, and that we must all pay it." In various anthologies of epitaphs, I have found many earlier references to Death as a debt. For example, James Jones's *Sepulchrorum Inscriptiones* (1727) has this from 1650, *On Mr. Samuel Bridges*:

> Receiver of this College Rents, he paid
> His Debt to Nature, and beneath he's laid,
> To rest here till his Summons to remove,
> At the last Audit, to the Quire above.*

Hervey, in his *Meditations*, contrasts the death of a soldier with the far greater sacrifice Christ made for all mankind, musing: "[The soldier] only yielded up a life, which was long before forfeited to divine justice; which must soon have been surrendered as a debt to nature, if it had not fallen as a prey to war."†

So the idea of death as the unavoidable price to be paid for life has a long tradition. But who, we can only wonder, took the step of rendering this commonplace observation into a concise, and widely popular, quatrain of funerary verse, which was then distributed, read, and used all across colonial New England?

Another popular example of the category is this consoling little verse for deceased children, "God thought/saw it best." One example in Agawam Center Cemetery can stand for countless others I have read in the course of my collecting:

> In Memory of 3 Sons of
> Mr. Jedediah & Mrs. Phebe Bliss
> {viz} Ithamar died Aug 6, 1774
> Aged 8 Years. Calvin died Sept
> 10, 1776 Aged 4 years.
> Luther died Sept 18, 1776 Aged 2 years
>
> *Sleep on dear Youths & take your rest*
> *God call'd you hence he thought it best*

Apparently some dreadful contagion struck Agawam in September 1776.

This reads like something from an anthology of "funeral verses appropriate for the loss of an infant." But who would own such a volume? Not a household, surely. Of the relatively few books a farming family might choose to own, would they pay for this one? More likely a minister or potentially a stone carver. This text again raises, in an especially sad circumstance, the question of who made the selection on behalf of the dead infant. The voice is meant to be that of a resigned mother consoling her child. But is this really a sentiment the grieving Phebe Bliss would have chosen herself, or might it have been chosen for her, to instruct her on the proper way to respond to the death of her three sons?

---

* Sadly, the college is not identified.
† Speaking of soldiers, in Shakespeare's *Henry IV Part 1*, on the eve of the Battle of Shrewsbury, Falstaff confides to Prince Hal: "I would 'twere bed-time, Hal, and all well." Hal chides the cowardly knight: "Why, thou owest God a death" and exits. Falstaff expresses a sentiment we all can recognize, but one these early New Englanders were trained to repress: "'Tis not due yet; I would be loath to pay him before his day. What need I be so forward with him that calls not on me?"

Other epitaphs turn up less frequently, but enough to indicate they were published and distributed to a greater or lesser extent. For example, consider this short verse from Longmeadow Cemetery:

> Mr. DAVID HALE
> Son of
> Mr. JOHN &
> Mrs. THANKFUL HALE
> died Aprl. 16th. 1759
> In His 26th
> Year
>
> *O! Time Supream*
> *How Swift thy Wings:*
> *On Time depends*
> *Eternal things.*

The same epitaph appears in Enfield, Connecticut (Hannah Olmsted, died 1766) and Hampden (Mary Chaffee, died 1774). This is one of the many verses I have read that are not especially brilliant but, by virtue of being chosen for a gravestone, obtain a certain resonance and gravity. There is something compelling in the idea that Time, which seems so fleeting, is a beam on which Eternity hangs.

One intriguing glimpse into the distribution of these recurring epitaphs can be obtained in the Berkshires, where we find two pairs of identical epitaphs, years and a few miles apart, carved in a single craftsman's hand. The first verse is used for two brothers in Richmond, Theophilus and David Rossiter (1766 and 1770), then again two decades later for Betsey Love (1790) in the Church on the Hill Cemetery in nearby Lenox:

> *Dust animated by a soul*
> *Appeard in beauteous form*
> *Just lept on this terrestrial ball*
> *Alas how soon called home.*

The image of birth as leaping onto the terrestrial ball is wonderful. The phrase "terrestrial ball" appears often in religious writing, but I have not found a source for this particular verse.

The second example appears on the stone of Thankfull Willard (1789), also in the Church on the Hill Cemetery in Lenox, then two years later and one town south in Stockbridge Cemetery, on the grave of Brigadier General Moses Ashley "who being in perfect health and in the midst of public business died in a sudden and unexpected manner" (1791):

> *Boast of thy conquest death o'er human things*
> *The pomp of empires and the pride of kings*
> *But know the saints shall burst their chains and rise*
> *To thrones celestial in their kindred skies*

This is a fine, hymn-like verse with smooth meter and commanding heroic couplets reminiscent of Pope. There is real skill in the contrast between the first couplet, which concedes the awesome power of death over kings and empires, and the second, which completely undermines the first. It may even be a sly dig at the pride of kings, who are conquered by death, at the expense of humbler but more virtuous saints, who will rise to thrones in Heaven. Again I cannot find a source for this text. Joel Barlow in his *Columbiad* uses the image of "kindred skies," though not in the context of saints on thrones. The identical verse also appears twice in Goshen, Connecticut (Deacon John Beatch, died 1773 and Abraham Parmelee, died 1795).

This pattern of repetition suggests a carver who had a collection of favorite epitaphs at his disposal, or at least two, for his customers to consider. The carver in Goshen must have had access to the same collection, or perhaps the same carver worked both in the central Berkshires and fifty miles south in Connecticut.

I came across another example of this category outside my core study area of Western Massachusetts, but it is too riveting to omit. The Colonial Dames of New Hampshire published a charming collection of old epitaphs including this remarkably developed and expanded articulation of The Classic from the gravestone of Robert Gilmore (d. 1782, aged 82):

> *Death steady to his purpose from ye womb,*
> *Pursues till we are driven to ye tomb.*
> *O, reader wisely lay this thought to heart,*
> *And seek an interest in ye better part.*
> *Then when you close in death your mortal eyes,*
> *Your soul may rise and reign above ye skies.*

I cannot find an original source, but the identical verse can be found at almost the same moment in time, in Bedford (James Lane, died 1783) and Worcester (Samuel Smith, died 1785). The image of Death steadily, purposefully, pursuing us every day of our lives is absolutely dreadful.

Here is a fine bit of poetry that appears up and down the Connecticut River valley and as far south as New Haven over a half-century, between 1740 and the 1790s. This example is from Hatfield's Hill Cemetery:

> In Memory of Mr
> Isaac Graves who died
> Septr 19th 1781 in ye 95th
> Year of his Age.
>
> *Youth glows and smiles in Prospects bright*
> *Mid life is doom'd to Care and Toil*
> *Old Age the lonely Eve of Night*
> *Quick Death writes Vanity on all*

Isn't this a well-crafted little verse? I hear an allusion to the Sphinx's riddle in its description of the three stages of life, then an Old Testament tone and vocabulary for Quick Death's sudden ending of it all.

I have seen the following ominous epitaph used three times, from the Berkshires to Marblehead, all in the 1780s, beginning in Stockbridge Cemetery:

> In Memory of John
> Son to Doctr. Erastus
> & Mrs. Elisabeth
> Sergeant. Who died
> March 26. 1781. in
> ye 11th Year of his Age.

> *Whom neither Youth nor worth*
> *Nor Friends could save:*
> *From the relentless Bondage of the Grave.*

There is not much of the comfort or consolation here, no promise of resurrection, just relentless bondage in the grave. Perhaps it will turn out to be an excerpt from a longer and more hopeful hymn—a pattern we have seen before.

Here's a tantalizing example of recurrence, a marvelously evocative vision of Resurrection Day found first in Sheffield's Plain Cemetery:

> Beneath this stone lies the body of
> the Rev. John Keep, A. M., pastor of the church
> in Sheffield, who died
> Sept. 3d, A.D. 1784, AEtat. 36, et ministerii 13,
> calmly resigning his mortal life in hope of
> a blessed immortality thro' the atonement of Jesus Christ.
> He was blessed with natural genius improved by education,
> and a benevolent heart, and was illustrious as a Divine,
> a Preacher, a Friend and a Christian.
>
> *When Suns and Planets from their orbs be hurl'd*
> *And livid flames involve this smoking world;*
> *The Trump of God announce the Savior nigh*
> *And shining hosts of angels crowd the sky*
> *Then from this tomb thy dust shall they convey*
> *To happier regions of eternal day.*[*]

This is stirring stuff—can't you see the planets hurled out of their orbits and red flames consuming the Earth, hear the trumpet, and feel the jostling of the crowd of shining angels? The identical verse appears on the gravestone of Captain Elkanah Ashley (d. 1803) in East Poultney, Vermont. How did this rousing text made its way more than a hundred miles from the southern Berkshires to central Vermont? I suspect a genealogist could explain. There are many Ashley graves in Sheffield. Elkanah himself was born in Rochester Massachusetts but it is possible some family connection made note of the distinctive memorial in Sheffield, and passed it along to Elkanah in Vermont.

I cannot find a source for the verse—it may be original though it sounds more polished than one might expect and may someday turn up somewhere in book of poetry or hymnody. I hear a thought-provoking echo of these lines in the Reverend Dodd's *Reflections on Death*:

> Picture the awful scene to your view.... See that earth, once the seat of all your cares and fears, now wrapped in universal flame: hark the heavens are passing away with insufferable noise; the sun is extinguished; the stars have started from their spheres.... The trump, the awakening trump hath sounded.

This is standard imagery of the Apocalypse, I suppose; there is no reason to conclude that whoever composed the Keep epitaph had read Dodd. But both writers clearly shared a common vocabulary for depicting the Last Day.

---

[*] This is sadly an example of a stone that is barely legible to the passing reader today. Reverend Keep's gravestone is a magnificent slab laying flat on the ground, but time and weather and lichens have almost entirely obscured the carving. Without an early historian's transcription, this memorial text would be entirely lost.

Here is a simple but effective little verse that had a significant distribution from the rocky crest of the Berkshire Barrier down to the Connecticut River valley and all the way to eastern Connecticut, across a span of thirty years. The earliest instance I have found is in the Longmeadow Cemetery:

> In Memory of
> Mrs. Lois Daughter of
> Mr. DAVID &
> Mrs. SARAH BURT
> Who died
> June 26th 1776
> In Her 21 Year.
>
> *Her Early Death*
> *and shorten'd Date*
> *Bids Youth and Age prepare*
> *Her lifeless Clay*
> *describes our Fate*
> *And shows us how frail we are*

The same verse (adjusted for gender) was chosen over the next thirty years in Hadley, Pomfret, Connecticut, Blandford, and Feeding Hills Cemetery in Agawam, right across the river from Longmeadow. It is not a particularly moving or spiritually instructive verse—the bidding to prepare recalls The Classic, but without much urgency. Still, like all the verses in this category, someone did in fact compose it and someone else published it. I include it here as the record of an episode of creativity and commerce that occurred two hundred and fifty years ago but left no trace of writer or book, except these few carved words.

A gently moving monument in Lee Center Cemetery has a solemn verse that I cannot identify (Figure 53). At the top of the stone are carved three solemn faces above the words NASCENTES MORIMUR.* Then comes to main body of the stone and the inscription:

> Jerusha died [illegible]
> 1781 aged 7 Months.
> John died Oct. 9th aged
> 5 Months—William died

Figure 53. Foot children stone (author's collection).

---

* This a phrase from the *Astronomica* generally attributed to Marcus Manilius (ca. 1st Century CE) that can be translated as "As we are born we die" or "We are born but to die." I have no idea how familiar anyone in the Berkshires was with Manilius's abstruse five-book didactic poem on the Zodiac and other celestial phenomena, but evidently the phrase was published, distributed, and fell under the reading eye of the Foots, their minister, or the gravestone carver.

Oct 1ˢᵗ 1792 aged 5 weeks.
The above were the child
ren of Mr. Jonathan Foot
& Mrs. Deliverence Foot.

Those guiltless charmes, those
marks of genius are surprest,
Which nurst the fondest hopes
in tender parents breasts

The identical verse is used for three-year-old Fanny Cochrane up in the nearby hills of Blandford, also in 1792, and one-year-old Ozas Morell in Lenox in 1794. The dates coincide and the distance between towns is not great, so there was surely some connection between the three stones, although they appear to be work of two different carvers. There is something impressive about the images evoked and the vocabulary used (guiltless charms, marks of genius); whoever composed this quatrain had skill.

This short verse was chosen twice in Longmeadow Cemetery, first in 1787:

In memory of
Mrs. ABIGAIL, Wife of
Mr. EBENZER BLISS,
Who died Oct, 6, 1787.
In the 57 Year of
her Age.

Long I,ve believ,d Gods Power to save
Cheerfull when calld go to ye Grave
My mould,rig flesh shall be his Care
And he will raise me strong & fair.

Interestingly that the last digit of "1787" appears to be a repair of a typographic error by the carver—he got the date wrong on his first try. This is another little piece of evidence of the delay between the time of death and the date of the carving. Who knows how long after 1787 this inscription actually was carved? Then some fifteen years later:

In memory of
Mrs. REBEKAH relict of
Capt. Simon Colton
who died July 21.
1803;
in the 87. year
of her age.

Long I,ve believd Gods power to save.
Chearful when called, go to the grave.
My mould,ring flesh shall be his care,
And he will raise me strong & fair.

Note the repeated use of commas instead of apostrophes—the designs on the stones are not identical but I assume both are the work of the same carver, or two carvers sharing a single text.

My first reaction is that this must be from a Watts hymn, but I have not been able to find a match. The closest I can come is a prose "discourse" by Watts (*Discourse IX, Faith built on Knowledge*) that contains some of the same imagery:

[Jesus] is governor of the land of blessedness, and the fittest guardian to whom I can commit my departing spirit. I leave also my poor remains of flesh to his care: These limbs I leave to moulder into dust, under the wakeful eye of his providence; for he is Lord of this lower world too, and he will raise my flesh to immortality, and rejoin it to my soul at the great day.

Interestingly, the same verse appears in the September 16, 1893, edition of *The Outlook: A Family Paper*, in an article by one Margaret Sutton Briscoe entitled "A New England Graveyard." The author takes a typically sentimental walk through a scenic and atmospheric old graveyard, and records various epitaphs that strike her fancy. Thus:

> Wander in and out among these ancient stones, you find a few inscriptions which, escaping the Puritan sternness, narrow as the grave, rise above it to a certain grandeur of thought. Here, for instance, is one which reads as a rude litany, and rings with the triumph of a certain faith:
>
> *Long I've believed*
> *God's power to save*
> *Cheerful when called*
> *Go to the grave.*
> *My flesh in dust*
> *Shall be his care*
> *And he will raise*
> *Me strong and fair.*

It is pleasant to think of someone else sharing my enthusiasm, so many years ago. Margaret Sutton Briscoe was a prolific writer of short stories, serialized fiction and miscellaneous articles whose work often appeared in *Harper's*. Her husband Arthur Hopkins was a professor of Chemistry at Amherst, and her papers are in the Amherst Archives collection. Sutton Briscoe does not specify the graveyard she describes, and I cannot identify it, though I expect it must be somewhere in the Connecticut River valley and clearly it could be Longmeadow. At any rate, this demonstrates that the verse was known and distributed some distance up and down the river. Until I find an actual hymn, I will guess that this is the work of a local author who knew his or her Watts.

This verse in Lanesborough Center Cemetery is repeated just a few times, and roughly regionally, but enough to confirm it was published and circulated in some form:

THIS MONUMENT
BESPEAKS A TEAR IN
FULL REMEMBRANCE
OF THE AMIABLE
MRS. ABIGAIL
CONSORT OF CAPT.
NATH. B. TORRY
WHO DEPARTED
THIS LIFE JAN. 22
1789. IN THE 32.
YEAR OF HER AGE.

Sleep on dear Spouse, till Jesus comes.
Till Gabriel's trump shall burst the Tombs.

> *Then may we wake in sweet surprise*
> *Releas'd from sin in transport rise.*
> *Unite again, and soar on high.*
> *No more to part no more to die.*

I quite like the happy alliteration of "sweet surprise" borrowed, I suspect, from Watts. Monterey's Old Center Cemetery has two repetitions of one fine little quatrain:

> In Memory of
> Mrs. MARY BREWER
> Wife of Col. Josiah Brewer
> was born June 29, 1751
> and died Feby. 17, 1799.
>
> *No more for me let tears of sorrow flow,*
> *Nor partial memory swell the tide of woe.*
> *but while my state remeans to thee unknown,*
> *Consider reader what will be thy own.*

And then:

> This
> monument is erected to
> perpetuate the memory of
> Lieut Joseph Bird who
> departed this Life June
> 23, 1811 AEt. 78 years.
>
> *No more for me let tears of sorrow flow,*
> *Nor partial memory swell the tide of woe.*
> *but while my state remains to thee unknown,*
> *Consider reader what will bee thy own.*

The identical verse is used twice in a dozen years with no other occurrences in between. I expect it was a local author; maybe Lt. Bird or his family had admired Mary Brewer's verse and made a note of it.

Read this carefully, and you will see it is a fairly nuanced composition. In the first two lines, the consoling voice of the deceased tells us not to mourn. I hear an echo of Scripture in the first line; Revelation 21:4 reads "And God shall wipe away all tears from their eyes; and there shall be no more death, neither sorrow, nor crying." In the second line, "partial" does not mean "in part" but rather "partial to, biased in favor of"—don't let your fond and favorable memories of me make you sad. So far so good, it sounds like the verse is meant to comfort us. But then the tone sharpens and we're back in the Calvinist world of The Classic: Right now, while you are alive, you don't know if I am saved in Paradise or damned to hell. My state remains to thee unknown. So don't waste your time thinking about me—you need to consider your own fate. This message is guaranteed to make you *un*comfortable.

My research into patterns of epitaphs by carvers led me to this stone attributed to Elijah Sikes in South Hadley:

> In Memory of Mr.
> JOHN GAYLORD who
> died 20. August 1798.
> in the 85 year of his
> age.

> *Farewell vain World,*
> *from hence I'm hurl'd,*
> *Your vanities are fled,*
> *I quit them all*
> *With this mean ball*
> *For regions of the dead.*

The identical verse appears in Palmer (Deacon David Spear, died 1800). Sikes also worked in Palmer, so this may be an example of a "house stock" verse of his—I have found only these two occurrences. The imagery of the poem is engaging and effective, with the speaker being hurled away from the world (neither buried, nor rising joyously) and its fleeting vanities. There is something fine in the declaration that the speaker is quitting this mean ball; "mean" as in ungenerous, spiteful, squalid. Apparently John Gaylord, at the age of eighty-five, had had enough.

The phrase "liv'd belov'd & lamented died" is a singular though elusive example of a published and recurring epitaph. Here it is in Old Hadley Cemetery, on the grave of Sarah Dickinson, 1799 age 92 (!):

> *Meek & affectionate in early pious life*
> *And free from envy and oppos'd to strife*
> *Esteem'd for virtue, free from vulgar pride*
> *She liv'd belov'd & lamented died,*
> *But why should we repine, & thus distrust,*
> *Lament a friend who reigns among the just.*

This is a terrific eulogy in verse. The heroic couplets recall Pope, though the scansion is a little rougher than the master's. It distills all the desirable attributes that run through countless devotional works of the time: meekness and piety; the avoidance of envy, strife and pride; the wisdom not to mope or distrust God's mercy. It is truly a sermon carved in stone, presenting a sterling example of one who lives forever among the just.

A good friend found the words chosen thirteen years earlier, in slightly different form, in Merrimack, New Hampshire, on the grave of Hannah Thornton (d. 1786). And in 1804, in "The Muses' Department" column of *The Boston Weekly Magazine*, the complete poem is published (as a sonnet, no less) entitled "On the Death of Mr. Charles B. Rich":

> Yes, he has gone, the dire disease prevail'd,
> And all the efforts of Physicians fail'd;
> The Great Jehovah's dread behest obey'd,
> *Rich* "in his narrow cell forever laid."
>
> We murmur not, "whatever is, is right,"
> And still we mourn his so untimely flight:
> Look wistful on his grave, and deep deplore
> His early exist to return no more.
>
> **Meek and affectionate, and full of life,**
> **And free from envy and oppos'd to strife,**
> **Esteem'd for virtue, free from vulgar pride,**
> **He liv'd beloved, and lamented died.**
>
> **But why should we repine, and thus distrest,**
> **Lament a friend who reigns among the blest?**

Sickness and grief, here to his lot were giv'n,
But now no pains disturb his rest in heav'n;

With untold pleasures blest, he dwells on high,
And thanks his Maker, he was born to die.

Evidently the survivors of Sarah Dickinson and Hannah Thornton, and editors of *The Boston Weekly Magazine*, all had access to a published version of this anonymous poem. Whoever composed it was well-read in devotional literature and familiar with Pope (who wrote "whatever is, is right") and the Restoration Poets and their couplets.

Another small but intriguing example of recurrence appears in Chester Center Cemetery, where the same verse is chosen five years apart, both times clearly by the same carver. Here is one of them (Figure 54):

In Memory of M^{rs}. Electa, wife of M^r. Hezekiah Nooney. she died. 14. Oct. 1802. in the 23. year of her age.

Their Infant son was born & died. 8. Oct. 1802.

Death's flying sickle
Cuts the flowers of time;
And virtues fairest Friends,
in youth expire.

Figure 54. Electa Nooney stone (courtesy of Bob Drinkwater).

The same verse was chosen in Dedham ca. 1805 (in the last line, "bloom" replaces "youth"), so the verse must have been published and distributed across the Commonwealth, though again I cannot identify a source text or author.* The imagery of the first line is really quite startling—it is horrifying to imagine a deadly sickle flying all around us. It recalls the Edward Young passage:

Each moment has its sickle…
[Time's] little weapon in the narrow sphere
Of Sweet domestick comfort … cuts down
The fair blooms of sublunary Bliss

This is one of the stones that pull me up short in my collecting. Pause, reader, and reflect on young Electa Nooney slowly dying over six days following the birth and death of her son.

A simple but, in its own way, powerful composition was chosen in Old Hadley Cemetery:

---

* A correspondent also sent me a picture of a gravestone in Griswold, Connecticut, with the same verse (Esther Benjamin, died 1768 at age 24). So the verse existed thirty years before it was used in Chester and Dedham.

> In Memory of
> Mr. Warham Smith
> who died October
> 30th 1802 in the
> 68 year of his
> age.
>
> *Lifes narrow circle soon is run*
> *The voige is quickly o'er*
> *Death points to us the race is done*
> *Eternity the shore*

This sounds to me like a hymn, but I cannot trace it to a source. It is not a great work of poetry—the metaphors of the narrow race-track and the sea-voyage to the eternal shore overlap and confuse each other, and the scansion is choppy. But the image of Death pointing at us, to signal that our race is finished, is terrifying. I have found the same verse just up the Connecticut River in Northfield (John Stratton, died 1805), so it enjoyed at least a modest local distribution.

A short, stern verse in Lee Center Cemetery appears all over New England in the course of some twenty-five years:

> In memory of Remem-
> ber Parker daut to Mr
> Jorge Parker who died
> june 26 1803 in the
> 19 year of her age
>
> *God is just supreme his power*
> *Mortals be silent & adore*

I also found it one town over in Becket's Center Cemetery (Elias Jager, died 1804), where several stones are identified as having been carved in Lee—there was clearly extensive commercial intercourse between the two towns. Recall that in 1798, Abigail Adams encouraged her relation to be silent and adore, so she must have read a version of this couplet too. It has an Old Testament ring to it, something Moses might have shouted to his unruly tribe.

A gravestone scholar friend brought my attention to two gravestones sharing the same epitaph, first in Hawley's Doane Cemetery:

> Mrs.
> Rebecca Mantor
> Wife of Mr. James Mantor
> Died Sept. 28
> AE. 1807
> in the 28 year
> of her age.
>
> *This stone repeats in plaintive tone*
> *Rebecca's dead, God takes his own.*
> *Dear husband and child, and friends adieu,*
> *Prepare for God will call for you.*

And then fifteen years later nearby in Charlemont:

> Mrs.
> Harriet Hanks

wife of Mr. Levi Hanks
Died October 3
1822
AEt. 26 years

This stone repeats in plaintive tone
Harriet's dead, God takes his own.
Dear husband and child, and friends adieu,
Prepare for God will call for you.

This is a nice composition in the tradition of The Classic, somewhat softened from its earlier language but still full of warning. This is the only example I have seen of the author having the deceased comment on her own epitaph, before addressing her bereaved loved ones. It is a subtle but quite poignant effect. This is also the only instance I have seen the same verse recurring with only the deceased's name changed. And I have not seen it outside of these two remote hill towns, Charlemont and Hawley. I assume it was the work of a local writer, not without skill.

Here is a slightly different type of recurrence, starting in the Monterey Old Center Cemetery:

In Memory of
Doct. ELIJAH FOWLER
Died March 21, 1812
aged 48 Years.

Ripe for heaven His soul assending
Flew and early bid this sinful world adieu
Short was his stay the longer his rest
In the eternal mantions
of the blest.

Granted, this is not great poetry—the scansion is uneven, and "short was his stay, the longer his rest" is an awkward mouthful to recite out loud. But it has some fine turns of phrase. "Ripe for heaven" an excellent way to describe a good life and a well-prepared soul, and it is consoling to think a loved one's early death just means their time in paradise will be longer than ours.

I read the identical verse in James Jones's *Sepulchrorum Inscriptiones* of 1727, transcribed from the grave of Mrs. Elizabeth Worthy (no date):

Ripe for Heaven her soul ascending flew
And early bid this sinful world adieu
Short was her time the longer be her rest
In the eternal mansions of the blest.

This is the second time I have found evidence that Jones's "curious collection" might have circulated in New England and been used as a source for epitaphs. I can discover practically nothing about the life and career of James Jones. Another Jones, John Jones, perhaps a relation, published a collection of *Sacred Poems* (London, 1760) which concludes with "Epitaph on Master David Langton; an Acrostick" that borrows the phrase from Elizabeth Worthy:

D esign'd **for heav'n, his soul ascending flew,**
A nd early bid this sinful world adieu.
V ain were the efforts to prolong his stay,

> I mmortal glory beckon'd him away:
> D eath, like a pitying friend, remov'd his pain,
> L ull'd him to rest, till Christ returns again,
> A nd bids his slumb'ring dust awake, and rise
> No more to die, but live beyond the skies.
> G rieve not, ye parents, when your babes expire,
> 'T is God commands, his will be your desire.
> O stop your tears, let them a passage find
> No more for them who're gone, but those who stay behind.

There was also an oft-anthologized epitaph of Elizabeth Carleton, daughter of a courtier in the court of James II who died in 1709 at age twenty-five:

> Had heav'n commission'd death to hold his hand,
> And virtue could the force of fate withstand,
> This beauteous virgin had been longer liv'd,
> Nor we so soon of her rich worth depriv'd;
> Her charming youth, her meekness, wit and sense,
> Her charity, her truth, her innocence.
> **But ripe for God, her soul ascending flew,**
> **And early bid this sinful world adieu.**
> Reader, make haste her graces to attain,
> That thou in bliss may'st ever reign.

The same verse was used as early as 1751 in Rehoboth, Massachusetts, and as late as the mid-nineteenth century in England. What an interesting little glimpse into the web of eighteenth-century editors and anthologists borrowing and re-cycling texts to serve the market for contemplative devotional readers, in the days before meaningful copyright laws!

Here is a locally-recurring verse in Lee, with the same text occurring three times over fifteen years, first in 1813 and finally:

> In
> Memory of
> Miss ELIZA HALL,
> Dautr of Mr Collins &
> Mrs Rebecca Hall, who
> died March 8, 1825
> aged 21 years
>
> *Farewell my weeping Parents dear*
> *Farewell my friends & sisters near;*
> *I wish you all to live in love,*
> *And make your peace with God above.*

This is not a sophisticated poem, but it reads well and the sound of the deceased imploring his or her survivors to live in love and make peace with God is quite touching. Consider, by the way, the relationship between this message and The Classic. Both call upon the reader to prepare their souls for eternity. But in The Classic, the need is urgent because death is imminent and the risk terrible. Here, we are granted a bit more time, enough to live for a while longer. We should prepare ourselves not through doctrinal exercise, but through love and making peace. I have found this epitaph only in this one village; given its apparent lack of wider distribution, it would appear to be the work of a local poet—one whose sentiments were relevant to mourners in town over a dozen years.

The most famous of all these unsourced but recurring epitaphs is "Affliction sore long time I bore." The earliest instance I have found is in Northfield Center Cemetery, in the 1770s (Figure 55):

> Here lies Buried
> M[rs]. Anne wife of Lieu[t]
> Eldad Wright who
> Died aug[st] 18 1777
> Aged 33 years
>
> *Affliction sore long time i bore,*
> *Physicians skill was vain,*
> *Till god did send Death as a friend,*
> *To ease me of my pain*

There are so many repetitions in Northfield that I stopped collecting them. It appeared in Enfield, Connecticut, in 1758 and 1763, decades before it found its way up the river to Northfield. There are also least three slight variations across fifty years in Lanesborough. An on-line search of "affliction sore long time I bore" turns up

Figure 55. Anne Wright stone (courtesy of American Antiquarian Society).

epitaphs everywhere from Yorkshire England in the 1760s (after this appearance in Enfield) to Hong Kong 1872 and everywhere in between.

It is so commonplace that it became a recognized cliché in popular culture. *Lippincott's Monthly Magazine* (May 1869) tells a short joke: an old woman demands that a carver use this on her stone. He refuses because, he tells her, some other carver has the copyright and he can't afford to get sued! Mark Twain winks at it as an example of the profusion of sentimental "Post-Mortem Poetry" in Philadelphia, in *The Galaxy* (June 1870). It even appears in *David Copperfield*, in a reference that Charles Dickens must have expected his readers to recognize: "I look up at the monumental tablets on the wall, and try to think of Mr. Bodgers, late of this parish, and what the feelings of Mrs. Bodgers must have been, when affliction sore, long time Mr. Bodgers bore, and the physicians were in vain."

My favorite reference occurs in a comic music-hall song from 1865 about the early days of oil wildcatting called "*Oil on the Brain*":

> Poor Mrs Jones was taken ill,
> The doctors gave her up;
> They lost the confidence they had
> In lancet, leech and cup;
> **Afflictions sore long time she bore,**
> **Physicians were in vain:**
> And she, at last, expired of
> Oil on the brain.

Clearly this little verse was distributed on a massive scale. And while the sentiments it expresses became trite, it evidently expressed the feelings of generations of mourners across the globe.

Though epically commonplace, its original source has never been identified. Charles Box, in *Elegies and Epitaphs* (Gloucester, UK 1892) speaks for us all when he writes: "It seems almost a pity that the author of this epitaph is not remembered among English writers, seeing that the above effusion has had a run of two centuries, and has found a place in probably more than half the churchyards and cemeteries of the kingdom." Hear, hear.

Bespoke

As mentioned in Part I, this category consists of epitaphs that are unique to one individual's death and as far as I can judge the work of a single writer—usually (though not always) unknown. We can begin with a series of bespoke epitaphs whose creator *is* known, a poetic parson with a flair for creative writing named Bunker Gay. The story of my discovery of the Reverend Gay's works is, in its own way, a perfect example of how the world of graveyard studies can work. Early in my studies, I came across a series of epitaphs in Northfield Center Cemetery and adjacent towns in New Hampshire and Vermont that appeared to share several distinctive characteristics. My trail started in 1770:

> In memory of Capt Samuel Hunt
> Who died very suddenly of an apo
> Plictick fit Feb 28th AD 1770
> In the 67 year of his age
>
> *Trust not in uncertain riches*
> *But in the living God.*
> *My children friends spectators all who view*
> *This marble stone this motto learn tis true*
> *Health wealth and honors all are empty things*
> *They fly with quicker speed than eagles wings*
> *Death sudden Death the Bubble quickly bursts*
> *And sinks the Owner instantly in Dust*
> *The industrious frugal Hand its action cease*
> *The cautious watchful Eye is clos'd*
> *Here sleeps my Body never more to wake*
> *Till Christ shall come and it in Glory take*

Certainly this impressive composition rewards careful reading. It is literally a sermon on stone, taking as its text I Timothy 6:17 "Charge them that are rich in this world, that they be not high-minded, nor trust in uncertain riches, but in the living God, who giveth us richly all things to enjoy." This suggests the hand of a minister accustomed to preaching on a Scripture reading. For length alone the epitaph suggests a wealthy individual, one whose estate could afford a substantial amount of carving. It also expresses the classic irony of these carvings: the poem is written or "spoken" in the first person, though we know the deceased did not write it or even choose it, because he died suddenly, of an apoplectic fit.

As far as I could tell this was created by an unknown hand specifically for Captain Hunt. Who wrote it? And who was granted, or assumed, the authority to put this lesson into the mouth of the departed Captain? Before attempting an answer, I read another long epitaph in Northfield of about the same vintage. This memorializes Captain Hunt's widow:

> Madam Anna Hunt
> Relict of the late
> Capt Samuel Hunt
> Obt May 6 1794 Aetat 90
>
> *To rise again the Sun goes down*
> *And in the furrow the grain is sown*
> *Beauties that sleep throu' winters reign*
> *When spring returns revive again*
> *Shall then the Friend o'er whom we mourn*
> *Never to Life again return*
> *Great Source of Light Love and Joy*
> *Let no such tho't our hope destroy*
> *Our lively hope that sometime hence*
> *Thro' the Redeemer's Influence*
> *On whom she plac'd her hope and trust*
> *She'll burst this Tomb shake off her dust*
> *Assend to where God hold his throne*
> *And Immortality put on.*

Note a hint of Ecclesiastes in the opening line. Throughout the verse, I also heard an echo of the parable of the grain of wheat and its message of resurrection after death (John 12:24–26): "Verily, verily, I say unto you, except a grain of wheat fall into the ground and die, it abideth alone: but if it die, it bringeth forth much fruit."

Overall this feels structurally similar to Captain Samuel's epitaph: twelve lines, rhymed couplets, a Scriptural "reading" to open the verse, then a middle section that serves as a commentary or homily, and finally an assurance of the resurrection to come. And sure enough, I learned there is a single source for both epitaphs. The author's identity was revealed in the *Vermont Historical Gazetteer, Volume V, 1891*. First, in a chapter on Vernon, Vermont, there is an article by one Cyrus Washburn M.D., concerning the late Lieut. Governor Jonathan Hunt, the son of Samuel and Anna, and his widow Lovina Swan Hunt. Washburn writes: "Gov. Hunt and his lady, with ample pecuniary means, with social and cordial manners, animated and sweetened with pleasantry, were entertaining and delightful companions with their numerous friends and acquaintances, among whom I should name Rev. Bunker Gay...."

Washburn then quotes the identical "To rise again the Sun goes down" text as the epitaph of "Mrs. Abijail P., wife of Rev. Bunker Gay, who died July 15 1792. AE 52 years" in (I believe) Vernon, Vermont. Dr. Washburn goes on to quote several more epitaphs, written in a similar style, all by the hand of the Reverend Gay. Could the Reverend be the author of this scriptural epitaph, and could his friend Governor Hunt have admired the verse, and then selected it for his mother's tomb, two years later? And might the same poetically inclined Reverend have been called upon to pen the father's epitaph, twenty years earlier? Washburn includes a few other epitaphs that Gay wrote, and closes the article with the suggestive comment: "The Rev. Bunker Gay wrote some rather famous 'poetry!'"

And indeed, in the same *Gazetteer* there is a chapter on the Stratton-Whithed family: "The following epitaphs, copied from the Stratton tombstones [in Vernon,

Vermont], were written by the Reverend Bunker Gay, ordained in 1764. Their quaintness has often attracted much attention":

EPITAPH
of
ENSIGN SAMUEL STRATTON

Reader, deny it if you can,
Here lies interred an honest man,
By Pope denominated rightly
The noblest work of the Almighty.

To men of all denominations,
Acquaintances, neighbors, and relations,
The rich and those who stood in need,
He proved himself a friend indeed.

He kept the faith, he kept his heart,
And well performed the Christian's part.
Had much to do, and did his best,
Fulfilled his charge and's gone to rest.

The path he trode with care pursue,
and you'll be crowned with glory too.

EPITAPH
of
RUTH STRATTON
Wife of Ensign Samuel Stratton

To rise again the Sun goes down
And in the furrow the grain is sown
Beauties that sleep through winters reign
When spring returns revive again

Shall then the Friend we mourn
Never again to life return?
Great Source of life, light, love and joy
Let no such thoughts our hope destroy.

Our lively hope that sometime since,
Through the Redeemer's influence,
In whom she placed her hope and trust
She'll burst this Tomb, shake off her dust,
Ascend to where God holds his throne
And Immortality put on.

Eureka! I thought, feeling very proud of myself: the Rev. Bunker Gay (1735–1815) is the author. Note the reference to Alexander Pope at the outset of the Samuel Stratton epitaph and The Classic at its conclusion. Evidently the Reverend was fond of reading and composing memorial verse, and his work was sufficiently admired to be widely reproduced over time and distance by friends, relatives, and strangers. For example, we find the opening quatrain in Old Hadley Cemetery:

In Memory of
Mr. Windsor Smith,
who died
December 31st, AD, 1788, in the

69th Year of his
age.

To rise again the sun goes down
And in the furrows grain is sown
Beaten that sleep thru winters reign,
When spring returns revives again.

A few years later, someone in West Rupert, Vermont, over along the New York border, was familiar with the same verse, and chose it for Molley Brown's epitaph (d. 1803, age 40). And the same *Vermont Gazetteer* has one more sample of the Reverend Gay's work. "In [the Whithed burial ground in Vernon], on the tombstone of Roxana, daughter of John and Roxana P. Stratton, is the following tribute from Rev. Bunker Gay":

What though on earth her days were few,
She now begins her life anew,
Disjoined and sheltered here,
In the deep grave her mortal part
Secure from guilt, and grief, and smart,
Will rest from year to year,
Until that all important day
When death shall yield up all its prey,
And from this putrid tomb,
Divinely polished she will rise
A spotless nymph to grace the skies,
Clothed in immortal bloom.

Here the poetic Reverend is showing off his craftsmanship and his capacity for creative imagery. First, note the deliberately intricate rhyme scheme: AAB CCB. Then admire the vibrant imagery, unexpected in a frontier graveyard: the putrid tomb, the divine polish, the spotless nymph. I sense the Reverend's knowledge of the Classics melding with a more traditional message of Resurrection.*

Back in Northfield, I read a similar-sounding memorial for a locally famous minister, the Rev. Benjamin Doolittle. Doolittle appears prominently in the frontier history of Northfield; the historian Francis Parkman offers this anecdote in his *A Half-Century of Conflict* (1892):

---

* A biographical sketch of Reverend Gay can be found in Duane Hamilton Hurd's *History of Cheshire and Sullivan Counties, New Hampshire*. (Philadelphia: J. W. Lewis. 1886): "Rev. Bunker Gay, born in Dedham, Mass., was educated at Harvard college, and was ordained a clergyman in the Congregational church. He came to Hinsdale [NH] in 1763, and was the first settled pastor of the Congregational church in the town. His ... parish embraced the whole town and Vernon, which was then included in Hinsdale. When Vermont became a state, and Vernon a separate town, that territory was taken from his parish, and left his church weak in members and property. He continued the nominal pastor during his life, and officiated at funerals and weddings, and preached until his old age compelled him to stop... Here he continued to live till his death, in 1815, aged eighty years. He was the father of five children; all died young and unmarried except his daughter Abigail..." I will add that he was born in Dedham and died and is buried in the Hooker Cemetery in Hinsdale, NH, with only a very short epitaph:
   Be thou faithful unto death
   And I will give thee a crown of gold.
   I have fought a good fight
   I have finished my course.
The first two lines are from Revelation, the second pair are from 2 Timothy. Perhaps a minister less poetically inclined than Bunker Gay chose these, when the great man's pen was exhausted.

At Northfield dwelt the Reverend Benjamin Doolitte, minister, apothecary, physician, and surgeon of the village; for he had studied medicine no less than theology. His parishioners thought that his cure of bodies encroached on his cure of souls, and requested him to confine his attention to his spiritual charge; to which he replied that he could not afford it, his salary as minister being seventy-five pounds in irredeemable Massachusetts paper, while his medical and surgical practice brought him full four hundred a year. He offered to comply with the wishes of his flock if they would add that amount to his salary,—which they were not prepared to do, and the minister continued his heterogeneous labors as before.

The Reverend Doolittle's epitaph is sixteen lines, not twelve, and does not open with a scriptural text. But the tone, tenor, and couplets are all comparable to the Hunts' epitaphs, and the closing image of rising to his reward in Heaven is perfectly similar (if hardly unique):

> In Memory of the Rev Mr. Benjamin Doolittle
> First Pastor of the Church of Christ in Northfield
> Who died Jany ye 9
> 1784 in the 54th Year
> of his Age and 30th
> Year of his Ministry
>
> *Blessed with good intellectual parts*
> *Well skilled in two important arts*
> *Nobly he filled the double station*
> *Both of a preacher and physician*
> *To cure men's sicknesses and sins*
> *He took unwearied care and pains*
> *And strove to make his patient whole*
> *Through in body and in soul.*
> *He lov'd his God lov'd to do good*
> *To all his friends vast Kindness show'd*
> *Nor could his enemies exclaim*
> *And say he was not kind to them*
> *His labors met a sudden close*
> *Now he enjoys a sweet repose*
> *And when the just to life shall rise*
> *Among the first he'll mount the skies.*

It is pure speculation, but surely plausible, that this could again Gay's work—a clergyman's epitaph with a good pithy moral lesson at the close. I can easily imagine the Reverend Gay, with an established reputation for erudition and epitaph-writing, being called upon (or volunteering, unbidden) to contribute to the memorial of a local fellow-churchman.

We should pause here and recall that while the Reverend Doolittle was given a great long memorial, and appears in Parkman, each epitaph we read is for someone who also lived a life (short or long), had an occupation, was known in his or her community, woke up in the morning and went about their affairs and went to bed at night ... just as we do. Every gravestone I have studied memorializes an individual life, whose story is most likely lost forever.

Back to Bunker Gay and Northfield Center Cemetery. Perhaps we can stretch this string of surmise to include the wife of Timothy Dutton Esq., who himself is memorialized as one "Who forty years did serve/In the church of Christ our Lord/His people to preserve":

> In Memory of Mrs
> Martha late amiable
> consort of Timothy
> Dutton Esq who de
> parted this life in hope
> of a Glorious immortality
> ye March 29 1802 in
> the 65 year of her age.
>
> *When You this monument behold*
> *O think by it what here is told*
> *That life is short and soon you'll be*
> *In an untry'd eternity*
> *I once stood with you on life's stage*
> *Life's busy scene did us engage*
> *But now in land beneath your feet*
> *Prepare your solemn change to meet*
> *For God above has called me home*
> *My tongue in dust now speaks to none*
> *But while you read and here me view*
> *Learn that the grave was made for you.*

It seems to me that someone not just literate, but learned, composed this, even if the poetry is not great (note the spotty scansion). There is a synthesis of The Classic—"Prepare your solemn change to meet" and "while you read … learn the grave was grave for you"—with a perhaps an allusion or two to *Macbeth* (strutting and fretting upon the stage, and ending in dusty death). Some of the writer's turns of phrase are much more than mere sentimental or theological doggerel, e.g., "My tongue in dust now speaks to none," preparing to meet changes "in land beneath your feet," the idea of finding yourself in "an untry'd eternity."

Can I push my luck (and your patience) even further, to include a husband and wife in the same graveyard? Once again, the deceased are a minister and his widow:

> Rev John Hubbard A.M
> Second minister of this town
> Died Nov 28 1794
> in the 69 yr of his Age
> and 45 of his ministry
>
> *A man he was to all his people dear*
> *And passing rich with* eighty *pound a year*
> *Remote from towns he ran his godly race*
> *Nor ever changed or wished to change his place*
> *In duty faithful prompt at every call*
> *He watched and wept he pray'd and felt for all*
> *He tryd each art reproved each dull delay*
> *Allured to brighter worlds and led the way.*
>
> Madam Anna Hubbard
> Relict of the late
> Rev John Hubbard
> and dau of the late
> Cap S. Hunt

Died March 11 1795
in the 59 year of her age.

With a mild lustre all her virtues shone
And nought but vice and folly felt her frown
She wept with the distressed their sorrows bore
And glanced with generous kindness to the poor
Beside the bed of trembling and dismay
She hope inspired and smooth'd deaths rugged way
But her best virtues to her friends were known
And her last triumph endless glories crown.

I concede these may be a stretch—the verses are shorter, more sing-song in meter, and there is a decidedly secular feel to the narrative. No Bible verse opens the epitaph, and the promise of salvation seems tacked on at the end almost as an afterthought. I am not sure I like these two; something may be lost in translation from the eighteenth-century poesy but observe that the minister had *eighty* pound a year (the italics are the carver's), and yet all his wife can do is glance with kindness to the poor, and weep at their distress. Sounds a bit worldly, and not overly charitable.

On the other hand, once again the compositions are certainly bespoke—these were written by someone who knew the ministers of Northfield and their wives. So whether the Reverend Gay monopolized the role of lyrical minister, or had several contemporaries, here is a trove of exceptional bespoke funerary verse in what was still a wild and dangerous corner of frontier New England.

The codicil to all of the above is as follows: Feeling very satisfied with myself, and thinking I would have credit for the discovery of Bunker Gay all to myself, later in my studies I came across an unpublished undergraduate thesis that highlights the "somewhat eccentric" minister's "well-known" work (Jonathan Tute, died 1777, age 10: "Here lies cut down like unripe fruit / A Son of Mr. Amos Tute").[*] Then I read a charming collection of New England epitaphs containing six examples of his work (including Jonathan Tute, but none of the others I collected).[†] I am appropriately humbled, like an amateur astronomer who thinks he has found a new heavenly body and runs to the local planetarium to brag about it, only to be told: "Yes, yes, we know all about it. We call it Jupiter."

Moving reluctantly along from the Reverend Gay, let me now draw your attention to other examples of bespoke epitaphs, beginning with this early instance in the Edwards Cemetery in East Windsor, Connecticut:

In memory of Mr.
Ephraim Wolcott who died
Decm^r ye. 18th AD 1762 in
the 47th year of his
age

The honours of his mortal Birth
Lie buried here where Repletes [?] dwell
His Heav'n born Soul could smile at Death
And triumph'd when his Body fell

---

[*] Catherine C. Macdonald, *The Dust They Left Behind: Community and the Persistence of Mortuary and Funerary Practices in the Connecticut River Valley, 1650–1850.* (Amherst College, 2006).
[†] Mann and Greene, *Over Their Dead Bodies.*

There is some nice work in the last two lines, juxtaposing the soul being borne upwards to Heaven and the body falling down to Earth. The use of "replete" (if I am reading the stone correctly) in the second line is curious. In entomology a replete is a worker ant with an expandable crop in which honeydew and nectar are stored for the use of the colony. Could it be this verse refer to ants, instead of the usual worms, keeping the dead body company? I need to find a 1760s dictionary to see if it is even possible. If so, what an astonishing expression from this anonymous author!

You can read this rich and evocative work on fine and solemn stone in Becket (Figure 56):

In Memory of Mrs. Ruth
Watson, late Consort to Mr.
William Watson jun^r who
died May 21st 1774 in the
39th year of her age.

Hear I am imbraced in Deaths cold arms
Injoying the sweetness of the tomb
But I shall rise in that blest morn
When Christ comes forth with rich perfume.
When youth was blushing on my brow
And Gilleads balm was fresh
I heard a whisper from my God
A ray from Gesus breast
My time pas'd sweetly on
To the meridian day
When bursting throw the cherry beams
My Soul was born a way

Figure 56. Ruth Watson stone (author's collection).

Where to begin? This is a lot of text—it completely fills the gravestone (indeed, several lines did not fit within the frame). The spelling is highly erratic, too. But no matter, what a wondrous verse, evocative of Easter with the Resurrection, the tomb, scents and perfume. It reads like a personal narrative of early conversion (a whisper from God, a ray—of what? Light? Love?—from Jesus's breast), after which the years passed sweetly along. Then came the day when the body died but the Soul burst through cheery sunbeams, borne away into eternity. This really is a marvelous work to find in a small hill town in 1774.

A short verse in Blandford Cemetery combines a specific historical reference with an expressive message to the living:

In Memory of Miss Eleanor
Ker who died March 27 AD
1778 aged 27 years. Daughte^r
of M^{rs}. Katharine relict of M^r.
William KER who was slain
by the Indians at fort George
in a morning scout, August
1757 Aged 46.

There fell the parent by the savage band
Here I was snatched by deaths unerring hand
Now gentle reader see what death has done
And humbly wait your own your certain doom

The unerring hand is a fearsome image. We have read elsewhere that Death is implacable, here Death is also incapable of error—the scythe never misses its target. The last two lines evoke The Classic, with humility specified as a key element of preparation. Finally, the cadence of "your own, your certain" has an arresting impact on the reader.

As seen in Northfield, a bespoke epitaph is often associated with a prominent member of the community, like the minister or a military leader. Such a personage would merit a personalized testimonial of virtue and worth. Here is a fine example from the Woods Cemetery in Monterey (formerly part of Tyringham):

> Sacred to the Memory of
> Revd. ADONIJAH BIDWELL, AM
> who was born at Hartford, Octobr. 18th, 1716,
> received an education at *Yale* College,
> was ordained Pastor of The Church of
> Christ in *Tyringham*, Octobr. 3rd, 1750,
> in which character he lived greatly
> beloved for his Christian friendship, can
> dour, charity, industry, sound judg
> ment, and strict integrity until June 2nd, 1784,
> and then calmly expired, in full
> hopes of a happy immortality, thro
> ugh the merits of the Redeemer.
>
> *Go, Reader,*
> *Follow his example,*
> *And live the life of the Rightous;*
> *That your latter end may be like his:*
> *For blessed are the dead, who die in the LORD*

The entire composition has a noble ring of authority, command, and above all confidence that the Reverend Bidwell's full hopes were fully realized. Note the reference back to the verse from Revelation.

This wonderful stone in Williamstown's South Lawn Cemetery displays a particularly wide variety of fonts, spelling and punctuation (Figure 57):

> Here Lies buried the Body of Capt.
> Hamlin Dwight who died on
> December the 18th AD 1786
> Etas 44 here lies the body of Hamlin
> Dwight *the Soul being seperated has*
> *took its flight to yonder Worlds unknown its*
> *waft its way beyond the Brilliant rays its out*
> *of sight no more to turn the Body to unite*
> *untill the Resurrection Day*

Figure 57. Hamlin Dwight stone (author's collection).

The imagery is startling, original, almost trippy, with the separated soul wafting its way out of sight beyond the sun. The uneven rhymes, scansion, and line breaks all suggest this was a local composition.

This epitaph from New Marlborough Old Center Cemetery was composed in the same year, but note the smoother, more polished poetry:

> Sacred to the memory of
> Jabez Ward Esqr.
> who died Aug. 17th 1786
> in the 52nd year of hi[s] age.
>
> *No lifeless Stone can tell the worth*
> *No tongue can set true merit forth*
> *Ye widow orphens and ye friends*
> *Weep for your selves weep not for him*
> *For when death comes the soul must fly*
> *Tis but the clay alone can die.*

Reading closely (perhaps, to be fair, more closely than the verse merits), I hear the timbre of Alexander Pope's heroic couplets. The first line contains a clear reference to Habakkuk 2:

> 18. What profiteth the graven image that the maker thereof hath graven it; the molten image, and a teacher of lies, that the maker of his work trusteth therein, to make dumb idols?
> 19. Woe unto him that saith to the wood, Awake; to the dumb stone, Arise, it shall teach! Behold, it is laid over with gold and silver, and there is no breath at all in the midst of it
> 20. But the LORD is in his holy temple: let all the earth keep silence before him.

The middle lines appear to have been influenced by Luke 23:27–28, when Jesus is being marched to Calvary: "And there followed him a great company of people, and of women, which also bewailed and lamented him. But Jesus turning unto them said, Daughters of Jerusalem, weep not for me, but weep for yourselves, and for your children."

The final couplet is the least resonant, comprising a fairly standard Graveyard sentiment. But taken as a whole, I call this a substantial and learned composition for its time and place.

Here is an odd and apparently original verse in Sturbridge Old Burial Ground:

> In Memory of
> JOHN Son of
> Capt. SAMUEL &
> M^{rs}. KEZIAH HANANT
> who departed this life
> Sepr 21: 1787
>
> *The body may, the power*
> *of mind Controul:*
> *Releas'd I thee below,*
> *on high best suits the soul*

Isn't this a complicated, knotty little piece of metaphysics? It invites slow consideration, out of proportion to its length. I am intrigued by the notion that the power of mind can control the body, not religion—though I suppose it is implicit that religion is what animates the power the mind. Still, there is a degree of ambiguity and allusive language that is uncommon on these stones.

In Stockbridge Cemetery I read this interesting composition; the anonymous poet's evident literary ambition produced mixed results at best:

> In Memory of
> Mrs. ABIGAIL BOUGHTON
> wife of
> Mr. HEZEKIAH BOUGHTON
> died August AD 1789
> Aged 58 Years
>
> *Here friends would weep a deluge o'er thy Urn*
> *And all the living world would pray for your return*
> *But Earth's maternal bosom no Compassion knows*
> *She's bury'd you in dust and us in woes*
> *Yet thy angelic nature to thy heirs is food*
> *Those never will be lost who died in doing good.*

There is a lot to unpack here. The poem aspires to the music of Pope's heroic couplets, but the scansion is sadly off. Some of the language is pedestrian—especially the opening two lines and the last line. But there are also some quite moving sentiments, well expressed: "Earth's material bosom no compassion knows" is a line worth remembering, "[Earth has] buried you in dust and us in woes" is nicely done, and the image of Abigail Boughton's angelic nature as a source of sustenance to her heirs is powerful.*

This notable eulogy in verse, well-composed but somewhat indifferently carved, is in Great Barrington's River Street Cemetery, a fine site that retains its gray dignity despite being wedged between the back side of a residential neighborhood, a pizza parlor, and a heavily-trafficked state road with a bike and snowboard shop across the way:

> S Sacred
> To the memory of
> Cpt AARON SHELDON
> Who Died April ᵗʰᵉ 22d 1792
> In the 30th year of his age.
> Much esteemed by his acquaintance.
>
> *Virtuous his actions and his tongue discreet*
> *His manners civil and his temper sweet*
> *To youthful providence had joind*
> *A frank and charitable mind.*
> *And tho hard fate's untimely dart*
> *Hath low hath perd his He*
> *Hath Laid him low hath pierc'd his heart*
> *Hath mingled SHELDON's dust with dust*
> *His spirit dwells among the just.*

Town histories inform us that an Aaron Sheldon ran a tavern on Main Street. I cannot be sure if this is the same person, but the dates appear to fit. Certainly Captain Sheldon was a citizen worthy of praise and had the good fortune to have a surviving

---

  * Incidentally, there is a blank space on the stone between "August" and "1789." Somehow the carver did not get around to inscribing the date. I have not observed this phenomenon on other stones.

admirer who could compose so eloquent an encomium. I am not sure he was as fortunate in the choice of carver; there are several irregularities. Note the stray "S" at the top, and evidence he completely messed up the sixth line and had to start over. One hopes the Sheldon estate was not charged for the wasted carving.

This lovely, well-composed tribute, very much in the tradition of devotional memorials, is in Old Belchertown Cemetery:

> In Memory of Mr.
> Joshua Dickinson of Hat-
> field who died at Belchet
> March 2d. AD. 1793. aged 84.
>
> *The word of God was his delight,*
> *A rule to form his Actions right:*
> *With this his Life did well agree.*
> *From Guile his Heart and Lips were free.*
> *He God did fear, Evil eschew,*
> *To man was kind, and just and true*
>
> E. Sikes Sculptr[*]

This has the tone and meter of something written for the tomb of the great and good, but I have not found it elsewhere, so for now I place it among the bespoke epitaphs. If truly original to Belchertown, then I commend the anonymous poet's ability to stitch together a range of quotations and allusions. The fourth line (and, roughly, the third) is from the third stanza of Watts's Psalm 32 *Blest is the man, for ever bless'd*:

> Blest is the man, for ever bless'd,
> Whose guilt is pardon'd by his God,
> Whose sins with sorrow are confess'd,
> And cover'd with his Saviour's blood.
>
> …
>
> **From guile his heart and lips are free**,
> His humble joy, his holy fear,
> **With deep repentance well agree**,
> And join to prove his faith sincere.

The fifth line refers to Job, a perfect and upright man who feared God and eschewed Evil. And the last line might refer to Philippians 4:8: "Finally, brethren, whatsoever things are true, whatsoever things are honest, whatsoever things are just, whatsoever things are pure, whatsoever things are lovely, whatsoever things are of good report; if there be any virtue, and if there be any praise, think on these things."

In Blandford Cemetery, this poignant memorial to a little girl bears strong evidence of a father's hand:

> In Memory of
> Sarah Daughter of
> the Rev[d] Joseph &
> M[rs] Lois Badger.
> She died Oct 27
> 1795 Aged 3 years
> 7 months.

---

[*] Here again we encounter the self-promoting Elijah Sikes.

> *The little Child was dear to me*
> *But just & right was that decree*
> *Which brought her to Eternity*

I have not found the lines elsewhere, and the phrase "dear to me" certainly indicates the voice of the bereaved father, the Reverend Badger. I see no reason not to attribute the verse to him. Think, then, what it took him to compose the next two lines. "Just and right" was a common legal term for an equitable decision; its use is significant in this context, asserting the fairness of God's decree that little Sarah must die. The choice of this epitaph—indeed the act of composing it—is surely an expression of her grieving parents' deep and committed faith.

This charming verse, combining original and borrowed material, is in the Sturbridge Old Burial Ground:

> Sacred to the memory
> of Mr. Henry Babbit, Son of Doctor
> Erasmus Babbit & Mary his wife;
> who died March 23 1795;
> AEtatis 23
>
> *Sweet in thy sleep, ages may roll away,*
> *Yet thou in placid silence shall remain,*
> *Till the almighty on the final day,*
> *Shall call thee home, to join the heavenly train;*
> *Then while the fates prolong our fleeting breath,*
> *Henry, thy bright example let us see,*
> *That we may learn to meet the stroke of Death,*
> *And share Eternal happiness with thee.*

The first four lines have a nice hymnodic meter. There is a poetic resonance to the opening image of ages rolling away while the young man sleeps sweetly, placidly. The last four lines are lightly edited from a poem that first appears in the London Magazine in February 1770. It is entirely anonymous, appearing with a handful of other poems under the heading of "Poetical Essays." The identical text appears in *The County Magazine for April 1786* (Volume 1 p. 60). There it is printed as follows:

To the Editor of the COUNTY MAGAZINE.

Sir,

By inserting the underwritten Elegy in your next Magazine, you will oblige a correspondent and constant reader,

H. W.
Salisbury, March 16, 1786.

ELEGY
To the Memory of Miss T. P------

In vain this tear, lamented maid, is shed,
In vain this breast may sorrow for thy doom;
The pang of woe can never reach the dead,
Nor pierce the sad recesses of the tomb.

Yet, sacred shade, the tributary sigh,
Which friendship pays, in tenderness receive;
'Tis the hard lot of excellence to die,
And must be nature's privilege to grieve.

> But here reflections easily may find
> The short duration of the human state;
> Since all the noblest virtues of the mind,
> Can ne'er exempt us from the stroke of fate.
>
> Time's rapid course mysterious appears,
> A new expansion of our days to lend,
> Yet ev'ry moment added to our years,
> Is sent to draw existence to an end.
>
> **Then, while the fates prolong my fleeting breath,**
> **Blest maid, thy bright example let me see,**
> **That I may learn to meet the stroke of fate,**
> **And share eternal happiness with thee.**

Apparently Doctor Babbit or some friend of the family read an anonymous poem anthologized in British magazines (and perhaps elsewhere, as yet untraced), made note of it, and had some skill as a writer when the time came to adapt it for their own use.

I read this short quatrain in the Church on the Hill Cemetery in Lenox. Much of the stone is sunk beneath the ground.* Little Caleb Walker's gravestone introduced me into a family of memorials—brothers, parents, aunts and uncles—and a series of original compositions:

> CALEB, Son of
> Esqr WILLIAM &
> MRS MARY WALKER
> died Dec^{br} 31^t 1796
> Aged 27 Hours
>
> *Death in quick successions*
> *Our dwelling place invades*
> *Blasts our fond hopes*
> *And plants deep anguish.*

It is a sad little epitaph; town records make clear the story is sadder still. William Walker and his first wife, Sarah, lost a son Richard in 1784, at the age of four. Richard's epitaph is a variant of The Classic: "Young friends behold me where i ly / and learn from hence you're born to die."† Two offspring of William and Sarah did survive childhood and led long lives (William lived to see eighty and Sarah lived to sixty-three). Sarah died in 1789 and is buried beneath an impressive grey stone:

> Sacred to the Memory
> of Mrs. Sarah Walker
> wife of William Walker Esqr
> who suddenly departed this life
> on the first day of Sept.
> Anno Domini 1789
> In the 40th year of her age.
>
> *The sacred Duties are perform'd*
> *The Soul with holy passions warm'd*

---

* I am indebted to Paul Pelky for his 1999 update of transcriptions gathered by Mabel Annie Parsons and Mira Katherine Parsons entitled *Lenox Church on the Hill Burial Grounds*. Pelky was foreman of the Lenox Cemetery Division of the Department of Public Works—another preserver of inscriptions that would otherwise be lost.

† The identical epitaph was also chosen a few towns over in Becket (Deborah Messenger, died 1783)

> *With eager haste ascends the Sky*
> *Where kindred Spirits stoop to meet*
> *The spotless Soul, and kindly greet*
> *And welcome it to joys on high*

I would not call the poetry fine: the phrases all have a familiar ring; there is nothing terribly original in its ideas; and the meter is a bit uneven. Yet it does conjure up a compelling picture of the passionately warmed soul hastening up into the sky where it encounters gentle, stooping, kindred spirits. They are much calmer and relaxed than the eager and hasty new arrival, at least in my mind's eye.

William remarried in 1790, but he and Mary had no surviving children. They lost two infant daughters, Mary in 1792 and Alice in 1795 (neither baby girl has an epitaph), then Caleb in 1796, followed by another son George in 1801, aged three weeks and one day. George's epitaph is quite touching, given his parents' harsh lessons in infant mortality:

> *Adieu, sweet babe,*
> *thy lovely form*
> *impress'd on our fond hearts,*
> *shall there remain,*
> *adored be the god of grace,*
> *whose covenant is sure;*
> *extending to our infant race,*
> *and ever will endure.*

So you see Caleb's epitaph truly tells a story; the phrase "quick successions" appears to speak for several of his little siblings. What a weight of sorrow and resignation William Walker carried to his grave in 1831 (at age 80) and Mary to hers in 1838 (aged 78).

William Walker's gravestone does not contain any epitaph verse, but he did merit a fine eulogistic inscription presumably composed by respectful townspeople on a substantial if somewhat squat obelisk memorial:

> Born at Rehoboth in the county of Bristol, He removed to this town in 1773, was an officer in the army of the revolution of 1776, a member of the convention which formed the constitution of this state in 1780, a judge of the court of common pleas, four and judge of probate twenty eight years. In all the relations of life, he sustained a character of unshaken integrity. He lived as a follower of Christ, was an able advocate of his doctrines, and died, rejoicing in a gospel hope.

Mary's gravestone has nothing but a simple inscription of her name, dates, and "Wife of the Hon. William Walker."

Let us stay among the extended Walker family just a little longer; nearby a husband and wife share an impressive monument. A double-headed stone would be more common for a couple, but in this case the stone is tall and slender, with a single tympanum, names and dates in two symmetrical side-by-side columns, then a shared epitaph:

> In Memory of
> HULDAH wife of
> Capt. CALEB
> WALKER

who died in March
1788 in the 33^d
Year of her Age

In Memory of
Capt. CALEB
WALKER
who died in
Canandarqua
in the State of
New York Aug. 10
1790 in the 38th
Year of his Age

Though scattered wide the kindred dust
Shall rise to life when Jesus comes
And triumph o'er the sable rust
Contracted in the lonely tombs
Then wing their flight to relms above
United in eternal love.

This is worth reading carefully, both as poetry and as a narrative that sheds light on the choice of epitaph and the selection of the gravestone itself. Apparently after Huldah died in 1788, her husband Caleb did not immediately commission a stone for her. Perhaps there was a temporary marker of some kind. Caleb was in the prime of his life, after all, just thirty-six years old. Then two years later, unexpectedly, while on a visit to upstate New York (business? family matters? seeking a second wife?) Caleb dies and it buried somewhere out there. His dust and Huldah's, though kindred, are scattered wide. They are collecting black rust in lonely tombs (note the plural).

I can do no more than speculate here, but is it not possible that William Walker, Esq., was Caleb's brother (and thus uncle Caleb the namesake of unfortunate little Caleb)? He could quite conceivably have commissioned a single stone to commemorate his late brother and sister-in-law, and perhaps also the verse, which appears to be bespoke. And, piling speculation upon speculation, if you read this epitaph and Sarah Walker's together, they have a strong similarity of diction and rhythm—it is conceivable that the same hand composed them both, William's or someone he knew. In contrast, the two children's stones, for George and little Caleb, are much less flowing, with choppy meter and irregular rhyming. They both might be the work of another poet. These stones are all trying to tell us a story, even if it is too faint now to hear clearly.

Here is a composition from Monterey's Chestnut Hill Cemetery that rewards our attention:

In Memory of
Mr. JAMES SMITH
who died June 21 1797
Aged 28 Years 3 months
& 7 days

Paws here a while ye spritely youth
Who may be passing by
Think well upon this awful truth
That you are born to die

> *A virtuous lover son and friend*
> *Though in his youthful bloom*
> *Is struck by Death's cold haggard hand*
> *And hastens to the tomb.*

The first quatrain is nothing special, a nice poetic variant of The Classic. The "awful truth" that we are born but to die is a recurring one in these graveyards, as we saw with Marcus Manilius. Note that in this context we can use the now-archaic definition of "awful" as "awe-inspiring," as opposed to "dreadful." Then the second quatrain suddenly captures our attention—the description of "virtuous lover" (not husband) seems full of unspoken drama and heartbreak, and the "cold haggard hand" is a powerful image conveyed with solemn alliteration. An admirable piece of work, out on a remote and tiny hill.

Two other epitaphs echo the same thought. In Longmeadow Cemetery, the epitaph of Thomas Bliss (1758) quotes a Watts hymn:

> In Memory of
> M^r.
> THOMAS BLISS
> who died
> Augst 12. 1758
> In His 85th
> Year
>
> *Our Life is Ever*
> *on the Wing*
> *And Death is Ever Nigh*
> *The Moment When Our Lives Begin*
> *We all Begin to Die.*

It is an interesting sentiment to ascribe to a wizened eighty-five-year-old—if he began to die when he was born, he took his time about it. Another example is in Blandford Cemetery, on a double-headed stone:

> In memory of
> William Wells
> Ferguson who
> died August 28
> 1802 aged 15 Mo
> & 5 days
>
> In memory of
> Alvah Ferguson
> Who died Sep^t.
> 9 1802 aged 3
> Years 8 Mo. &
> 11 days.
>
> These were the Children to Mr.
> William & Mrs. Sarah Ferguson
>
> *How soon our Sun drops down the western skie*
> *Soon as our souls began to live our bodies are doomed to die.*

The sun dropping down in the west is surely appropriate for a graveyard in this hilltop town. The choice of language and resulting tone is poignant: these children did not just *begin* to die at birth, they were *doomed* to die. Consider, too, the aching sorrow implicit in the statement "These were the children of…"—not "two of the children" or even "children," which might imply surviving siblings. That brutal definite article implies that this was their entire family. What dreadful contagion killed these two brothers in just two weeks? The winter that followed must have been unbearable for William and Sarah Ferguson.

Let us turn now to a long, original composition in Palmer Center Cemetery that borrows from various epitaphic traditions to create a very loving tribute (Figure 58):

> *Life is Short*
> In Memory of Miss LUCINDA
> daughter of Lt. DAVID & MRS.
> MOLLY KING she died 12 June AD
> 1798. in the 19 year of her age.
>
> *If worth departed claims one heartfelt tear*
> *O stop and let it flow profusely here.*
> *where humbly lies what once had every art*
> *To soothe to chear to captivate the heart.*
> *Lucinda the young the gentle and the gay*
> *When call'd by Jesus must no longer stay.*
> *Heaven lent her to us but for 18 years*
> *The call'd her home and left her friends in tears.*

Lucinda's name could have been inserted into a source poem, but I can't find these lines anywhere, so it is likely bespoke. Whoever wrote it borrowed from a few different sources or traditions: the phrase "worth departed" appears in several other funeral poems; the "if [good qualities of the deceased] … then [shed a tear, or death would have been averted]" formulation is quite common in these epitaphs. So too is the conceit of the dead as only having been loaned to us for a period of time. I like the cadence of three attributes in lines 4 and 5 (soothe / cheer / captivate and young / gentle / gay). It may not be poetry for the ages, but some loving and creative survivor put time and talent into this.

Figure 58. Lucinda King stone (courtesy of American Antiquarian Society).

Parenthetically, the same "attribute" lines reappear from just a few years later up in Northfield:

> Mr William
> Swan Lyman de
> Ceased Feb 26 1801 in the 26
> Year of his age
>
> *The young the gay*
> *The noble and the brave*
> *Must quit this Life*
> *To moulder in the grave*

Very similar sentiments, when you read these two together.

The "if/then" device was used again in this quite moving epitaph in Sharon, Connecticut:

> In memory of Mrs. BULA MOULTON
> the amiable consort of
> Capt. Wm. Moulton,
> who having endeared herself to
> her friends and acquaintances
> by an exemplary and virtuous life,
> died a few days after the birth
> of her only child,
> July 5th, 1783
>
> *Could modest worth elude ye grasp of death,*
> *This virtuous fair had ne'er resign'd her breath.*
> *Could beauty's grace, or virtue's sacred charm;*
> *Could nuptial bliss the cruel foe disarm;*
> *Could ye deep anguish of an husband's love,*
> *Or infant cries, the fatal sting remove;*
> *She ne'er had wing'd ye long, ye glorious flight*
> *To seats of bliss, to realms of sparkling light.*

The first four lines also appear on a gorgeously-carved stone in Bennington, Vermont (Sarah Hubbel, died 1797). What a compelling, conflicted composition this is. It begins with a doomed plea that modesty, virtue, beauty, nuptial bliss, a husband's love, or a baby's cries might fend off the grasp of the cruel foe, the fatal sting. But then it resolves into a comforting vision of the deceased wife winging her way to a glorious, blissful, sparkling paradise. This composition is typical of formal eighteenth-century epitaphs, where restrained grief is elegantly redeemed by faith in religion; I have to believe I'll find it someday in an anthology of odes and eulogies.

In Sheffield's Barnard Cemetery, an earlier monument inverts the "if/then" formula and asserts directly that the presence of these virtues was not enough to prevent death:

> SACRED
> to the Memory of
> Mrs. Elisabeth Sedgwick
> Wife of Theodore
> Sedgwick Esq:
> she died 12 April
> 1771 AEtat. 26
>
> *Neither religion, virtue, beauty, youth;*
> *The most unblemish'd Heart, distinguish'd truth*
> *Could from the rigor of relentless death*
> *Purchase one moment of expiring breath*

It sounds like a quotation from an elegantly-crafted Ode or Elegy, but I have not been able to identify an author. The source may be lost in piles of forgotten eighteenth-century verse, or this may be the work of a local poet with a good ear for the genre. I find the last two lines quite powerful: Anyone who has ever sat by a loved one's death-bed can appreciate the value of purchasing one moment of expiring breath.

Here is another apparently original verse from Southbridge that manages to combine several evocative images into just a few lines:

> In memory of Mr.
> Jeremiah Shumway
> who died Octr 24th 1801
> in ye 40th year of his age
>
> *Alas how short is life*
> *how subtle human breath,*
> *Every health hangs quivering*
> *o'er the verge of death.*
> *Wee mount the stage life's*
> [illegible] *explore*

The gravestone is dominated by masonic symbols (which I have seen occasionally on these stones, but not often). It contains several distinctive touches: the use of "subtle" to describe our mortal breath, the use of "health" instead of "life" as the opposite of death, and the idea of mounting a stage to participate in life. The image of well-being hanging quivering over the brink of death certainly recalls Jonathan Edwards. All in all a busy and carefully crafted fragment.

I encountered this rare example of an identified author in Old Hadley Cemetery. The compiler of a collection of epitaphs explicitly states: "[Lines written by President Dwight, in whose family the deceased (18-year-old girl) had been an inmate.]" This must be the Rev. Timothy Dwight, whom we have already encountered. Note here the archaic use of the word "inmate." I assume that means she was in the employ of the Dwights—unless it is a misspelling of "intimate."

> This Stone is erected to the
> Memory of Miss MARY KELLOGG,
> Only daughter of Doct. Giles C. Kellogg,
> Who died Nov. 11, 1802,
> In the 18th year of her age.
>
> *Stay, thoughtful mourner, hither led*
> *To weep, and mingle with the dead;*
> *Pity the maid, who slumbers here,*
> *And pay the tributary tear.—*
> *Thy feet must wander far to find*
> *A fairer form, a lovelier mind;*
> *An eye that beams a sweeter smile:*
> *A bosom more enstrang'd from guile,*
> *A heart with kinder passions warm'd,*
> *A life with fewer stains deform'd;*
> *A death with deeper sighs confess'd*
> *A memory more belov'd and bless'd.*

I cannot help noticing the irony of using the present tense when listing the qualities of the deceased young woman. Mary Kellogg is dead; her eye no longer beams, her heart is no longer warm, the mind is dark and the bosom decayed. One could argue that coming from a Yale scholar and minister, this is not a particularly great elegy. It strikes an almost cloying sentimental note (the tributary tear, the deep sighs). No doubt it sounded differently to its contemporary readers, and who am I to criticize? The poem's sincerity and affection offset any shortcomings as literature.

Lee Center Cemetery contains a gravestone with an astonishing original composition that merits a careful reading:

>Mrs. Nancy Fessenden
>departed this life June 23, 1813
>aged 34½ years; The Wife of
>Cornelius T. Fessenden
>
>*She's gone nor angels could prevent her flight*
>*Her lovely soul has winged its way to regions of eternal light*
>*There gentle spirit may you find,*
>*That happiness denied you here,*
>*There peace and harmony are joined,*
>*Nor can detraction enter there.*
>*There no aspersing tongue can send,*
>*It's venom to thy feeling heart,*
>*Jesus is thy immortal friend,*
>*Nor will he e're depart*
>---o---
>*But where, O where, shall her poor husband find*
>*One beam of light to cheer his drooping mind*
>*All sad he wanders round the earth & skyes,*
>*But no soft solace meets his falling eyes.*

This is an unusually long epitaph; it would have been an expensive commission. The first section does not occur anywhere else that I can find, which suggests it is the work of a local poet. It contains from fine elements: The meter of the first few lines is a little rough, but the imagery is both lofty and affectionate (with maybe a touch of Milton?); and the concluding lines provide a succinct yet comforting affirmation of Christian faith.

The final quatrain, much smoother and more gracefully written, is a reworked passage from Reverend Dwight's *The Conquest of Canäan*:

> **And where, O where shall poor Selima find**
> **One beam of light to cheer her drooping mind?**
> **All sad, I wander round the earth, and skies;**
> **But no soft solace meets my failing eyes.**
> To friends I fly: those weeping friends I see
> Sunk in the deep despair, that buries me.
> For him, O kindest, tenderest mother! rise
> Thy heart-felt anguish, and they hopeless sighs.
> Thy tears, all-gentle fire! resistless shed,
> Approve my grief, and weep the hero dead.

Apparently whoever composed this epitaph had read his Timothy Dwight. An educated man then, maybe from Yale, perhaps a clergyman himself.

Now read the middle section again. What is happening here? The epitaph suddenly becomes a highly personal, almost anguished, message to a woman who suffered unhappiness in the village of Lee, her peace and harmony denied by aspersion and detraction of venomous tongues.

Put the two passages together we see an original work, written by an educated, well-read, and religious person who knew and cared deeply for Nancy Fessenden—maybe the widowed husband. I would like to learn more about Cornelius and his decision to carve this damning message for his neighbors to read in perpetuity.

I am intrigued by the allusions in this charming composition from Old Center Cemetery in Monterey:

>Sacred
>to the memory of
>Mr. JOHN BREWER
>Son of Col. Josiah Brewer
>who died March 24th 1816
>aged 30 Years.
>
>*Heaven gave the blow in* [illegible] *called him home*
>*from pain and woe to its recompence.*
>*Adieu dear saint may thy example prove*
>*Lessons of good to those thou here didst love.*

Candidly, I do not know what to make of the first line, not least because it is partly illegible. The second line is a Scriptural reference to the Gospels of Luke and Matthew, both of whom quote Jesus's teaching that the reward or recompense for the just will be great in Heaven. So clearly the writer holds John Brewer's virtue in the highest regard. The third line is especially suggestive. This may be a stretch, but I hear two echoes from Shakespeare's Romeo and Juliet II:2, the famous balcony scene, wherein first Romeo assures Juliet:

>My name, **dear saint**, is hateful to myself,
>Because it is an enemy to thee

And Juliet then says to Romeo:

>This bud of love, by summer's ripening breath,
>**May prove** a beauteous flower when next we meet.

It is the merest speculation, but isn't it nice to imagine that someone loved both Shakespeare and John Brewer, and used the language of one in addressing the other? There is certainly a discernible shift in the writer's voice from the first two lines which use the third person (called *him* home) to address us all, or the passing reader; to the more intimate use of second person (*thy* example, *thou* didst love). Now the writer is talking directly to the deceased. The last line is wonderful valediction that brings together in perpetuity John Brewer and the edifying example he set, the bereaved loved ones he left behind, and us, the readers who come and experience this memorial years later.

One fine autumn day, shuffling through dry fallen leaves between the irregular rows of old stones in Monterey's Chestnut Hill Cemetery, I read this splendid verse:

>IN memory of Mr.
>THEODORE ADAMS
>Who Died Dec 7th. 1826
>Aet 29 years
>
>*There needs no art or spicy dust*
>*To embalm the memory of the Just*
>*True piety more odour yields*
>*Than all the sweet Arabian fields.*

This is a gob-smacking, exotic, Orientalist composition. Who could have imagined and composed such a message? "Spicy dust" for embalming may refer to myrrh and Christ's tomb, but whence these fantastic images of incense and Arabian fields? I don't suppose I'll ever know. What was his or her literary frame of reference? Let's just say we have wandered wondrous far from Jonathan Edwards and The Classic, into the world of the *Arabian Nights*.

Here is a lovely bit of verse from Hancock, from a later, more lyric and sentimental era than where we began. Note how the meter spills over from one line to the next. It sounds like a hymn, but I have not found it elsewhere (though the phrase "weep not for me" is common in hymnody. It elegantly evokes John 23, which we earlier encountered in Scripture: "Weep not for me, but for yourselves and for your children.")

> In
> Memory of
> SIBYL A. CRANSTON
> who departed this
> Life June 14th 1832
> in the 22 second year
> of her age.
>
> *Oh weep not for me I am safely conveyed,*
> *To these hills of immortal delight,*
> *I rest from the dangers and toils of the way*
> *That lead to these mansions of light.*
> *O why should we weep since the spirit that's fled*
> *From the earth has gone up to its rest,*
> *Since the pains and* [illegible]

I can only speculate here, imagining linkages between disparate threads of devotional literature, but indulge me for a moment. The great work of Thomas Stackhouse (1677–1752), an English theologian, was his *New History of the Holy Bible from the Beginning of the World to the Establishment of Christianity* (1733). In it, discussing Christ's temptation in the desert, he quotes *Barnes on the Gospel*: "Scripture is silent as to the precise manner in which the tempter **conveyed** our Saviour to the top of the temple" and a few lines later, cites a Mr. Maundrell's journey from Jerusalem to Jordan: "From the tops of **these hills of desolation**, we had … a delightful prospect of the mountains of Arabia, the Dead Sea, and the plains of Jericho." Perhaps, somewhere in the shadow of the Taconics, an anonymous minister, steeped in Scripture and Stackhouse and countless other Bible commentaries, along with (who knows?) a collection of elegies and epitaphs of the good and great, put together this lyric pastiche.

Or, alternatively, this text was written in London or Boston or New York, by a now completely unknown and forgotten poet, and an enterprising publisher put it in an anthology or almanac where one day it was read by an approving minister or carver or inspired farmer, whereby we can read it today, in a tiny abandoned family cemetery, all overgrown with trees. Whatever the case, here is a lesson for us all regarding the level of literacy and eloquence that was available to mourners in these rural hill towns.

Here is another apparently bespoke verse from the 1830s that is worth a careful reading. It is from the Monterey Old Center Cemetery:

> IN memory of
> Col. JOSIAH BREWER
> Born August 28th 1744
> Died June 12th 1830 AEt. 86.

*Reader trust not the
treacherous marble but let
your deeds like his who lies
beneath bespeak your praise*

This has the tone of a finely-crafted epitaph from a century earlier in England, but I have not found it any such anthology. I am intrigued by the way the composer inverts the usual formula of "Reader! Pay attention to this inscribed message!" and instead instructs us to distrust the very words we are reading. "Treacherous marble"—what a terrific conceit: even the most solemn words on the most impressive monuments are just words, and they might be false. Far better, we are told, to concentrate your attention on Colonel Brewer's deeds. Finally, note how the writer contrasts those deeds, which we might be inclined to mistakenly think of as transient or ephemeral, with the material but unreliable marble and body lying beneath. There is a good bit of philosophy compacted into these four lines.

Let me share the engrossing story of an epitaph that started out as a bespoke verse composed at the point of death. It subsequently appeared throughout western New England, including on the memorial of a gravestone carver. Two friends, a couple who take beautiful photographs of gravestones, shared this from the Old Bloomfield, Connecticut, Cemetery (Figure 59):

In Memory of
HEZEKIAH GOODWIN
A.M. & Preacher of y^e
Gospel. Son to M^r. Stephen & M^{rs}. Sarah Good
win: who departed this Life
Jany. 19th A.D. 1767; in y^e 27th
Year of his Age. His Epitaph
compos^d by himself; upon his
Death bed is as follows

*How short, how precarious, how
uncertain is life! How quick y^e
Transition from life to Eternity!
A Breath, a Gaspe, a Groan & lo
We're seen no more! And yet on
this point, Oh alarming Thought!
On this slender point
swings a vast eternity.*[*]

Figure 59. Hezekiah Goodwin stone (courtesy of Betsy and Al McKee).

---

[*] Researching the potential sources of these epitaphs constantly yields delightful parenthetical nuggets. In this instance I came across this un-signed item in the *Overland Monthly and Out West Magazine* (July 1885):

It was my fortune to spend a portion of the summer of 1884 in a quiet little New England village, away from the whirl and bustle of busy life... [O]ne day I strolled into the grave-yard... I copied some epitaphs, among which [was] ... the epitaph of a clergyman who died at the age of twenty-seven, which was, as is certified on the same stone, composed by himself on his death-bed, reads as follows: 'How short, how precarious, how uncertain is life! How quick the transition from time to eternity. A breath, a gasp, a groan, and lo, we're seen no more. And yet on this point, oh alarming thought, on this slender point swings a vast eternity.'

This is an absolutely compelling composition. Consider the setting: a young minister confronting his own imminent death, compelled to apply to himself the doctrines he has been trained to teach his flock. He has already learned them, and bitterly—next to the Reverend's grave stands a single stone with four tympana or "heads," one for each of his four young children who died before him. Now he recognizes that he himself is living (and dying) evidence of the conventional message we have heard over and over, that life is short and eternity is long. He is clearly incorporating ideas from Edwards and Hopkins, who emphasized how thin a thread keeps us from dropping into the pit at any minute. Yet he transforms them into an arresting image of eternity itself swinging on the Transition's slender point. The use of "point" is ambiguous and suggestive, combining the notion of a point in time and point as a locus or crux. Recall a similar image from another bespoke epitaph: "On Time depends / Eternal things." I also find the cadence of "a breath, a gasp, a groan and lo" very rhythmic and effective. This is an inspired and skillful piece of work.

Someone noticed the Reverend Goodwin's work and admired it enough to reproduce it, with slight variations, in the Colchester, Connecticut, Burying Ground just a few years later:

> In Memory of Mr.
> ELIPHALET GILLET
> who departed this life
> May ye 2nd AD 1790
> in ye 57th Year of his Age
>
> *how soon the thread of*
> *life is spun a breath a*
> *gasp a groan or two*
> *and we are seen no more*
> *yet on this brittle thread*
> [illegible]

Note that someone has added a new image, the thread of life, borrowed from the classical story of the Fates.

I will end this section with the gravestone of Jonathan Burt, a known stone carver, in the Longmeadow Cemetery. This epitaph that combines both prior versions into one (Figure 60):

> In Memory of
> Adj^t. JONATHAN BURT
> who departed
> this Life in a sudden
> and surprising manner,
> April 18 1794:
> in his 50th year.
>
> *How short, how precarious, how*
> *uncertain is life! How quick the*
> *Transition from life to Eternity!*
> *How soon the thread of life is spun:*
> *A breath a Gasp a Groan or two*
> *and we are seen no more.*
> *Yet on this brittle thread of life*
> *hangs a vast eternity.*

As is so often the case, I do not know who chose Jonathan Burt's epitaph, but I can easily imagine he encountered it in Connecticut in the course of his professional work. I do not know the details of his "sudden and surprising" death, and the local Historical Society's guide to the graveyard professes ignorance, too.* But this provides a segue into a section on epitaphs that memorialize just such departures from life.

Figure 60. Jonathan Burt stone (courtesy of Betsy and Al McKee).

---

* An AGS correspondent from Longmeadow pursued the question further, and concludes that Burt died while traveling between Longmeadow and East Longmeadow, most likely of cardiac arrest or a stroke. She reports that according to Genealogybank, Burt:
> was found dead—In the road, in Longmeadow, on Saturday morning last. He was a well man the preceding evening—and said to have been a worthy citizen—a tender husband, and an indulgent, instructive parent. He corpse was brought to the meeting-house in Longmeadow, on Sunday afternoon last, where a judicious and well adapted discourse was delivered by a Rev. Mr. Howard, of this town, from these words "Man that is born of Woman, is of few days, and full of trouble"— after which his remains were decently interred.

Sudden Death

As mentioned in Part I, this category consists of bespoke epitaphs that describe an individual's sudden and unexpected demise. Here is a striking example in Agawam's Old North Burial Ground, spare and blunt, delivering the familiar lesson under dramatic circumstances:

> Here is Buried ye Body of Lamberton
> the Son of Dr. Lamberton Cooper
> Who was taken out of the World by Lightining
> July 8 1747 in the 17th Year of his age
>
> *With awful Terror and*
> *Surprize, Death comes*

That, gentle reader, is all there is to say. Comfort have I none.

Lightning struck again in Sheffield twenty years later, as noted in the Bow Wow Cemetery (Figure 61):

> In memory of
> Mr. SIMON WILLARD
> He was instantly kill^d. Oct. 19.1766.
> In ye 60 year of his age
> He was born in Concord Aug.7.1706.
> and removed to Sheffield 1720.
>
> *Stop here ye Gay*
> *& ponder what ye doath*
> *Blue Lightnings Flew &*
> *swiftly seized my Breath*
> *A more tremendous*
> *Flash will fill the skies*
> *When I and all that*
> *Sleep in death shall rise.*

Some anonymous writer was inspired by poor Simon's fate and created a compelling composition that combines the enduring message of The Classic with dramatic touches like the blue lightning, the last gasp for breath, and the more tremendous flash to come on Judgment Day.

Figure 61. Simon Willard stone (author's collection).

An astonishing memorial in Townsend Connecticut's God's Acre cemetery not only provides a poetic description of sudden death, but also incorporates a very clear religious lesson for the survivors (Figure 62):

Figure 62. Levi Caschet stone (courtesy of Betsy and Al McKee).

> In Memory of
> M[r]. Levi Cashet
> who Departed this life
> Dec[r] the 29th 1784;
> Aged 38 Years & 1 Day
>
> *Surprizing stroke: Who Could Expect*
> *That hour the moral Wound*
> *Yet Did the Lord the Tree Direct*
> *to Crush him to the Ground.*
> *Watch Y[e] that live for Y[e] Don't Know*
> *How near Y[e] are to Death*
> *Or What may Give the Fatal Blow*
> *To stop your fleeting breath*
> *Death is in all the Paths we tread*
> *Mocks Ev'ry art we try*
> *Outstrips our Unavailing Speed*
> *Or meets us as we fly.*

Surely this is the work of a local minister. It is clearly bespoke to the occasion of Levi Cashet's death, and it is equally clearly designed to instruct his survivors—and all future readers—in the old Classic lesson to prepare for death at any hour. The final quatrain in particular is a very effective composition, showing us Death blocking our path, mocking us, catching us from behind, or waiting in front of us, all with great clarity of image and economy of language.

Powder mills were terribly dangerous places to work, as can be seen in Lee—three times:

> In
> memory of
> Mr. EDMUND HINCKLEY,
> who died Sept. 20 1824,
> aged 25 years
> In consequence of the
> explosion of a
> Powder Mill
>
> *How quick and sudden was his flight,*
> *To yonder world unknown!*
> [illegible] *blaze,*
> *How small the spark that caus'd the* [illegible]
> *That sent him to his tomb.*

> In memory of
> JESSE SPARKS

who was
instantly killed in
a Powder-Mill, Sep 18,
1824, aged 19 Years

In memory of
HORACE H. LEWIS,
who was blown up in
a Powder-Mill Dec 14
1825 and died the 27,
in the 29 year of his age.

Farewell my friends and Children dear
Prepare for death while I sleep here.

Two fatal explosions in two years.[*] I cannot imagine Horace Lewis's suffering as he lingered for thirteen days. Nor what his children made of his admonition from beyond the grave (or, rather, the admonition that was chosen for him), to prepare for their own deaths. This was a recurring Congregationalist theme as we have seen many times, but doesn't it sound a bit out of place at this later date, and under these dire circumstances?

Hunting has always posed the risk of accidents; here is a tragic example from Becket, memorialized on a plain stone (Figure 63):

In memory of
Micah Higley,
who was shot, & died
Instantly, Decr 19*th*
1778. *in the* 35*th* year
of his age.

Deaths arrows are often
unexpected and unseen

Figure 63. Micah Higley stone (author's collection).

---

[*] I wonder if perhaps Horace Lewis's gravestone (or the transcription of it) contains an error, and he too died in the 1824 explosion. A history of the Berkshires contains this harrowing account:

In September, 1824, a scene of most appalling desolation was exhibited in this town. It was the explosion of an extensive powder factory, owned by Messrs. Laflin, Loomis & Co. At the time, it was estimated that there were about 5 tons of power in the different buildings. On a very pleasant morning when the workmen thought all things were going on securely, in a moment every building was razed from its foundation with a tremendous explosion. Three of the unfortunate workmen were instantly killed, and a fourth, who was thrown into the river, lingered for a short time till death, like a friend, relieved him from his pains. Every house and building in the neighborhood was more or less injured, and every breast was shocked. Such was the consternation produced in the minds of the inhabitants, that they universally protested against the rebuilding, and, the feelings of the proprietors coinciding, the site and water privilege were soon after sold, and an extensive paper-mill erected.

That paper mill stands to this day, though it is now being developed for new uses.

The Findagrave.com entry for this stone contains a dramatic account of the accident, which I presume is from a family genealogy or local town history (no citation is provided):

> Married Olive Adams January 5 1774. Micah purchased a home in Becket, Mass. His sister Sarah, who had married James Rudd less than two months previously, also removed with her husband to Becket, the two families living [as] neighbors. The married life of Micah and Olive Higley was cut short in a little less than five years by a distressing accident. On the morning of December 19 1778, a light snow having fallen in the night, Micah and his brother-in-law, Mr. Rudd, went to the woods to shoot deer, neither of them knowing that the other was out. Micah wore a deer-skin cap. Mr Rudd, while stealthily watching about, caught glimpse of a moving object behind a fallen tree top, and supposing it to be a deer, took aim and discharged his gun. To his horror on approaching his game, as he thought, he discovered that he had shot and killed his brother-in-law, Micah Higley. The fatal accident caused a great shock to the neighbors and friends, and plunged Mr. Rudd into bitter emotions, but regrets were fruitless. The interment took place in the old Becket burial-ground.... His widow, Olive (Adams) Higley, was left with two young sons, Micah Jr. and Benjamin.

The epitaph sounds like a minister's cautionary choice, tacitly implying that preparation is essential. The sentiment and imagery would be familiar from countless sermons, including those of Jonathan Edwards ("The arrows of death fly unseen at noon-day; the sharpest sight cannot discern them") and John Logan ("death comes unexpected; the arrow is still unseen that strikes through the heart"). As epitaphs go, this one offers little in the way of comfort to Olive and her two children.

A stone in Springfield Cemetery tells a compelling, dramatic story in simple verse:

> In Memory of 2 sons of
> Mr. ELLIS RUSSELL,
> Who were both drowned together May 23 1783,
> Vis. Mr. STEPHEN RUSSELL, in ye 31 year of his age,
> and ARCHELAUS, in ye 13 of his age.
>
> *Reader beware, and venture not too far,*
> *To save one drowning, lest my fate you share.*
> *The second I ventured in to save,*
> *A brother drowning, brought me to my grave.*

The first-person voice is a simple artifice, reminiscent of The Classic "as you are now, so once was I" formulation. In reality this is the grieving father warning us: "Don't put a second life at risk. Losing one of my boys would have been bad enough; losing both is devastating."

A stone in Hadley's Hockanum Cemetery merits several observations (Figure 64):

> In Memory of SETH
> Son of
> Mr. ELIJAH LEE Junr.
> and Mrs. SALLEY LEE
> who was Drowned
> April 16: 1792
> aged 15 Months & 12 Days

*If ardent prayers,
If flowing sorrows shed,
In all the bitterness of faith could plead
Our prayers bless'd babe
Would have revers'd thy doom*

First, consider the circumstances: what terrible accident led to the drowning of a fifteen-month-old toddler? A tragedy in a bath? A boating disaster on the Connecticut River? Second, note that the epitaph employs the touching "if/then" formulation we have already encountered: "If prayer, or love, or virtue, or godliness, or whatever worthy attribute were enough to avoid death, you would still be alive … but in fact they aren't enough." Almost the very same lines appear in an 1833 edition of the Rev. P. Doddridge's *Paraphrase of the New Testament*, in a memorial poem for the late divine:

> If ardent pray'rs, if flowing sorrows shed
> In all the bitterness of soul, could plead,
> Our pray'rs, bless'd DODDRIDGE, had revers'd thy doom,
> And tears of thousands wept thee from the tomb.

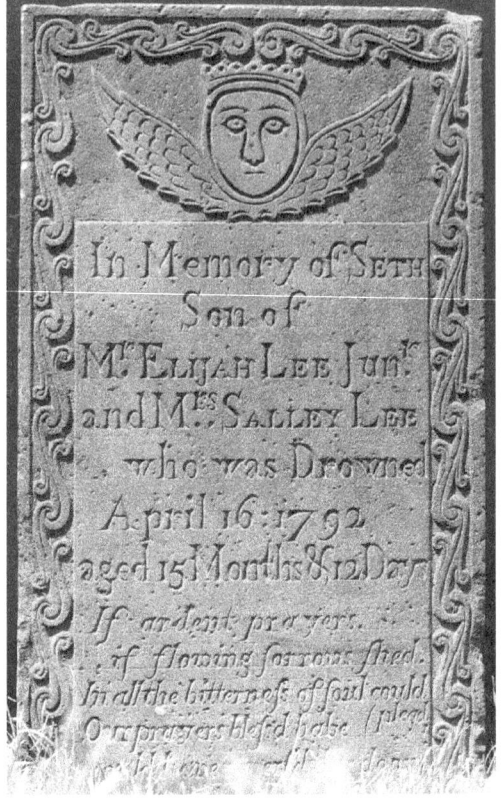

Figure 64. Seth Lee stone (courtesy of American Antiquarian Society).

Doddridge's *Paraphrase* was intended to be more "family-friendly" and readable text than the language of the King James Bible. I expect both the panegyric to Doddridge's memory, and little Seth Lee's epitaph, share a common source that will turn up someday in a collection of old English memorials. And the as-yet-undiscovered author of *that* verse may have recalled consciously or unconsciously that in *King Lear*, Kent pleads with Lear to "reverse thy doom / And in thy best consideration check / This hideous rashness."[*]

Here are three more examples, all from Lanesborough in the early 1800s. First, another death while wood-cutting, this time a mere boy, just a month after Isaiah Leach:

> Daniel C. Norton,
> son of Gideon and Lucy,
> died Feb. 24, 1816,

---

[*] Incidentally, *Murray's English Reader* has a verse written by Doddridge that would serve well as an epitaph; I am somewhat surprised I have not seen it used:
> Seize, mortals! seize the transient hour;
> Improve each moment as it flies:
> Life's a short summer—man a flow'r;
> He dies—Alas! how soon he dies!

> *by having his body crushed*
> *beneath a slead loaded with wood*
> *and expired in two hours,*
> *age 12 years and 5 months*

I fear the following may have been the disastrous consequence of a lethal eleventh birthday gift:

> Stephen, son of
> Mr. Jason and Mrs. Abigail Newton
> *Was killed by the accidental explosion of a rifle*
> *Sep. 6, 1836. Age 11 years and 9 days*

The next one appears to be a case of an Independence Day celebration gone tragically awry:

> Samuel Brenton,
> son of Rev. Samuel B. and Caroline F. Shaw,
> was suddenly killed at early dawn July 4, 1842
> by the explosion of a small cannon.
> Age 15 years and 18 days.
>
> *This monument is the voluntary and honorable testimonial*
> *of numerous friends to the memory of one whom all loved*
> *and whose virtues and talents and acquirements*
> *were sure indications of future usefulness and eminence.*

Perhaps it was written by the bereaved father, the Rev. Samuel Shaw. Certainly the list of attributes and the tone of the composition indicate a well-educated, articulate, and devout author.

Two stones in Westfield's Old Burying Ground tell sad stories of sudden death in everyday circumstances. First, a man out riding in his sleigh of a snowy January evening:

> ZENAS ATKINS,
> Was suddenly killed while riding in a sleigh,
> And coming in contact with another turning a corner,
> On the evening of Jan'y 14th, 1816, aged 34

And then a boy walking to school:

> James N.
> Eldest Son of Ira and Lucy Yeomans,
> who was instantly killed when on his way to
> School, by the slide of a bank of earth,
> Nov. 20, 1840, AE 7 1–2 years

You can understand why these people so often focused on the brevity and uncertainty of life in their choices of epitaph. Lee's Center Cemetery has several similar examples, as gruesome in detail as they are commonplace in circumstance:

> ELIEL:
> Last member of the
> Family of Mr.
> NATHAN & MRS. LUCY
> TOBEY,

> *died of a wound*
> *Rec'd by a rakes-tail*
> *on sliding from*
> *a hay-mow*
>
> Decm 29
> 1809 AE 16 years
>
> CORNELIUS B.
> son of
> Horace & Experience
> Lewis
>
> *who was instantly killed*
> *in consequence of*
> *the falling of a Cart*
> *Body that was set up*
> *against an Appletree*
>
> Dec. 6, 1826;
> AE. 5 Y's. 1 Mo.
>
> JAMES H.
> son of
> Moses & Hannah
> Culver
>
> *who was drowned in*
> *consequence of falling*
> *into the floom of a*
> *Saw-mill*
>
> April, 6, 1831
> AE 6 Y's

And finally this:

> EMMA JOSEPHINE
> daugh[t] of
> M. & D.A. PETERS
> DIED
>
> *In consequence of being*
> *burnt, by her clothes taking*
> *fire.*
>
> Oct. 16, 1850
> AE. 6 Y's. 2½ M's.

Presumably while helping her mother prepare dinner at an open hearth. Note the repeated use of the phrase "in consequence of"—perhaps there was a single writer for each of these. A legalistic one, at that. One friend commented dryly that these verses read like a coroner's report.

Finally, almost every graveyard contains grim accounts of infants dying at birth or very young, and often the mother dying with them. Here are a few notable examples; you have already read several others, and I could provide dozens more. We start in Longmeadow (Figure 65):

> In Memory of
> M[RS]. NAOMI;

wife of M^R
RITCHARD
WOOLWORTH
who died aug^st.,
22^d, 1760, aged 30
Years; also IOSEPH
their son died the same Day
aged 6 days.

Darkness & Death
Make hast at once
[illegible]

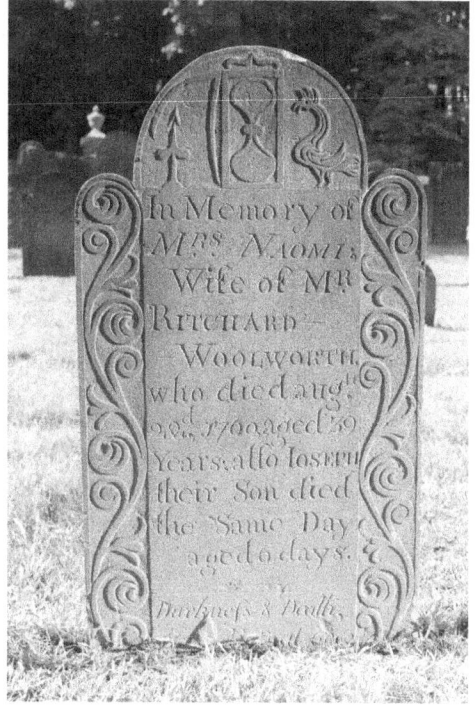

Figure 65. Naomi Woolworth stone (courtesy of Betsy and Al McKee).

The iconography is arresting: On the left of the tympanum, an old-fashioned single-arm clock points to midnight. In the center, an hourglass is fully run down. On the right is a crowing rooster, perhaps a herald of resurrection. Then as short and dreadful an epitaph as I have come across, an anguished cry, permanently carved in stone, from the grieving husband and father whose wife and new-born son died together after six days of suffering. It is tersely declarative, yet powerfully suggestive, evoking the Gospel tradition of the sky darkening when Christ dies on the cross. If religion brought Richard Woolworth solace for his losses, I do not read it here.

In contrast, consider this equally short but quite different message in Old Hadley Cemetery a generation later, on the stone of Benjamin Colt Porter (1793, 1 year):

Sleep in Innocence

Grief is still expressed, but in a gentle and affectionate tone, not a tortured cry. This strikes me as a loving parent's personal theological statement, taking a clear position opposed to any proposition that a one-year-old might be depraved by nature and doomed to die in a state of sin.

From Dedham's Old Village Cemetery, I read a remarkably powerful memorial to a woman and her twin girls who all died within three weeks of birth. I hear the voice of the minister in the didactic (though sympathetic) explication to the reader of this sad lesson:

Here lies interr'd the Body
of Mrs SALLY POND, Consort
of Capt. ELIPHALET POND who
Departed this Life Janry 1st
1774. Aged 31 years.
Likewise two of there children. Viz
ABIGAIL aged 20 & Sally Aged 21 Days.

Under this stone confin'd doth lie
Three subjects of Death's Tyranny.

> *The mother who in this close tomb*
> *Sleeps with the offspring of her womb.*
> *Whereby we see Death's cruelty*
> *In cutting off both fruit and tree.*
> *Yet all his malice will prove vain.*
> *For tree and fruit shall spring again.*

An earlier version can be found in Barnstable:

> HERE LYS INTERRED YE BODY OF MRS
> ANNA RUSSELL CONSORT TO MR. JOSEPH
> RUSSELL WHO DEPARTED THIS LIFE FEBRY
> YE 5 1729 30 IN YE 23D YEAR OF HER AGE
> AND IN HER ARM THEIR SON LEONARD
> DIED YE SAME DAY AETATIS 17 DAYES
>
> *Beneath this Marble Stone doth Lye*
> *Two Subjects of Death's Tyranny*
> *The Mother who in this Close Tomb*
> *Sleeps with the Issue of her Womb*
> *Here Death deals Cruely you see*
> *Who with the Fruit cuts down the Tree*
> *Yet is his Malice all in vain*
> *For Tree and Fruit shall Spring again.*

The later version reads a little more smoothly; the scansion and syntax are a bit more polished. But the message remains unchanged; in both, Death is a cruel tyrant but his malice is ultimately in vain. Whoever chose these epitaphs had a deep and unequivocal faith that still rings clearly in our ears today. The source text must be English, ca. seventeenth century. A 1794 anthology of monuments and epitaphs "chiefly in the eastern part of Kent" has the last quatrain from 1682:

> Here lieth the body of Joanna, the wife of John Hunt, of this towne
> Who died in childbirth of a daughter buried with her on the 18th of
> April, 1682, in the 24th year of her age, and left issue one son.
>
> *In this death's cruelty you see,*
> *Who with the fruit shakes down the tree.*
> *Yet is his malice all in vain.*
> *For tree and fruit shall spring again.*

A verse in Harvard Center Cemetery contains a memorable turn of phrase—the baby becomes the mother's death, and mother the baby's tomb (Figure 66):

> In memory of M^{rs}. Nancy
> Worster, wife of M^r. Samuel
> Worster, who Died in
> Child-birth. Septr ye 21
> 1776 Aged 24 years
> 8 months & 21 Days
>
> *though she was fair, while she had breath*
> *and on her Cheeks the Rose did Bloom*
> *yet her Dear Babe became her Death*
> *while she became the Infant's Tomb.*

What a lovely, sorrowful, and sophisticated composition. This is an elegant metaphysical conceit, the work of a thoughtful, gifted yet entirely unknown writer.

To conclude, consider this later epitaph in Lanesborough Center Cemetery:

Jeremiah Bull, Esq.
died Dec. 22 1815. Age 77 years,
and his wife, died Sept. 16 [illegible]
Age 71 years,
and a daughter stillborn, 31st of July 1769,
and a stillborn son, Oct. 22, 1770,
and a son born and died, Aug. 19, 1771,
and a son stillborn, June 8, 1774.

They died for Adam sin'd
They live for Jesus died.

Figure 66. Nancy Worster stone (courtesy of American Antiquarian Society).

These two short lines, in a little graveyard in the heart of the Berkshire hills, eloquently capture the grief that Mr. and Mrs. Bull experienced at the loss of four infant children in five years, but also the devotion and faith that sustained them for decades until their own time came.

Bibliography

Epitaph Collections and Transcriptions

Rev. Timothy Alden, *A Collection of American Epitaphs and Inscriptions* (New York, 1814).
Ethel Stanwood Bolton and Eva Johnston Coe, *American Samplers* (Boston, MA: The Massachusetts Society of the Colonial Dames of America, 1921).
Thomas Bridgman, *Inscriptions on the Grave Stones in the Grave Yards of Northampton and of Other Towns in the Valley of the Connecticut* (Northampton, MA: Hopkins, Bridgman & Co., 1850).
Mrs. Josiah Carpenter, *Gravestone Inscriptions Gathered by the Old Burial Grounds Committee of the National Society of the Colonial Dames of America in the State of New Hampshire* (Cambridge, 1913).
Ephraim Eliot, *Commonplace Books, ca. 1783-ca. 1825* (Unpublished MS in Boston Athenaeum).
Nathaniel Frobisher, *New Select Collection of Epitaphs* (London, 1795).
Josephine C. Frost, *Cemetery Inscriptions from Lanesboro, Massachusetts* (Unpublished MS of typewritten transcriptions, 1910).
Diana Hume George and Malcolm A. Nelson, *Epitaph and Icon: A Field Guide to the Old Burying Grounds of Cape Cod, Martha's Vineyard, and Nantucket* (Orleans, MA: Parnassus Imprints, 1983).
Cynthia Tryon Hoogs, *Cemetery Inscriptions, Monterey, Massachusetts* (Monterey MA, 2013).
James Jones, *Sepulchrorum Inscriptiones* (Westminster UK: Ciuer, Campbell, and Creake, 1727).
Catherine C. Macdonald, *The Dust They Left Behind: Community and the Persistence of Mortuary and Funerary Practices in the Connecticut River Valley, 1650–1850*. (Amherst College, unpublished undergraduate honors thesis, 2006).
Thomas Mann and Janet Greene, *Over Their Dead Bodies* (Brattleboro, VT: Stephen Greene Press, 1962).
Alfred Noon, *Ludlow: A Century and a Centennial* (Springfield, MA, 1875).
Henry S. Nourse, *The Early Records of Lancaster, Massachusetts* (Clinton, MA, 1884).
Robert Pike, *Granite Laughter and Marble Tears* (Brattleboro, VT: Stephen Daye Press, 1938).
John Stevens, *John Stevens, his book, 1705* (Newport, RI: Preservation Society of Newport County, 1953).
R. S. Storrs, *Proceedings at the Centennial Celebration of the Incorporation of the Town of Longmeadow* (Longmeadow, MA: 1884).
J. H. Temple and George Sheldon, *A History of Northfield, Massachusetts* (Albany, NY: Joel Munsell, 1875).
William Toldervy, *Select Epitaphs* (London, 1755).
Don Van Nostrand, *Stone Poets* (North Hampton, NH: Mindstar Media, 2018).
Charles Wallis, *Stories on Stone* (New York: Oxford University Press, 1954).
Thomas Webb, *A New Select Collection of Epitaphs* (London, 1775).
Dorvil Miller Wilcox, *Gravestone Inscriptions, Lee, Mass. Including All Extant of the Quarter Century 1801–1825* (Lee, MA: Press of the Valley Gleaner, 1910).
Dorvil Miller Wilcox, *Gravestone Inscriptions Lee, Mass. Including All Extant of the Quarter Century 1826–1850* (Lee, MA: Press of the Valley Gleaner, 1910).
Dorvil Miller Wilcox, *Records of the Town of Lee from Its Incorporation to A.D. 1801* (Lee, MA: Press of the Valley Gleaner, 1900).

Gravestone Iconography and Carvers

James Bachowicz, *From Slate to Marble: Gravestone Carving Traditions in Eastern Massachusetts* (Evanston, IL: Graver Press, 2006).
Peter Benes, *The Masks of Orthodoxy: Folk Gravestone Carving in Plymouth County, Massachusetts 1689–1805* (Amherst, MA: The University of Massachusetts Press, 1977).

Theodore Chase and Laurel K. Gabel, *Gravestone Chronicles* (Boston, MA: New England Historic Genealogical Society, 1990).
Harriet Merrifield Forbes, *Gravestones of Early New England and the Men Who Made Them (1653–1800)* (Boston, MA: Houghton Mifflin Company, 1927).
Laurel Gabel and Theodore Chase, "James Wilder of Lancaster, MA" in *Markers IV: The Journal of the Association for Gravestone Studies; David Watters, Editor* (Lanham, MD and London: University Press of America, 1987).
Allen I. Ludwig, *Graven Images: New England Stonecarving and Its Symbols* (Middletown, CT: Wesleyan University Press, 1966).
Nancy Jean Melin, "Samuel Dwight: Vermont Gravestone Cutter" in *Markers IV: The Journal of the Association for Gravestone Studies; David Watters, Editor* (Lanham, MD and London: University Press of America, 1987).
Daniel W. Patterson, *The True Image: Gravestone Art and the Culture of Scotch Irish Settlers in the Pennsylvania and Carolina Backcountry* (Chapel Hill, NC: The University of North Carolina Press, 2012).
Kevin M. Sweeney, "Where the Bay Meets the River: Gravestones and Stonecutters in the River Towns of Western Massachusetts, 1690–1810" in *Markers III: The Journal of the Association for Gravestone Studies; David Watters, Editor* (Lanham, MD and London: University Press of America, 1985).
Dickran and Ann Tashjian, *Memorials for Children of Change: The Art of Early New England Stonecarving* (Middletown, CT: Wesleyan University Press, 1974).
John S. Wilson, "Purchase Delay, Pricing Factors, and Attribution Elements in Gravestones from the Shop of Ithamar Spauldin" in *Markers IX: The Journal of the Association for Gravestone Studies; Theodore Chase, Editor* (Worcester, MA, 1982).

Religious and Cultural Context

Rev. Moses Baldwin, *The Ungodly Condemned in Judgment. A Sermon Preached at Springfield, December 13 1770. On the Occasion of the Execution of William Shaw, for Murder* (Boston, 1771).
Richard D. Birdsall, *Berkshire County: A Cultural History* (New Haven, CT: Yale University Press, 1959).
Paul Leicester Ford, ed., *The New-England Primer: A History of Its Origin and Development* (New York: Dodd, Mead, and Company, 1897).
David D. Hall, *Worlds of Wonder, Days of Judgment: Popular Religious Belief in Early New England* (New York: Alfred A. Knopf, 1989).
Charles P. Hanson, *Necessary Virtue: The Pragmatic Origins of Religious Liberty in New England* (Charlottesville, VA, and London: University Press of Virginia, 1998).
Rev. Jonathan Homer, *The Mourner's Friend, or, Consolation and Advice Offered to Christian Parents in the Death of Their Little Children* (Boston, 1793).
Rev. Samuel Hopkins, *An Inquiry Concerning the Future State of Those Who Die in Their Sins* (Newport, RI, 1783).
Rev. Alvan Hyde, *A Sermon Delivered at Stockbridge (Massachusetts) September 17th, 1804; Being the Day of the Interment of Mrs. Elizabeth West and her Nephew Henry W. Dwight, Esq.* (Stockbridge).
_____, *A Sermon, Preached at Lee, Massachusetts, December 20th, 1807: Being the Next Lord's Day After the Interment of Mr. Jonathan Thacher, Who Departed This Life December 14th, 1807—Aged 27 Years.* (Pittsfield, MA, 1808).
R. DeWitt Mallary, *Lenox and the Berkshire Highlands* (New York: G. P. Putnam's Sons, 1902).
David E. Stannard, *The Puritan Way of Death: A Study in Religion, Culture, and Social Change* (New York and Oxford: Oxford University Press, 1979).
Harry S. Stout, *The New England Soul: Preaching and Religious Culture in Colonial New England* (New York and Oxford: Oxford University Press, 1986).
Douglas L. Winiarski, *Darkness Falls on the Land of Light: Experiencing Religious Awakenings in Eighteenth-Century New England* (Williamsburg, VA: Omohundro Institute of Early American History and Culture, 2017).

Hymns and Psalms

Allan I. Ludwig and David D. Hall, "Aspects of Music, Poetry, Stonecarving, and Death in Early New England," *Puritan Gravestone Art II: The Dublin Seminar for New England Folklife Annual Proceedings* (1978).
Christopher N. Phillips, *The Hymnal: A Reading History* (Baltimore, MD: Johns Hopkins University Press, 2018).

Colonial and Early American Book Ownership and Reading

William J. Gilmore, *Reading Becomes a Necessity of Life* (Knoxville, TN: The University of Tennessee Press, 1989).

Kevin J. Hayes, *A Colonial Woman's Bookshelf* (Knoxville, TN: The University of Tennessee Press, 1996).

Elizabeth Pope, *"Mary Hascall, Her Book": A Colonial Rhode Island Woman's Commonplace Book* (Worcester, MA: unpublished MS).

Index

accessing source texts 26–30, 105, 109, 141, 145, 178, 184, 191, 198
Adams, Abigail 141, 175
Addison, Joseph 39, 117
Agawam, MA 81, 100, 145, 186, 189, 193
Alden, Timothy 146
Alford MA 21, 81
Alsop, Richard 142, 144
American Antiquarian Society vii, 26, 29
Amherst MA 7, 54, 57, 108, 136, 154
Association for Gravestone Studies vii, viii, 2, 27, 36, 38, 229
Attleborough MA 51

Bacon, Francis 64, 127–8
Baldwin, Moses 69, 86
Barbauld, Anna Laetitia 17, 136–7, 151
Barlow, Joel 142, 168–70, 191
Barnstable, MA 238
Barre MA 23
Baxter, Richard 27, 38, 116–7
Beattie, James 135–6
Becket MA 85, 139, 199, 211, 217, 232–3
Bedford, MA 191
Belchertown MA 74, 107, 115, 215
Bennington VT 26, 109, 222
Bernardston MA 31, 85
Bespoke epitaphs 23–25, 204–39
Bible verse epitaphs 12–14, 24, 56–69; *Corinthians* 103, 107; *Ecclesiastes* 13, 138, 205; *Exodus* 65; *Genesis* 62; *Habakkuk* 213; *Isaiah* 24, 65; *Job* 13, 15–16, 23, 31–2, 57, 59–60, 64, 76, 131, 132, 172, 215; *John* 63, 205; *Lamentations* 13, 64; *Luke* 213, 225; *Matthew* 61, 63; *Philippians* 215; *Proverbs* 52, 58–9, 61; *Psalms* 13, 14, 24, 57–8, 64, 65, 66, 112, 138, 215;

Revelation 13, 56, 58, 61, 166, 196, 207n., 212; *Romans* 41; *1 Timothy* 65, 103, 204, *2 Timothy* 207n.
Bidwell House museum 26
Blair, Robert 20, 160–1
Blake, William 153, 160, 171
Blandford MA 7, 185, 193, 194, 211, 215, 220
Bond, Edmund 159–60
The Book of Common Prayer 67–8
Boston Athenaeum 11, 29, 145
Bradford, MA 121
Brainerd, David 93–4
Brandon, VT 53–4
Brattleboro VT 51, 151
Bridgman, Thomas 8, 54
Brookfield MA 20
Burns, Robert 16, 34, 109, 115

Campbell, Thomas 17–9
Canton, MA 51
Carter, Elizabeth 17, 122–5, 135, 151
carvers 22, 23, 28, 32, 35–40, 151, 186, 196
Caulfield, Dr. Ernest 9
Charlemont, MA 199–200
Chester, MA 198
choosing epitaphs 30–2, 42, 64, 68, 72, 93, 113, 138, 189, 204
The Classic epitaph 10–2, 41–2, 48–55
Cleaveland, John 144–5
Colchester, CT 43, 228
Coleridge, Samuel Taylor 113–4, 115
Collins, William 130–1, 160
Collyer, William Bengo 1, 95–6
Colonial Dames: Massachusetts 28; New Hampshire 191
Colrain, MA 60
commonplace books 29, 38, 54, 70, 156
Concord, MA 37–8
Cotton, Nathaniel 138–9, 148

Cowper, William 26, 33, 110–1, 138
Creech, Thomas 118
Crossman, Samuel 38, 121

Dartmouth College 97–9
Dedham MA 198, 237
Deerfield, MA 7, 20, 50, 60, 173
Dodd, William 27, 28, 72, 156–9, 193
Doddridge, Philip 234
Dorchester, MA 152
Dryden, John 112, 115, 118
Dublin, NH 146
Dwight, Timothy 142, 223–4

East Bridgewater, MA 51
East Derry, NH 52
East Poultney, VT 192
East Randolph, VT 53
East Windsor, CT 210
Edwards, Jonathan 11, 12, 16, 93, 94, 142, 182, 223, 226, 228, 233
Eliot, Ephraim 29–30, 139
Enfield, William 96
Enfield, CT 65, 118, 185, 186, 190, 202, 203
epitaph anthologies 8, 189

Fairfield, CT 121
Falmouth, MA 115
Farber Gravestone Collection 2, 9, 38, 77
Fawkes, Francis 119
Flavel, John 27, 115–6
Forbes, Harriet Merrifield 9, 36
Francis, Philip 118–9
Frost, Josephine 9, 187
Frost, Robert 48

Gay, Bunker 204–10
Goshen, CT 191
Granby, CT 119
Granby, MA 43, 45, 115
graveyard poetry epitaphs 19–21, 148–84
Gray, Thomas 20, 21, 167

245

246 Index

Great Barrington, MA 12, 71, 182, 188, 214
Greenfield, MA 178
Griswold, CT 198n.
Groton, CT 121

Hadley MA 15, 16, 54, 58, 76, 87, 171, 182, 197, 198, 206, 223, 233
Hancock MA 41, 56, 88, 187, 226
Hart, Joseph 90–1
Hartford Wits 142, 144, 168, 170
Harvard, MA 37, 238
Harvard College 26, 29, 119, 146, 207
Hatfield MA 13, 65–6, 191
Hawley, MA 199
Hemans, Felicia 138
Hervey, James 11, 27–9, 38, 72, 106, 153–6, 158–9, 179, 189
Hoogs, Cynthia Tryon 9, 95
Hopkins, Samuel 11–2, 228
Horace 39, 117–9
Hyde, Alvan 1, 6, 12, 21–2, 45, 55, 148, 150
Hymns and Psalms as epitaphs 14–6, 70–99

Johnson, Samuel 16, 38, 101n., 112, 113, 134n., 135, 137, 157
Jones, James 9, 189, 200

Keteltas, Abraham 146
Knox, Vicesimus 26–7, 123, 180; *Elegant Extracts* 27, 86, 123, 139, 160, 171, 180, 184

Lancaster, MA 15, 21, 33–4, 36n., 42, 51, 59, 61, 65, 66, 105, 109, 120, 153, 164
Lanesborough, MA 8, 9, 17, 19, 34, 66, 81, 92, 94, 105, 112–3, 125, 145–6, 153, 154, 174, 187, 188, 195, 202, 234, 239
Lee MA 7, 8, 12, 21–2, 41, 45, 49, 63–4, 65–6, 102, 105, 114, 137–8, 148, 160–1, 167–8, 186, 193, 199, 201, 224, 235
Lenox MA 7, 35, 76, 82, 133, 190, 194, 217
Logan, John 26, 131–3, 160, 233
Longmeadow MA 7, 8, 27, 49, 56–7, 60, 64, 72, 121–2, 133, 155, 159–60, 164–6, 180, 183, 186, 190, 193, 194–5, 220, 228, 229n., 236
Ludlow MA 7, 58, 156
Ludwig, Allen 16, 36, 41

Marcus Manilius 118, 193, 220
Mather, Cotton 28n., 189

Merrimack, NH 197
Milton, John 16, 26, 27, 107–8, 115, 170
Monson, MA 141, 173
Montague, MA 31, 172, 176
Monterey, MA 8, 9, 10, 24, 26, 56, 90, 95–6, 102, 196, 200, 212, 219, 225, 226
Montgomery, James 1, 28, 162–6
More, Hannah 17, 27, 135
Moschus 119
Murray, Judith Sargent 17, 39, 140
Murray, Lindley 27; *English Reader* 27, 106, 139, 160, 234n

The New England Primer 27, 43, 45, 69, 120, 146, 172, 171, 184
New Haven, CT 6, 7, 116, 191
New Marlborough, MA 66, 71, 70, 213
Newton, John 11, 133
Norfolk, CT 126
Northampton, MA 7, 8, 12n., 13, 20, 58, 73, 80, 93, 111, 113–4, 131–3, 142, 172–6, 182
Northfield, MA 8, 14, 50, 71–2, 78, 106, 174, 199, 202, 204–5, 207–10, 212, 221

Old Bloomfield, CT 227
Orleans, MA 119
Otis, MA 67, 76, 106, 166
Oxford University 68–9, 130, 153, 170

Palmer MA 57, 81, 86–7, 197, 221
Parnell, Thomas 148–50
Pittsfield, MA 7, 130
poetry in epitaphs 16–9, 100–47
Pomfret, John 125–6
Pomfret, CT 193
Pope, Alexander 16, 17, 27, 28, 38–9, 100–7, 112, 115, 118, 121n., 128, 130, 137, 150, 190, 197–8, 206, 213, 214
Pope, Elizabeth 29
Prior, Matthew 28, 106, 120, 121n., 134, 151n., 157
Provincetown, MA 177–8

recurring but unattributed epitaphs 21–2, 185–203
Rehoboth, MA 201
religious context 11–2, 40–2, 54–5, 145n.
Richmond, MA 103, 179, 190
Rowe, Elizabeth Singer 17, 29, 37, 38, 151–2, 171

Salem, MA 115
Samplers 28–9, 70
Shakespeare, William 16, 26, 109, 189n., 225
Sharon, CT 222
Sheffield MA 8, 33, 51, 62, 68, 110, 117, 121n., 123, 129, 135, 144, 152, 179, 182, 192, 222, 130
Shelburne, MA 180
Shelburne, VT 134
Sheperd, Thomas 92–3
South Hadley, MA 7, 186, 196
Southbridge, MA 223
Springfield MA 7, 60, 76, 233
Stackhouse, Thomas 226
Steele, Anne 91–2
Sterne, Laurence 38, 129
Stockbridge MA 7, 33, 88, 103, 110, 174, 181, 190, 191, 214
Storrs, Richard 26, 133, 184
Sturbridge MA 213
sudden death epitaphs 25–6, 230–9

timing the choice of epitaph 32–5, 76
Toldervy, William 159–60
Townsend, CT 231
Tyringham MA 7, 80–1, 96–9, 138–9

Virgil 39, 117–8

Waller, Edmund 134
Watts, Isaac 14–6, 26, 27, 28n., 29, 37–9, 70–88, 91, 122, 127–8, 151n., 154, 168, 194–5, 196, 215, 220
Webb, Thomas 9
Wesley, John 41, 88–90
West Rupert, VT 207
West Stockbridge, MA 114, 164
Westfield, MA 7, 52, 100, 107, 127–9, 140, 178, 185, 186, 235
Wilbraham, MA 61
Wilcox, Dorvil Miller 8
Wilkinson, Henry 68–9
Williamstown, MA 7, 81, 86–7, 91, 186
Worcester, MA 191
Worthington, MA 62
Wrentham, MA 111
Wright, George 72, 157–60, 179

Yale University 26, 36n., 119, 142, 168, 223, 224
Young, Edward 20–1, 26, 38–9, 152, 170–184, 198

www.ingramcontent.com/pod-product-compliance
Lightning Source LLC
Chambersburg PA
CBHW060339010526
44117CB00017B/2893